The Weight of Evidence

New Scientific Discoveries
Support
a
Supernatural Creation

by

Lyle Francisco

Promise Publishing Co.   Orange, California 92865

The Weight of Evidence

Francisco, Lyle

Copyright 1998 by Promise Publishing Co.

Library of Congress Cataloging-in-Publication Data

Francisco, Lyle

The Weight of Evidence

ISBN 0-939497-50-6

The Weight of Evidence

A book providing nearly 300 quotes to support the following:

- The Anthropic Principle—a fine-tuned universe and earth-sun system was planned for mankind's existence by a personal, caring God.

- The Genesis biblical account of Creation is in complete harmony with science.

- The geological fossil record supports special Creation, not gradual evolution.

- The unparalleled complexity, design and information content of a single cell demands an infinite, intelligent designer.

- Homology (similarity of species) supports typology (cladistics) which says that no species can be considered ancestors to another.

- New discoveries on the molecular level show irreducible complexity of design and defy a gradual evolution while supporting a planned Creation.

- Atheistic Evolutionary indoctrination of the last fifty years is responsible for the moral breakdown in America.

- The real basis and origin of American democracy was the Bible's gospel of the grace of God.

- Creation science **can** legally be brought back into science and social studies classes.

- The time has come for Bible-believing Americans to take back American culture, beginning in the classrooms of our country.

About the Author

Lyle Francisco's "Damascus Road" experience came after he was hit on the head with a football, but he was so energized by his newfound relationship with Jesus that he not only gave his heart to the Lord, but also gave Him his life. He entered Biola University in La Mirada, California, for Bible training after pitching professional baseball in the Cleveland Indian farm system for two seasons.

The B.A. degree in Bible that he earned at Biola, and the B.A. degree in History and Social Studies that he earned at Pasadena Nazarene College were the foundation for the M.A. degree in Education and the secondary teaching and administrative credentials he earned at Whittier College, also in California. Then, he taught High School Social Studies for 25 years in the Chaffey Union District while he and his wife raised their two children. His Social Studies teaching took him into Ancient, Modern European and Western Civilization specialities and he did curriculum development at the district level. Training, experience and research give him a solid basis for his observations and comments.

The trends he has seen in the California School system are part of the overall school ... and public ... trends in thinking and the flaws of one are the flaws of all. Students and the public alike need to bring their philosophy of life in line with current scientific discoveries instead of living by what we were taught years ago. The new discoveries tell us a far different story than we were led to believe in the past.

Let's look at the facts ... and follow wherever they lead!

Dedication

To my mother,

Emma Francisco,

who in difficult times

raised my sister, **Barbara,** and me virtually alone.

And to my sister for faithfully caring for our mother

who is 93 and still going strong.

Acknowledgments

My thanks and appreciation go to:

- my wife, Dorothy, for her support, encouragement and patience;

- author, Jeanie Gordon, for giving me professional direction and confidence;

- author, speaker and former director of Hume Lake Conference Grounds, Ken Poure, for pushing me on in this project;

- editors, Norm Rohrer and Mary Belle Steele for organizing and refining my manuscript;

- typist and computer expert, Cary Nakamura, for coping with my muddled handwriting;

- the many scientists, historians, apologists and theologians whose knowledge and wisdom give life to this manuscript.

Table Of Contents

Foreword

In the past forty years of work among young people, there is one question that has come to me hundreds of times. The question comes in many forms, but the bottom line is, "What is causing America to come apart at her moral seams?" Lyle "Skip" Francisco offers a fresh, contemporary, apologetic system that is the heart of the answer. In his timely book, Lyle has revealed a major flaw in the California public education system that is producing disastrous results leading already confused students to moral and spiritual bankruptcy. That flaw is the new state framework on science which teaches organic evolution as a fact, further bolstering secular humanist philosophy.

As an evangelical, Lyle uses the Bible, science and history as his primary weapons. After discrediting atheism and evolution and their byproducts — relativism and humanistic thought — he provides irrefutable evidence for Creation by almighty God. He also presents a case for the need to get Creation science and the Judeo-Christian heritage back in our public schools.

I commend the reading of this much-needed book to:

- parents concerned about the teaching of evolution (molecule-to-man) as fact and its devastating consequences,

- believers desirous of bolstering their faith, and

- unbelievers or agnostics as a challenge to their positions.

Lyle has all the qualifications for such an extensive undertaking. He not only has an in-depth historical and biblical perspective but has also had the unique opportunity of teaching World Religions to high school students thus encountering speakers from all the major religions, cults and ideological systems including evolutionary based existentialism and secular humanism. This valuable experience has enabled him to gain unique insights into the weaknesses and contradictions of their movements.

I've known Lyle since his college days in Compton. His ability to debate and ask heavy questions in his early Christian life has become a part of his lifestyle and, coupled with his 35 years of teaching in public high schools, Lyle has put it all together in his book "The Weight of Evidence" I commend its reading to you and personally believe that it contains the TRUTH that will overcome the BIG LIE…evolution.

Yours for youth,

Ken Poure
Director at Large
Hume Lake

Preface

Since its inception in 1989, a new comprehensive state science framework, teaching organic evolution as a fact from kindergarten up to and including high school, has gradually been implemented in California, and other public schools throughout America are following suit. Americans **must** ask themselves whether or not they want their children to be indoctrinated into evolutionary philosophy. There are few questions of greater significance than this, "Is mankind a cosmic evolutionary accident as secular humanists claim, or is he the product of an all powerful, benevolent creator who is alive and providentially controlling history as recorded in the Bible?" That's what this book is all about.

The Evolution–Creation controversy has been going on for about a hundred years since the publication of Darwin's *Origin of Species* in 1859. In the last twenty years, there has been increased interest in the United States as a result of legislative proposals in many states demanding the teaching of creation as well as evolution in public schools. The importance of this subject, however, is timeless. The question of origins has a universal appeal to all ages who seek to satisfy innate curiosity. Even children with their first words ask, "Where did I come from?" The solution of this question is vital to all ages for formulation of a life philosophy and consequently, the answer to this question affects life itself. Because of our current social problems, many concerned citizens are asking: "Is time running out for our young people?" "Is time running out for our nation?" Quite possibly, these are the most crucial questions of our day.

Introduction

Before we begin, a definition of creation and evolution would be appropriate. Dr. J. P. Moreland, Professor of Philosophy at Biola University and author of the book *Christianity and the Nature of Science: A Philosophical Investigation*, gives the following abbreviated definition of creation science.

"'Creation-science' means the scientific evidences for creation and inferences from those scientific evidences. Creation-science includes the scientific evidences and related inferences that indicate: (1) **Sudden creation** of the universe, energy, and life from nothing; (2) The **insufficiency of mutation** and natural selection in bringing about the development of all living kinds from a single organism; (3) Changes only **within fixed limits** of originally created kinds of plants and animals; (4) **Separate ancestry** for man and apes."

Dr. Philip E. Johnson, law professor at U. C. Berkeley, California, in his book *Darwin on Trial* (1989), gives the following clarion definition of evolution. He states,

"The key to understanding what is at stake is to know what scientists mean by evolution. Nobody doubts that a certain amount of evolution occurs. For example, bacteria develops resistance to antibiotics and bugs to insecticides. Evolution in this narrow sense can be demonstrated, and so it is uncontroversial.

"Evolution, however, also stands for a much bigger idea. To Darwinists, it means an all-embracing philosophical system in which microorganisms evolved from non–living chemicals and eventually became plants, insects, reptiles, monkeys and humans — with no divine input whatsoever. The tree of life grew of its own accord, by random genetic changes and survival of the fittest, without guidance from any creator. As the notable Darwinist George Gaylord Simpson put it: 'Man is the result of a purposeless and natural process that did not have him in mind.'"

The above definition is the so–called "molecule-to-man" theory of evolution or "Macro-evolution". "Micro-evolution" or little changes as Dr. Johnson relates, is a fact. There are many different kinds of dogs, cats, birds and fish but there are always limits of variation—a bee remains a bee, a grape remains a grape. Species as we see them today are well-defined. Creationists don't have a problem with micro-evolution, but maintain that there is insufficient scientific evidence to support macro-evolution.

Dr. Johnson maintains that the need for a creator is ruled out by the theory of evolution as Julian Huxley, former world famous biologist, has dogmatically stated,

"Darwinism removed the whole idea of God as the creator of organisms from the sphere of rational discussion, Darwin pointed out no supernatural designer was needed..."

Carl Sagan in *Cosmos* also stated,

"The universe is all that there is, all that there has been, and is all that there ever will be, and we are part of the stuff of the stars."

Many evolutionists would say, "Evolution has nothing to do with religion." Oh, yes it does, as the above quotes clearly show. When you discuss ultimate origins, you are moving into the realm of religion, and atheism is just as much a religion as theism. Neo-Darwinism (belief of Darwinists) is **non**-theistic in its position that all things have come about by purely naturalistic, mechanistic causes. Evolution is not just a scientific theory (as it is being justified in science and social studies classes in California) but in essence as the legal scholar Philip E. Johnson has stated,

"Evolution is a metaphysical, grand theory of life."

In his booklet entitled *Evolution as Dogma,* he states,

"The important claim of 'evolution' is that life developed gradually from nonliving matter to its present state of diverse complexity through purposeless natural mechanisms that are known to science. *Evolution in this sense is a grand metaphysical system that contradicts any meaningful notion of creation, because it leaves the Creator with nothing to do. Contemporary neo-Darwinism rules out theistic or 'guided' evolution just as firmly as it rejects direct creation ex nihilo.*

"It is this universal, naturalistic version of evolution that Darwinists are preaching (the word is appropriate) in the schools and colleges, with more or less clarity depending on the circumstances. As William B. Provine rightly says, 'Liberal theologians and Darwinists share a common interest in obscuring the anti-theistic implications of Darwinism.'"

The philosophical implications of the question of origins are enormous. Was mankind specially created by almighty God or is mankind an accident of the universe? It *matters* how we answer this question.

Dr. Michael Denton, Ph.D. in molecular Biology, in his book *Evolution: a Theory in Crisis* (1986), further defines neo-Darwin evolution and gives the revolutionary consequences to the Western world adopting this theory. He states,

"All the designing order and complexity and eerie purposefulness of living systems of life are the result of a blind random process–natural selection. Before Darwin, many believed that a providential intelligence had imposed its mysterious design upon nature, but now chance ruled supreme. God's will was replaced by the capriciousness of a roulette wheel.

"Darwin's theory was entirely materialistic and mechanistic. 'Pure chance—absolutely free but blind— is the foundation of evolution.' It was a revolutionary claim. Where once design had been the result of God's creation, it was now put down to chance.

"Victorian England (19th century) was shocked by the theory of evolution which resulted in a revolutionary decline in religion. England, which was formerly biblical fundamentalists, now came to the end of the theological and anthropocentric view of nature. 'Man is a cosmic accident.' Chance and design are antithetical concepts. Intellectuals became anticlerical and religious. *Darwin's theory broke man's link with God and set him adrift in a cosmos without purpose or end. Its impact was so fundamental that it's considered the greatest intellectual revolution in modern times.*"

As Dr. Denton relates above, evolution is the foundation for the secularization of the western world in the 20th century. Bringing it close to home, I believe it is the bottom line cause for the moral decline of our great nation that could bring about our demise.

After England adopted the theory of evolution, the theory quickly spread all over Europe and finally it became vogue in the United States after the defeat of the creationists in the Scopes Monkey Trial of 1925. From that time on, this atheistic theory began to take over our educational institutions and is now being taught *as fact* in California's public schools.

The new California framework on the teaching of natural science (Elementary, Jr. High, High School) was adopted by the State Board of Education on January 13, 1989. This framework, in spite of the latest scientific findings **against** the theory of evolution (which I believe are conclusive), has made the strongest statement in the history of the state supporting evolution. The state framework, of course, is the official guide for science teachers and textbook makers, and it states categorically that evolution "molecule-to-man" *is a fact* — no more controversial in scientific circles than the theories of electron flow or the laws of gravity — as it states. The only part that is theory, the authors claim, is *how* it happened. The state framework on natural science relates,

> "Evolution is both a pattern and a process. It is also both a fact and a theory. It is a scientific fact that organisms have evolved through time...for example, the first birds evolved from small carnivorous dinosaurs, so birds are properly considered members of the dinosauria, regardless of how they are traditionally classified. Similarly, humans evolved from other apes–tailless primates–and are, in turn, apes, primates, mammals, amniotes, vertebrates and so forth.

> "The mechanisms, patterns and processes by which this evolution has occurred constitute the theory of evolution."

I believe the above statements (along with much of the contents in the framework given by the State Board of Education) are outdated, often false, ethically irresponsible and potentially dangerous. The state framework could encourage Elementary, Junior High and High School teachers to be dogmatic in highly speculative areas.

As a former teacher of World Religions, I have seen many students come into my class actually brainwashed and unable to consider alternative points of view. In making a critical analysis of their own philosophical position, they would either become inflamed or the information given was shed like "water off a duck's back".

My concern is that the general public (including many science and social studies teachers) is not only unaware of the "bankrupt" state of the theory of evolution, but they are also unaware of the extensive and comprehensive state programs for teaching the theory of evolution. Legal scholar, Philip E. Johnson of U.C. Berkeley, an expert in the current Evolution/Creation controversy, in his booklet, "Evolution as Dogma", *The Establishment of Naturalism,* states,

> "For now, things are going well for Darwinism in America. The Supreme Court has dealt the creationists a crushing blow, and state boards of education are beginning to adopt 'science frameworks'. These policy statements are designed to encourage textbook publishers to proclaim boldly the fact of evolution—and therefore the naturalistic philosophy that underlies the fact—instead of minimizing the subject to avoid any controversy. Efforts are also underway to bring under control any individual teachers who express creationist sentiments in the classroom, especially if they make use of unapproved materials. As ideological authority collapses in other parts of the world, the Darwinists are successfully swimming against the current."

This is true throughout America as public schools across our country follow the lead set in California. However, teaching evolution as a fact and not allowing alternative points of view is not only *unethical* but also *illegal* because of the following Supreme Court rulings and guidelines.

- Evolution-based Secular Humanism has been ruled as one of the atheistic religions, along with Hinayana Buddhism and Taoism (Supreme Court 1961). Also, the Supreme Court has said that religious concepts need deal only in ultimate realities such as Man's nature and his place in the Universe.

- Teaching only one point of view not only violates the principle of academic freedom and the free exchange of ideas, but doesn't follow the Supreme Court guidelines of presenting a variety of theories, as long as they are based on established fact (Supreme Court, 1987).

I believe that Neo-Darwinism has lost its legal footing in the classroom, for it can now be shown that it is not based on established facts.

The impression given by the State Board of Education is that the entire scientific and academic communities are in unison in their affirmation of Macro-evolution, and the only debate is how it happened. Nothing could be further from the truth. In fact, many scientists (not only creationist scientists) do not hold to this position, the field is literally in an uproar. They're not only debating how it happened but whether or not there's been any kind of evolution (Macro-evolution) at all! *The debate is not reaching the general public and much of the significant scientific information (which is talked about "behind closed doors") is not being made available to the general public nor is it being made available in school textbooks and materials.*

Chapter 1

— The Evidence —

The Universe and the Earth

Twenty to thirty years ago, scientists were convinced that outer space held the key to unlocking the mystery of origins. In the last thirty years, they have attempted, by use of radio–telescopes, to contact life in our universe but they have come up with no evidence of intelligent life anywhere. The millions of dollars spent in search of intelligent radio messages from outer space proved fruitless. Also, the investigation of our solar system for primitive organic life has provided no evidence of life evolving. Explorations of the moon, Mars, Venus, Jupiter and Saturn have only produced negative results and many scientists are giving up, convinced that there is no hope of ever finding extra-terrestrial life in our solar system. In the midst of the dry, barren waste planets, our "fishbowl" earth stands uniquely alone. Of course, this evidence alone is not conclusive, however significant.

- Evolutionary theory states that, given the right conditions, formation of life is the inevitable consequence of chemical processes on any planet. This, by the way, would include our own planet. In other words, if evolution is true, we should be witnessing new life (including new species) coming into being today. This is not the case in our solar system — including planet earth.

- Evolutionary theory states that out of an eternal universe and unchanging natural laws, all things have come about; however, the latest scientific findings support a beginning to our universe which demands an answer to a first cause.

Evidence for a Beginning to the Universe

Almost all scientists today accept the fact that there was a beginning to the universe which agrees with the Genesis account of creation. Dr. Robert Jastrow (former evolutionist—now agnostic), the renowned astrophysicist who was founder and former director of NASA's Goddard Institute for Space Studies related,

"A careful study of the stars has proved as well as anything can be proved in science, that the universe had a beginning. Now, we see how the astronomical evidence leads to a biblical view of the origin of the world. The details differ but the essential elements in the astronomical evidence and the biblical account of Genesis are the same. The chain of events leading to man began suddenly and sharply, in a definite moment of time, in a flash of light and energy. The astronomers are so embarrassed by this that for the scientist who lived by his faith in the power of reason, the story ends like a bad dream. He has scaled the mountain of ignorance, he is about to conquer the highest peak when he finds himself face to face with a group of theologians who have been there for centuries!"

The following is an outline of the mounting evidence provided by astronomy and other branches of science for a beginning to the universe.

- Our most powerful telescopes have proved (through measurement of the red shift of the spectrum, for example) that we live in an expanding universe in which all the galaxies around us are moving away from us at enormous speeds. The closest galaxies are traveling one million miles an hour and galaxies further out, over 100 million miles an hour.

- Radio astronomy has demonstrated that our expanding universe is actually blowing up before our eyes as if in the aftermath of a gigantic explosion. Using the most sensitive radio astronomy antennas, scientists have discovered a constant faint signal of noise pervading all space and a faint glow of radiation coming from all directions. The radiation discovered has exactly the pattern and wave lengths expected for the light and heat produced in a great explosion. Also, Cal Tech astronomers have discovered large wispy clouds along the furthest edges of the observable universe.

- Einstein's equation of general relativity (1915-1916) predicted an expanding universe. Einstein was disturbed by the notion of a universe that expands because it implies a beginning, a first cause and a primal mover (creator). Einstein believed in a God, something like an active force that was a part of an orderly eternal universe (static universe or steady-state theory) but because of the mounting evidence, he changed his position and came to believe that there was a beginning and a first cause creative agent of superior reasoning power. The concluding evidence was provided in

1929 by Edwin Hubble. His measurements of forty different galaxies demonstrated that the galaxies were expanding away from each other and the expansion was in the same manner predicted by Einstein.

- A five-year study led by a team of California Institute of Technology astronomers and other scientists around the world concluded about fifteen years ago that there was one initial explosion or creation. In other words, the universe will expand forever and not contract back into another explosion.

James E. Bunn of Cal Tech has related,

"After reviewing the velocities of distant galaxies, the average density of matter throughout the cosmos and other factors, we've reached the conclusion that the expansion of the universe cannot be reversed."

In an article entitled, *Big Bang Gets New Adjectives— Open and Hot,* printed in his publication, Facts and Faith (First Quarter, 1998), Dr. Hugh Ross states:

"A big bang universe is a universe that began. A *hot* big bang implies one beginning only; that is, a universe where no rebounding or reincarnating is possible because the level of entropy (efficiency of radiation release) is extremely high. An *open* big bang implies a universe that never stops expanding because its mass is insufficient to halt it. If we could run time backward, like a movie film, we could trace the open hot big bang to a singular beginning in finite time, as the Bible declares.

"Powerful assurance of the validityof this origin scenario comes from five different research groups all at the same time. Five sets of results independently and simultaneously confirm an open hot big bang creation. Each came up with the same measure for the universe's mass, expansion rate and age."

- The two laws of thermodynamics demonstrate that ultimately the universe will end, and thus there must have been a beginning. These two laws, being the most testable of the available scientific evidence, are the strongest evidence for a beginning and the need for a first cause, creative agent.

The laws of thermodynamics state that the universe is being preserved or conserved and not recreating itself (although changing in form—the first law), and that the universe is going from order to disorder, dying out and running down, like a battery in a watch (the second law). In other words, the universe (like our sun) will eventually die a heat death. The conclusion is obvious. If there is going to be an end to our universe, then there must have been a beginning, as the universe could not have been eternally dying out. The fact that the universe is still here proves there was a beginning. To put it another way, the most basic and universal laws of science, the first and second laws of thermodynamics, speak of a finished cosmos not recreating itself, being conserved quantitatively, but decaying qualitatively. These laws point directly to a primeval creation.

Dr. Duane T. Gish (Ph.D. in Biochemistry, University of California at Berkeley), in an article in *Impact* September 1991, ably elaborates on the laws of thermodynamics and demonstrates the agreement between science and the Bible concerning these two laws. He states:

"First, let us consider the science of thermodynamics: In Psalm 102:25,26, we read, 'Of old hast Thou laid the foundation of the earth: and the heavens are the work of Thy hands. They shall perish, but Thou shalt endure: yea, all of them shall wax old like a garment.'

"In verse 25, we find, restated, the fact that God is the Creator of all that exists. Verse 26 then tells us something highly significant, not about the initial, created state of the universe, but about the present state of the universe. According to this Scripture, written three thousand years before the dawn of modern science, we learn that the universe is like a suit of clothes that is wearing out. In other words, the universe is running down, deteriorating, constantly becoming less and less orderly.

"Everywhere we look, from the scale of the galaxies down to the scale of the atom, we find a universal, natural tendency of all systems to go from order to disorder; from complexity to simplicity. Thus, clusters of galaxies are dispersing as the galaxies move away from one another.

"The rotation of the earth is slowing; the magnetic field of the earth is decaying. Erosion constantly wears down the features of the earth. Our bodies wear out; we die and decay to a pile of dust. Our houses, our machines wear out and are finally abandoned and replaced.

"Each star, including our own sun, is constantly burning up billions of tons of fuel every second. Eventually, every star in the universe, unless God intervenes (which we are certain He will), will exhaust its fuel and become dark and cold. The universe would then be cold and dead, and, of course, all life would have ceased long before the last death throes of the universe. Even now, every so often a nova or supernova occurs, and a star very rapidly becomes less orderly, in a gigantic explosion. The natural tendency towards disorder is so all-pervasive and unfailing that it has been formalized as a natural law — the Second Law of Thermodynamics.

"If there is a second law of thermodynamics, there must be a first law, of course. Indeed there is, and this natural law confirms another scientifically testable statement found in the Bible. The First Law of Thermodynamics states that the total quantity of energy and matter in the universe is a constant. One form of energy may be converted into another, energy may be converted into matter, and matter may be converted into energy, but the total quantity always remains the same.

"The First Law of Thermodynamics, the most firmly established natural law in science, confirms the biblical statement concerning a finished creation, as found in Genesis 2:1,2: 'Thus the heavens and the earth were finished, and all the host of them. And on the seventh day God ended His work which He had made; and He rested on the seventh day from all His work which He had made.'

"If it could be shown that somewhere in this universe matter or energy was coming into being from nothing, then this biblical statement of a finished creation would be falsified. The opposite is true. It has been precisely verified. Once again, a biblical statement has withstood scientific test."

In *Dr. Einstein and the Universe,* Einstein related that the universe was running out of energy. Dr. Lincoln Barnett pointed out that Einstein's basic argument in his great advances in physics led him to state time and time again, "The second law stands: everything tends to entropy; therefore, we are living in a circular finite universe and it's running down!" He concludes, "God does not play dice with His universe."

Sir James Jeans (mathematician, physicist, astronomer) compared the universe to a clock that is running down which brings up the question, "Who wound it up in the first place?" Two internationally acknowledged authorities on thermodynamics, Sontag and Van Aylen, in their widely-used, two-volume textbook say,

"...The Authors see the second law of thermodynamics as Man's description of the prior and continuing work of a creator, who also holds the answer to the future destiny of man and the universe."

Genesis 1:1 reads,

"In the beginning God created the heavens and the earth."

"Ingenious design demands an ingenious designer"

The Bible (unlike other religions—Hinduism, Buddhism, paganism, etc.) teaches that God is transcendent and exterior to his creation and, as Einstein has stated, we live in a *circular finite* universe that is expanding, but has an end. The question (using the scientific method of Cause and Effect) is, "Who made the universe, and how powerful and ingenious is this first cause, creative agent?" Science has discovered that there are a 100 billion stars in our own galaxy and estimates that there are billions of other galaxies. The entire universe with its moons, planets and suns, moves in precise orbits inside their own galaxies as the galaxies move in precise orbits inside the universe!

Dr. Hugh Ross (astrophysicist and Ph.D. in Astronomy from Toronto University and also former researcher on quasars and galaxies at Cal Tech), in his book *The Fingerprint of God* (1991), relates that because of mounting scientific evidence for a beginning to the universe supporting the "Big Bang" theory and the fact of ingenious design throughout the universe, most astronomers now believe in God.

New Discoveries Make Old Theories Obsolete

In the 18th and 19th centuries (before Darwin), most cosmologists followed the non-theistic view of Immanuel Kant (father of Cosmology) of an infinite universe. Because of the telescopes of that day and other factors, the universe seemed to have no end and so scientists deduced that it must be infinite and eternal with no beginning and consequently there would be no need of a first cause—God. Then with the advent of Darwin (1859), the whole package of a steady-state (eternal universe) became the accepted language and dogma of the scientific community. Everything seemed to fit. Now mankind had a scientific explanation of origins replacing the so-called biblical myth story and also, with an infinite universe in which you could "throw the dice" as many times as you want, you would eventually come up with the evolution of all things. However, in the 19th and 20th centuries with more sophisticated and powerful telescopes and better scientific research, everything changed as Robert Jastrow stated, "A careful study of the stars has proved as well as anything can be proved in science that the universe had a beginning."

The Big Bang Theory

- ### Einstein's General Theory of Relativity

The universe has been proven by Einstein's theories of relativity to be like the result of a gigantic explosion. Using the analogy of an exploding hand grenade, the universe is expanding and also decelerating. It's being blown apart, and it is slowing down. Deceleration and expansion together imply that the universe is exploding out from a single point. Through the equations of general relativity, we can trace that explosion backward in time to its origin, an instant when the entire physical universe burst forth from a single point of infinite density called Singularity. Thus, the universe is **finite** not infinite and has a creation date. The questions confronts us, "Who was there (**before** Creation) to create matter and to put it into motion?"

Concerning the origin of space and time, Dr. Ross states,

"In 1966 and 1970, Einstein's work was further developed when three British Astrophysicists, Stephen Hawking, George Ellis and Roger Penrose applied the equations of General Relativity to include Space and Time. Their space-time theorem of General Relativity demonstrated that space and time originated in the same Cosmic Bang that brought matter and energy into existence."

- **The Laws of Thermodynamics**

Dr. Ross states,

"Arthur Eddington and other theoreticians pointed out that the second law of thermodynamics had all along demanded the disintegration of the universe. For the universe as a whole, disorder must continually increase and energy must irreversibly flow from hot to cold bodies. In other words, the universe is running down like a wound up clock. And, if it is running down, then there must have been a time when it was fully wound up."

Thus, classical thermodynamics, observational astronomy, and general relativity joined forces in confirming the maturing of the universe — a maturation with obvious reference to a beginning point and to finite spatial limits. This convergence of research findings was hailed as one of the great triumphs of modern science.

- **Helium Abundance**

Dr. Ross states,

"In 1966, Peebles calculated that the observed abundance of helium precisely matches what would result from nuclear fusion taking place during the first four minutes of the Big Bang, given the radiation temperature measured by Penzias, Wilson and others. Peebles' conclusion was confirmed independently by more elaborate calculations done by Robert Wagoner, William Fowler and Fred Hoyle."

- **Radiation Background**

Dr. Ross states,

"Recent data (1990) from the COBE satellite reveal a uniformity in background radiation that in orders of magnitude are higher than any previously measured—further proof that the universe began with some kind of hot big bang."

- **Big Bang Relics**

Since 1984, scientists with the Hubble satellite telescope have measured and mapped out the Universe. It is extremely significant that we are the first generation to witness the measuring of the Cosmos. From the COBE satellite, we have even taken a picture of the outer edge of our galaxy providing new evidence that it started with a "Big Bang".

On April 24, 1992 in the headlines of *The Los Angeles Times,* there was an article entitled "Relics of 'Big Bang' seen for the first time." The picture of the outer rim of our galaxy was taken by the NASA COBE satellite. It showed the earth's galaxy as the thick center band and pink and blue patches that reflect slight temperature variations that represent wisps of gas—"Big Bang" relics.

These relics represent massive wisps of gas more than 500 million light years long. Physicist Joel Primack of U.C. Santa Cruz stated "It was one of the major discoveries of the

Century…in fact, it's one of the major discoveries of science."
British physicist Stephen Hawking related that "… the discovery of
the century, if not of all time …" had been made. Science historian
Frederic Burnham related that it made belief that God created the
universe "… a more respectable hypothesis than at any time in the
past 100 years." George Smoot (U.C. Berkeley astronomer and
project leader for COBE satellite) states,

> "What we have found is evidence for the birth of the
> universe …. It's like looking at God."

Dr. Ross states,

> "One year ago in Facts & Faith (vol. 6, no. 2), I wrote
> about the first ever detection of fluctuations in the
> temperature of the cosmic background radiation—a
> finding headlined around the world as proof for the hot
> big bang. The importance of that discovery, announced
> in April 1992, was that it chased away a lingering cloud
> of uncertainty about the big bang, uncertainty about how
> a smooth burst and expansion of radiation could account
> for galaxy formation, which requires at least a little
> bumpiness (ripples). COBE detected that bumpiness,
> slight fluctuations in the temperature of the cosmic
> background radiation (radiation leftover from the initial
> bang).

> "No reasonable shadow of doubt hangs over the hot big
> bang model…. The only possible explanation for such
> extreme entropy is that the universe really did experience
> a hot big bang origin.

> "Together these Hubble and COBE discoveries have
> helped us solve the problem of how galaxies and clusters
> of galaxies form out of a big bang. The level of
> irregularity in the background radiation observed by the
> COBE satellite fits the rough values and ratio of exotic to
> ordinary matter derived from the Hubble measurements.
> And these findings fit the observed abundances of

deuterium, boron and beryllium as well as the observed clumping of the galaxies. Everything fits.

"It is all quite wonderful. In fact, I have rarely, if ever, seen physicists and astronomers so ecstatic. Their work is far from finished. But its focus is much sharper. Some eye specks, such as the hypothesis of an infinitely old, uncreated universe (dredged up for a last gasp in Eric Lerner's book, *The Big Bang Never Happened*), have been cleared out of the way."

Dr. Ross further relates that not only do most astronomers believe in God, but the creation and creator of the universe has now become an area of active research in physics. In his book, *The Creator and the Cosmos* (1993), Dr. Ross states,

"Much more is going on, however, than mere talk by astronomers about the design of the cosmos for life support. Words such as *somebody fine-tuned nature, superintellect, monkeyed, overwhelming design, hand of God, ultimate purpose, God's mind, exquisite order, very delicate balance, exceedingly ingenious, supernatural Agency, supernatural plan, tailor-made, Supreme Being, and providentially crafted* obviously apply to a Person. Beyond just establishing that the Creator is a Person, the findings about design provide some evidence of what that Person is like."

Dr. Ross concludes with a pertinent message for the divided world of creationists. He states,

"Ironically, many Christians still feel compelled to fight the fact of the Big Bang. For some strange reason, they call it a 'godless myth' even though non–theistic scientists have despised it for its potent theological ramifications. I suspect that the persistent problem of the age of the universe and the length of the creation days is once again getting in the way.

"My prayer and my hope is that at least some of these fellow believers in Christ will begin to see Genesis 1:1 as the most eloquent statement of the Big Bang ever penned. Rather than some kind of random explosion, the Big Bang was a carefully controlled burst of matter, energy, space and time from a reality which exists beyond. The more we learn about the burst, the more we see the hand of the transcendent God of the Bible in it. As if we needed yet more reason to believe in Him, He has graciously provided it."

Evidence Refuting the Steady-State Model

The steady-state theory was almost universally accepted in the 19th century and is still stubbornly held by a few scientists.

The Steady-State theory implies that the universe is eternal (has always existed). As it expands, it never completely thins out because it is continually recreating itself, filling the spaces. To put it more succinctly, the universe is generating hydrogen from nothing in order to maintain energy without running down. This has been going on from eternity past, they say.

Dr. Ross provides the following scientific facts, rendering the Steady-State theory as fallacious:

- The lack of very old galaxies in the vicinity of our galaxy negates an infinite age for the universe.

- The lack of very young galaxies in the vicinity of our galaxy negates continual spontaneous creation.

- The lack of red shifts beyond z = 4 implies a real limit for the universe.

- A steady-state universe lacks a physical mechanism (such as the primeval explosion) to drive the observed expansion of the universe.

- The observed microwave background radiation (perfectly explained by the cooling off of the primordial fireball) defies explanation in a steady-state universe.

- The enormous entropy of the universe makes no sense in a steady-state system.

- In a steady-state universe, spontaneously generated matter must come into being with a specified ratio of helium to hydrogen, and that ratio must decrease with respect to time in an entirely ad hoc fashion. Instead, the measure of helium abundance for the universe has exactly the value that the big bang would predict.

- The observed abundances of deuterium, light helium and lithium have no physical explanation in a steady-state universe. (Again, a hot Big Bang precisely predicts them.)

- Galaxies and quasars at distances so great that we are viewing them from the remote past appear to differ so substantially in character and distribution from nearby, more contemporary galaxies and quasars as to render steady-state models completely implausible.

Evidence Refuting the Oscillating Universe Model

The Oscillating Universe Theory implies that the universe is eternal and that it expands, "runs out of energy", comes back to another primordial ball, blows up and expands again. This has been going on from eternity, they say. Dr. Ross states,

"Given a hot Big Bang, theoreticians went to work yet again to distance themselves from the dread beginning. They hypothesized a cycle of expansion and contraction for the universe. An infinite number of cycles might remove any need to deal with an ultimate origin for the universe. However, observational evidence suggests that the universe has insufficient mass to force a collapse. Moreover, thermodynamic arguments show that even if the universe were massive enough to collapse, entropy would prevent a rebound. Instead of a bounce, there would be a crunch.

"The observed density of the universe appears to be at most only one–half of what is needed to force a collapse.

"No physical mechanism is known that could realistically be expected to reverse a cosmic contraction.

"As noted earlier, the universe, with a specific entropy of about a billion, ranks as the most entropic phenomenon known. Thus, even if the universe contained sufficient mass to force an eventual collapse, that collapse would not produce a bounce. Far too much of the energy of the universe is dissipated in unreclaimable form to fuel a bounce. Like a lump of wet clay falling on a carpet, the universe, if it did collapse, would go 'splat.'"

Evidence of Purposeful Design in the Universe

- The universe is expanding at just the right rate. If it were expanding faster, no galaxies would have formed; if slower, it would have collapsed back into a primordial ball.

- The work energy in the universe is in perfect ratio with the radiation level (non–reversible heat energy) for the formulation of stars and galaxies. The entropic level is about a billion to one—very extreme but, if any smaller or larger, the universe would be devoid of stars and thus life.

- All stars move in precise orbits and are all just the right distance from each other; if closer, gravity would disturb the orbit of the planets, in fact, they would be ripped out of their orbits and drawn into the stars.

- The velocity of light can be expressed as a function of any one of the fundamental forces of physics. Any real changes in the velocity of light would alter all constants. Thus, the slightest variation, up or down, would negate the possibility of life in the universe.

- The mass and energy of the universe is perfect for sustaining life. If the mass were slightly larger, extra deuterium would cause stars to burn too rapidly to sustain life; if smaller, no helium would be generated during the cooling of the Big Bang for life. If the universe were any smaller or larger, not even one planet like earth would be possible.

- The age of the universe is perfect for sustaining life. If the universe were just a couple of billion years younger no environment suited for life would exist. However; if the universe were about ten billion years older, there would be no solar-type stars in a stable burning phase in the right part of the galaxy for life to exist.

Dr. Ross states that this list of sensitive constants is by no means complete. Only 6 of the 17 constants given by Dr. Ross are listed here, and yet it demonstrates why a growing number of physicists and astronomers have been considering the possibility that *the universe was not only divinely caused but also divinely designed.*

Dr. William Swann, a leading authority on cosmic radiation stated,

"The man of science likes to separate fact from speculation. Now viewing the universe as a whole, I cannot escape the fact that it is of intelligent design. By this I mean that the universe shows on a magnificent scale the same kind of interrelationship of its working and efficiency of planning as an engineer strives to achieve in his smaller undertakings."

Wernher von Braun, the brilliant German rocket expert, stated,

"Why do I believe in God? Simply stated, the main reason is this: anything as well ordered and perfectly created as is our earth and universe must have a maker, a master designer. Anything so orderly, so perfect, so precisely balanced, so majestic as this creation can only be the product of a divine idea. There must be a maker; there can be no other way."

Dr. Warren Weaver, mathematician and scientist, similarly stated,

"Every new discovery of science is a further revelation of the order that God has built into His universe. God gains in dignity and power through manifestations of His reason and order."

American astronomer George Greenstein (who does not claim to be a Christian) expresses his thoughts on the subject:

"As we survey all the evidence, the thought insistently arises that some supernatural agency—or, rather, Agency—must be involved. Is it possible that suddenly, without intending to, we have stumbled upon scientific proof of the existence of a Supreme Being? Was it God who stepped in and so providentially crafted the cosmos for our benefit?"

British physicist Paul Davies was the 1995 winner of the Templeton Prize because of his work which is bridging the realms of science and religion. Dr. Davies was formerly an atheist but, because of recent discoveries, is now entertaining thoughts about a creator. In the Los Angeles Times (March 11, 1995), he states,

"It is impossible to be a scientist, even an atheistic scientist, and not be struck by the awesome beauty, harmony and ingenuity of nature. How can one accept a scheme of things so cleverly arranged, so subtle and felicitous, simply as a brute fact, as a package of properties that just happens to be?"

In his latest book *Cosmic Blueprint* (1988), he states,

"The laws of physics seem themselves to be the product of exceedingly ingenious design. The temptation to believe that the universe is the product of some sort of design, a manifestation of subtle aesthetic and mathematical judgment, is overwhelming. The belief that there is 'something behind it all' is one that I personally share with, I suspect, a majority of physicists."

Dr. Ross concludes,

"Speaking from the perspective of an astronomer, now that we have measured the limits, dimensions and parameters of the universe, we've discovered something amazing. If jiggled ever so slightly, life would not be possible in our solar system or anywhere else in the universe. The universe must be exactly the size, the mass that it is and the age that it is for life to be possible. Given the laws of physics that God has established, it must be exactly the mass, size, age and must be expanding at exactly the right rate. The delicacy of such balance has been described by a secular scientist—a non-Christian. He says its like 50,000 pencils standing on their points and not falling over. That's how delicately balanced are the parameters and design. Why all the billions of galaxies and trillions of stars? So we

could be here; It tells us something about the love of God
for us."

The Earth-Sun System

As with the ingenious design of the universe, the fantastically
delicate balance of the earth-sun system raises the obvious
question, *"Where does the weight of evidence lie*—in atheism, in
blind, accidental evolution or in creation?" In layman's language,
consider the following:

- If our earth were not situated two thirds out from
  the center of our galaxy, life would not be possible.
  If it were closer to the sun, everything would burn
  up—including us.   If further away, everything
  would freeze.

- If there were no ozone, the ultraviolet rays would
  destroy all life in minutes.

- If the earth's orbit around the sun were irregular,
  we would either freeze or burn —or both.

- If the orbit of the other planets were irregular, our
  planet would be pulled out of its orbit and we
  would either freeze or burn.

- If the earth didn't rotate on its axis, we wouldn't
  have seasons and life wouldn't be possible. The tilt
  of the orbit of 23 degrees is perfect. If it were
  more, seasons would be too extreme, if less there
  would be no seasons.

- If the rotation of the earth were too fast we would
  have winds perhaps a 1,000 miles an hour like on
  Jupiter. If too slow, the night temperature would
  freeze us.

- If the atmosphere surrounding the earth were not the perfect mixture of gases, we would all choke to death.

- If the mass and size of the earth were not perfect and did not provide the perfect gravitational force, we would all drift off or be crushed.

- The moon with its gravitational force keeps our atmosphere just right. It also keeps our 23 degree tilt perfect. Without these constants, life would be impossible. Also, if the moon were not the perfect size and distance away from the earth, the tides would inundate the continents and we wouldn't have to worry about it the second time around.

- If the atmosphere thinned out and didn't remain constant, many of the meteors that normally burn out in our atmosphere would bombard us and we would have to live underground.

- Even with our atmosphere, if we didn't have the massive planet Jupiter as our neighbor, with its huge gravitational force which sucks meteors, asteroids and comets into itself or out of orbit, we would be bombarded and life wouldn't be possible. If Jupiter were smaller, we would be bombarded; if bigger, we would be sucked out of our perfect orbit and life wouldn't be possible.

- If the ocean floor were any deeper, carbon dioxide and oxygen would be absorbed and no vegetable life could exist.

- Our sun must be the perfect mass; if bigger, the heat output would be unstable, if smaller, our planet would be pulled closer to the sun, making gravity stronger and the tidal forces too great, our days would slow down to months and we would either freeze or burn.

- If the age of our sun were too young or too old (not middle-aged—as it is) the luminosity of the sun (intensity of light) would not be consistent and all life would be destroyed.

- If our earth's crust were too thin, volcanic activities would be too great, polluting the atmosphere and life would not be possible.

The Anthropic Principle

Scientists have recently discovered the Anthropic Principle—the observation that the universe and the solar system reflect the exact characteristics necessary for life. Scientists are now cataloguing distinct characteristics of the universe that must be fine-tuned for any kind of life to be possible. So far, there are about 75 components of our galaxy and solar system that must be in careful balance to explain earth's capacity to support life. The chance of all these components coming together by random processes is one chance in trillions, thus demonstrating the absurdity of neo-Darwin atheistic materialism.

Dean C. Halverson (general Editor of the book, *The Compact Guide to World Religions* in his chapter on Secularism) states concerning the fine tuning necessity at the initial Big Bang,

"Scientists understand that the universe was tuned at its inception to a precision of greater than sixty decimal places, which is a precision equal to the number ten multiplied by itself more than 60 times. Unless the universe had been finely tuned, it would not have 'worked'. But all known natural processes are not tuned that finely, only to several decimal places. Only a First Cause with supreme intelligence could have produced such phenomenal accuracy."

Newsweek (July 20, 1998) in their feature article, Science Finds God, by Sharon Begley, provides another example of the Anthropic Principle:

"Physicists have stumbled on signs that the cosmos is custom-made for life and consciousness. It turns out that if the constants of nature—unchanging numbers like the strength of gravity, the charge of an electron and the mass of a proton—were the tiniest bit different, then atoms would not hold together, stars would not burn and life would never have made an appearance."

What about all these vast laws and forces at work? What about the purposes and rhythm of it all? How could you have the precise and immutable laws with no intelligence?

All of the above—the complexity, the harmony and beauty, the exquisite fine-tuning—demonstrate that the universe, the earth-sun system was designed for Man by a creative agent who must be personal because only a person has the capacity for purposeful design.

"The fool hath said in his heart there is no God"

Many people would say, "I believe in some kind of creative or active force, but I can't think of a God as a being or person like some celestial 'big brother' in the sky." No doubt, the perception of God as the bearded old man in the sky or someone driving a flying saucer is erroneous, but does He have a personality?

Dr. J. P. Moreland, in his book, *Scaling the Secular City*, gives evidence for the First Cause being personal. He states,

"Events have a definite beginning and end, and do not happen without something causing them. By contrast, God does not need a cause, since He is neither an event nor a contingent being. He is a necessary Being and such a being does not need a cause. In fact, it is a categorical fallacy to ask for a cause for God since this is really asking for a cause for an uncaused being.

"The principle that something does not come from nothing without a cause is a rational principle verified time and again in the course of daily life.... The cause for the beginning of the universe was personal. The first event arose spontaneously from an ontologically prior state of affairs which was timeless, spaceless and immutable. Physical causation has mutability and temporal sequence built into it. When the necessary and sufficient conditions for an effect are present, the effect occurs immediately. Only a personal agent could spontaneously act to generate a first event from a timeless, spaceless, immutable state of affairs."

We've already seen that purposeful design implies a personal God. Also, the fact that humans have personality implies a personal God. Francis Schaeffer in his book, *The God Who Is There*, gives a good illustration of this truth. He tells a story of two boys who hiked to the top of a mountain and discovered a beautiful lake. They were up about 12,000 feet and they wondered what the source of the lake was and where the water came from. One of the boys looked off the edge of the mountain and saw a river, and cried, "There's the source of the lake about a thousand feet down." His partner promptly straightened him out with a science lesson on the fact that water does not run uphill. The point of the story is, "How could an impersonal god, or a force, or even evolution create personality?" This is like saying that the source of a lake is lower than the lake itself, or that something inferior created something superior.

Dr. Henry M. Morris in his book, *The Bible and Modern Science,* states,

"How, then, can it be possible, even by an interminable process of evolution to produce intelligence, to produce feeling, emotion, will—in short, to produce personality (which is beyond doubt an effect observable in a universe and in our own self-consciousness), if the cause is not itself possessed of personality?"

If there is an all powerful personal God, is He moral? Is this a moral universe? The apostle Paul says (Romans one) that man knows within himself that there is a God and that man has a moral conscience within himself. Thus, going by the principle of cause and effect, even though it can't be measured scientifically, *this is a moral universe.*

We can safely say that all cultures and people have a standard of behavior and laws, or rules, of fair or decent behavior. No doubt, a person's conscience is greatly affected by his environment, but the *idea* of right and wrong is intrinsic to man's nature.

Francis Schaeffer, in his book, *The God Who is There*, supports the biblical position and illustrates it with another story about two boys all alone fishing in a river high in the mountains. They were casual friends who had just met. One boy falls into the river and is stranded in the middle on a rock. The boy on shore realizes that if he does not rescue him quickly, the boy will drown. There is no time to get help. He also realizes that there is a fifty-fifty chance he will drown, too, if he attempts a rescue. While contemplating what to do, he has two conflicting emotions. One is that he is afraid he will die (self-preservation)—the other, an equally strong emotion, is his conscience that tells him he *ought to do the right thing.* He should try to save the boy. This is the built-in knowledge of good and evil.

Dr. Henry M. Morris states,

"There is something in our own finite personalities that we call conscience or a moral urge. Whatever it is, each individual, however benighted, recognizes something in him that tells him he ought to do the thing that is right morally and ought to shun the wrong even though individual standards as to what constitutes right and wrong seem to vary somewhat with time and place. As far as personalities in the universe are concerned, at least it is a moral universe. Therefore, the Creator is a moral being, who has placed in his creatures a moral consciousness."

The Death of the "Old Scientism"

The dilemma of men, women, teenagers and children in our modern world today stems, not from modern science but from the "old scientism" of the past which says that man cannot know ultimate reality or the nature of being. The erosion of metaphysical faith started in the 19th century with evolution and scientific naturalism (Darwin, Freud, Nietzsche) which denied the supernatural or invisible reality. The old modernist school of theology of the late 19th or early 20th century adopted and developed this basic thesis of naturalism. Philosophers and theologians such as Kant, Hegal, Whitehead, Brunner, Sartre and Bultman, accepting the scientific world view of the day, developed modern existential thought which, in essence, surrendered ontological knowledge about God with the basic premise that reality cannot be grasped as a rational system. In other words, mankind does not and cannot have a cognitive knowledge of God.

Bultman reinterpreted the Bible (following the science of his day), taking out all the miraculous and was a forerunner of the modernist theology which relegated most of the Bible to being a myth. Carl F. H. Henry, former editor of *Christianity Today* in his book *Evangelicals at the Brink of Crisis* related that the old scientism of blind naturalism and the nebulous existential school of thought are now giving way to true science and the revival of absolute thought. Thus, not everyone is in despair because of the old scientism, evolution, existentialism or the modernist school of thought and many people are finding hope based upon sound logical reasoning, new scientific evidence and the Bible.

"I won't believe it unless I can see it!"

"No man has seen God at any time...."

"God is a spirit...."

John 1:18; 4:24

Dr. Bernard L. Ramm, in his book *Questions About the Spirit* states:

> "Whatever the great philosophers have said about spirit, the average man to the contrary feels that he is a sense-bound creature. What is real to him is what he touches, hears, tastes or bumps into.

> "But is it that simple? Consider the following experiment. A beam of light is passed through a prism and reflected on a white sheet of paper. We see the typical rainbow spectrum. If we put a thermometer to the right of either end of the spectrum where we see no colors, the temperature of the thermometer rises. That means that there are waves in the electromagnetic spectrum our eyes cannot see. Yet these invisible rays are as real as the visible ones. It would be wrong to say that the only rays that exist are the ones we can see. In fact, we know that the human eye sees only a small segment of the electromagnetic spectrum. Some of the most dangerous rays are invisible to the naked eye.

> "What about our ears? A dog hears a person or a car approaching before we humans do. Evidently he is picking up sound waves that humans cannot hear. How bats guide themselves has been a mystery for centuries. Now we know that bats emit high-frequency beeps that create echoes which they can hear and enable them to

navigate. But, the unaided human ear cannot hear these beeps. How premature it is to claim that the only sound waves that exist are those waves heard by the human ear!

"Gravity is an equally bewildering phenomenon. There have been many theories about how the sun influences the trajectories of the planets. We all live in this powerful gravitational field. We know how many millions of pounds of thrust it takes for a space ship to escape the earth's gravitational pull. Yet we cannot feel, taste nor smell this powerful gravitational field in which we all live.

"But, the story does not stop here. Sir Arthur Eddington used to talk about two tables: the first table was the table of ordinary perception, and the second was the table of modern physics. The first table was hard, solid and compact. The second was a fantastic ballet of atomic particles and was more than 99 percent pure space! How much more we have learned of that second table since the days of Eddington! We have learned that there are many kinds of these subatomic particles; that they move at incredible speeds; and that they pack enormous power. The enormous power of atomic bombs is the conversion of a fraction of their mass into pure energy. We are also overcome by the extremely small size of these particles. For example, in one gram of hydrogen there are 300,000,000,000,000,000,000,000 hydrogen molecules. Or to put it in reverse terms, one hydrogen molecule weighs 0.0000000000000000000000033 grams!

"What an odd claim it must now be that the only things that exist are what man can grasp directly with his senses! The truth is that the bulk of the materials and events of the universe in which we live are beyond our powers of immediate perception. Yet, the average man goes through the average day in his sense-bound way thinking that what he sees and hears is reality and that reality is what can be seen and heard! To him, this is the real world!"

Can Everything Be Measured Scientifically?

The examples given by Dr. Bernard L. Ramm demonstrate the many realities inaccessible to man's senses and, although we cannot feel, see or hear such phenomenon, nevertheless it exists. Scientists agree that there is much more ingenious "goings on" still inaccessible to mankind and, of course, this includes the very real possibility of the existence of God and the spirit world. Just because you can't see, hear or measure all the other dimensions, doesn't mean that they don't exist. To put it another way, scientists admit, because science is limited by the scientific method (naturalistic, materialistic world and universe), there are abstract concepts of reality inaccessible to science such as love, truth, beauty, ugliness, good and bad, right and wrong. God also is outside the domain of science—He can't be put in a test tube. But, we know He exists because of what we observe in the universe and nature as well as in our own personalities. Also, as we saw through the quotes of imminent scientists, as science discovers the many new mysteries of the universe and nature, many more scientists are beginning to believe in a master designer.

Internationally known author and lecturer, Dave Hunt, in his book, *A Cup of Trembling* (1995), quotes eminent scientists on the possibility of a non-materialist reality. He states,

> "Like many other top scientists today, [Robert] Jastrow, though an agnostic, repudiates scientific materialism and acknowledges that the universe may very well extend beyond matter into a nonphysical dimension of spirit beings. Nor is he alone in this conviction; Jastrow is joined by many of the world's most eminent scientists from every field."

Philosophy-of-science professor John Gliedman interviewed top scientists throughout Europe and America and reported his results in *Science Digest*:

"From Berkeley to Paris and from London to Princeton, prominent scientists from fields as diverse as neuro-physiology and quantum physics are... admitting they believe in the possibility, at least, of... the immortal human spirit and divine creation."

In agreement are such celebrated scientists as Nobel Laureate Eugene Wigner, known as "one of the greatest physicists of the century", Sir Karl Popper who has been called "the most famous philosopher of science of our age", and the late mathematician and quantum mechanics theorist John von Neumann, who has been described as perhaps "the smartest man who ever lived". Nobel Laureate Sir John Eccles has put it rather succinctly:

"But if there are bona fide mental events—events that are not themselves physical or material—then the whole program of philosophical materialism collapses. The universe is no longer composed of 'matter and a void' but now must make (spaceless) room for (massless) entities [i.e., nonphysical intelligence]."

In *Science and the Unseen World*, Sir Arthur Eddington, one of the greatest physicists of all time, wrote that to imagine that consciousness is ruled by the laws of physics and chemistry "... is as preposterous as the suggestion that a nation could be ruled by... the laws of grammar." Ken Wilbur reviewed the writings of the greatest physicists of this century and discovered that they virtually *all* believed in a non-physical dimension of reality. Based on their writings, he concluded, "There is no longer any major physical-theoretical objection to spiritual realities.... [T]his view ... in all likelihood marks final closure on that most nagging aspect of the age-old debate between the physical sciences and religion...."

In complete agreement, Arthur Koestler declared:

"The nineteenth-century clockwork model of the universe is in shambles and, since matter itself has been dematerialized, materialism can no longer claim to be a scientific philosophy."

Dr. Robert Jastrow, one of the world's leading astronomers (whom I just quoted), shocked his colleagues by admitting at a national conference of the Association for the Advancement of Science, that contrary to the article of faith in the scientific profession, evidence seems to demand an intelligent creator of the universe.

Is Life Only on Planet Earth?

During the Renaissance, the Roman Catholic Church persecuted Copernicus and Galileo for giving accurate concepts of the universe and our solar system (sun-centered, not earth-centered). The church demanded that they recant the position that says the earth is not the center of God's universe where He sent His only Son and also the implication that life might exist elsewhere in the universe. Then, with Immanuel Kant and the astronomy of the 18th and 19th centuries, the position of an insignificant earth and life elsewhere in the universe seemed to be confirmed.

Now, with the advances of modern science, everything is changing. The big shock is that life on planet earth is now considered by many scientists to be the equivalent of a miracle and that there's only a remote chance of life being anywhere else in the universe. Dr. Ross related that with the continuing new discoveries, parameters (conditions necessary for life) have been found to be so numerous and sensitive all over the universe and the earth/sun system, that life is probably only on planet earth. He relates that there is less than one chance in a trillion of finding even one planet having all the parameters necessary for sustaining life.

Conclusion—the whole universe seems to be designed by God for mankind. Further, is it possible that planet Earth is center stage in God's universe where the grace of God is being displayed? The Apostle Paul, in the New Testament, related that the created angels of God have their attention focused on the earth to learn about the grace of God.

What about a first cause? Science is based on causality. Evolutionary scientists who hold to an uncaused universe—that the universe came from nothing or that it has always been here —are violating the fundamental law of science for causality since these views require scientists to believe in events happening **without** a cause. For every effect, there must be an adequate cause! An adequate cause means a primal mover and a cause adequate to account for all the incredibly balanced design features.

Dr. Hugh Ross gives the theological impact of the great scientific discoveries of the past few years with which virtually all astronomers agree. He states,

> "*Fact:* The universe can be traced back to a single, ultimate origin of matter, energy, time and space (with the dimensions of length, width and height). *Theological significance*: The cause of the universe—i.e., the Entity who brought the universe into existence— existed and created from outside (independent) of the matter, energy and space-time dimensions of the universe.

> "*Fact:* The universe, our galaxy, and our solar system exhibit more than sixty characteristics that require fine-tuning for their very existence, and for the existence of life as we know it. *Theological significance*: The Entity who brought the universe into existence must be personal and intelligent for only such a Person could design and manufacture what we see; caring, for only care could explain the enormous investment of creative effort, the attention to intricate detail, and the comprehensive provision for needs."

Chapter 2

—The Evidence—

Science and Genesis

We have seen the incredible evidence of design in the universe and earth and thus the need of an ingenious designer. The next question that arises is, "If God has revealed himself through His creation, has He also revealed Himself to mankind in a written record?" More specifically, "Does the Genesis account of creation agree with the findings of science as we would expect it to if God is the author of both?"

Before looking at Genesis and the creation account, we'll briefly examine the nature of biblical reporting of scientific information. Remember, the Bible was written about two to three thousand years ago, communicating to people who lived in pre-scientific times. Consequently, the Bible doesn't use modern scientific, technical language.

Josh McDowell, in his book, *Reasons Skeptics Should Consider Christianity* (1981), gives some important introductory points concerning science and the Bible. He states,

"Where the Bible speaks on matters of science, it does so with simple yet correct terms devoid of absurdities.

Where non-biblical accounts of the formation of the universe and other scientific matters border on the ridiculous, the Scriptures nowhere are guilty of this. It is not what could be expected from a book written by men during pre-scientific times.

"Matters dealing with science also are written with restraint (such as the Genesis account of creation). The biblical narrative is accurate and concise in direct contrast to the crude Babylonian story which contends the earth was made from a dismembered part of one of the gods after in-fighting in heaven.

"Likewise, the flood of Noah's day is given in simple but accurate terms which are sensible scientifically. The clarity and restraint which the Bible shows toward the scientific is exactly what we should expect if this book were inspired by God."

Dr. Hugh Ross (astrophysicist and Ph.D. in astronomy from Toronto University) in a significant and interesting handout, *Biblical Forecast of Scientific Discoveries*, gives some examples of the simplicity and scientific accuracy of the Bible which we'll look at before we embark on the evolution/biblical creation controversy and the question of the agreement between science and Genesis. He states:

"Not only is the Bible filled with the fundamentals of science, but it is as much as 3,000 years ahead of its time. The Bible's statements in most cases directly contradicted the science of the day in which they were made. When modern scientific knowledge approaches reality, the divine accuracy of the scriptures is substantiated. For example:

Biblical Statement	Science Then	Science Now
*Earth is a sphere. (Isaiah 40:22)	Earth is a flat disk.	Earth is a sphere.
*Number of stars exceeds a billion. (Jeremiah 33:22)	Number of stars totals 1,100.	Number of stars exceeds a billion.
*Every star is different. (I Corinthians 15:41)	All stars are the same.	Every star is different.
*Light is in motion. (Job 38:19-20)	Light is fixed in place.	Light is in motion.
*Air has weight. (Job 28:25)	Air is weightless.	Air has weight.
*Blood is a source of life and healing. (Leviticus 17:11)	Sick people must be bled.	Blood is a source of life and healing.
*Winds blow in cyclones. (Ecclesiastes 1:6)	Winds blow straight.	Winds blow in cyclones.

Below is a partial list of other fundamentals of science explained in the Bible:

- Conservation of mass and energy (Ecclesiastes 1:9; Ecclesiastes 3:14-15)

- Water cycle (Ecclesiastes 1:7; Isaiah 55:10)

- Gravity (Job 26:7; Job 38:31-33)

- Pleides and Orion as gravitationally bound star groups (Job 38:31) (NOTE: All other star groups visible to the naked eye are unbound with the possible exception of the Hyades.)

- Effects of emotion on physical health (Proverbs 16:24; Proverbs 17:22)

- Control of contagious diseases (Leviticus; Numbers 19; Deuteronomy 23:12-13)

- Importance of sanitation to health (Leviticus; Numbers 19; Deuteronomy 23:12-13)

- Control of cancer and heart disease (Lev. 7-19)

"In the crucible of scientific investigation, the Bible has proven invariably to be correct. No other book, ancient or modern, can make this claim; but then, no other book has been written (through men) by God."

Dr. Ross, as an astronomer and astrophysicist, is well qualified as an expert in this area, not only in reporting his own findings but the findings of other eminent astronomers. In reporting the very latest scientific findings concerning cosmology, he is resurrecting among creationists the "Day Age" and Big Bang theories, not for Evolution as defined in this book or for Theistic Evolution, but for Special Creation.

The importance of the question of a recent or an old creation concerning education in our public schools is monumental. I believe many scientists and science teachers as well as other educators know of the many "holes" in the theory of evolution, molecule-to-man, but could never accept a creationist's position of a universe only six to fifteen thousand years old, or even fifty thousand years old. All of science testifies against this thesis. This point of contention is probably the greatest obstacle against creation science being considered in science classes. Scientists and science teachers many times reject the entire creationist package because of this insistence on a creation of six literal 24-hour days. However, there is perfect agreement between a universe of billions of years and the Bible's depiction without violating the normal, literal interpretation of the Bible.

"In the beginning God created the heavens and the earth."

Scholars readily admit that the Genesis account of the origin of the universe and earth and man is majestic, logical and can be fitted into the findings of science. Genesis is unique over all other religious books in that Genesis (as well as the rest of the Bible) speaks of one all-powerful, personal God who is transcendent to His creation and who created all things by divine fiat, out of nothing. *The Bible is also unique in that it is the only book in the world that tells where everything came from.* All other religious accounts start with matter and energy already here, then many gods emerging out of some kind of watery chaos. Genesis 1:1 states that the God of the Bible created matter, energy, length, width, height and time in the first verse.

Time Had a Beginning

The Bible is unique in that it is a multidimensional book and the only holy book that tells us that time is finite—it had a beginning. This was considered to be unscientific prior to 1970, but the Bible says,

"This grace was given us before the beginning of time (II Timothy 1:9).

" ... which God who does not lie promised before the beginning of time" (Titus 2:1).

In one time/space dimension, you must have a beginning, but not with more dimensions. God, who is infinite, and works outside His creation, works in at least eleven dimensions since scientists tell us that at the point of the Big Bang, there had to be at least ten dimensions in operation. Two examples of extra-dimensionality would be:

- If we had one dimension more than the four that we have (height, width, length and time), we could remove the inside of an orange out without distrubing the peeling.

- Jesus, after His resurrection,　appeared to His disciples who were behind locked doors without benefit of a key or anyone opening the door.

John 1:1 and Colossians 1:16,17 tell us that Jesus (like God) was before all things and, as God, He created all things. Genesis 1:1 and 1:26 show us that the Trinity (Father, Son and Holy Ghost— three persons and also one being; in essence, a multi-dimensional being) created all things. The Bible is the only multi-dimensional book in existence. All other holy books relate only to our four dimensional world, thus demonstrating that they are of human origin. They also contain scientific and historical contra-dictions and absurdities. They are not supernatural as is the Bible.

Genesis is remarkable in that it was written about 1,500 B.C. in an age of cosmological ignorance and superstition. Much of the science of the time was erroneous and there were many "wild superstitions and even grotesque accounts" concerning the origin of the universe, earth and man. The following are some examples:

Greek Cosmology

Zeus implanted his seed in the goddess Seneclae without meeting her. Seneclae felt she should meet her son's father and so went to Zeus after he was born. Zeus then put the boy on Earth saying he would be the god who would rule the Earth. But the Titans who were on the Earth ate him. Zeus rescued the heart of the boy and swallowed it. Zeus had a girl named Dionysus. Zeus then turned the Titans into dust, and that's where humans came from.   The Earth was carried by elephants standing on turtles. When they shook, earthquakes occurred.

The Chinese, Egyptians and Mesopotamians

The Chinese believed the earth was square with China in the middle. The sun and moon were gods.

The Egyptians believed the earth was a rectangular foundation of the universe. A goddess rested her hands and feet on the four corners of the earth which permitted the sun and moon deities to glide daily over her back, legs and arms.

The Mesopotamians believed the earth was a floating vessel on the waters of the deluge. The heavenly lights were thought to be eternal deities, creators of the universe.

Babylonian Creation Myth

The earliest written account, according to scholars (about 2,600 B.C.), is the "Enuma Elish" Babylonian cosmological myth. According to this myth, the original state of the universe was one of watery chaos. The watery chaos consisted of sweet water, sea water and cloudy mists. All three types of water were mingled in a large undefined mass. (The myth doesn't tell where the watery chaos or mass came from). Then out of the watery chaos, two gods come into existence—Lahau and Lehemu. Other gods also came out of the chaos and began fighting and killing one another— among other activities. The god Marduk, whom Hammurabi (King of Babylon) believed was the one true god and himself Marduk's spokesman, eventually gained control and proceeded to create heavens, earth and man. Man was believed created from the blood of one of the slain gods.

Some scholars of the past actually believe that this unscientific, illogical, grotesque myth (because it was written before the Bible) was the one from which Moses got his ideas for Genesis one and two. This story of origins makes no more sense than the Greek belief about the earth which was written after Moses. Pagan stories of origins are all ludicrous as well as evolutionary in that out of an eternal, watery mass emerge the gods. They are also always polytheistic stories. Genesis, on the other hand, is an entirely unique telling of one all-powerful, personal God who is outside His creation and who created all things from nothing.

The purpose of the book of Genesis was not to give an elaborate scientific exposition of the origin of things. It's main purpose and scope concerns God's dealing with man—man's fall and God's message of redemption to fallen man. This is also the main message of the entire Bible—God's message to fallen man. The Old Testament told man what he needed to know for salvation and a relationship with God from the fall to the coming of Christ. The New Testament was the completion of God's redemptive message to man. The origin of things is taken up only in the first two chapters of Genesis and the remainder of Genesis (the main bulk of it) has to do with God's dealing with Abraham, the founder of the chosen people through whom the Savior would come. In this respect, Genesis is foundational to the whole Bible without which the rest of the Bible would make little sense. We would not know about the origin of all things or about the dilemma of mankind because of the Fall, and his need for redemption.

The Bible doesn't address such issues as the origin of the dinosaurs and the so-called hominids. It doesn't even mention such animals as giraffes, insects or amphibians. It only provides a highly abbreviated summary of God's creation and puts emphasis on the coming of mankind.

The first two chapters are the introduction to the Bible and their purpose is to declare that God Almighty created all things and that the original creation was perfect, complete and good, being an expression of God himself. It also follows that mankind, having received the gift of life, should be grateful and responsive to God. The account provides true knowledge of the origin of things, but it is not exhaustive knowledge; God simply didn't tell mankind everything about origins but instead, He disclosed all that man needs to know. It is good to keep in mind that the Bible is not a science book, but a historical and spiritual book. For example, the Bible touches on angels but it is not a book about angels. Genesis likewise is also spiritual in nature and not intended to be a complete scientific explanation of origins.

The Growing Controversy Among Creationists

From the beginning of the church age, some of the church fathers believed in long creation days—Origin, Justin Martyr, Augustine and later, St. Thomas Aquinas. But, in the United States, prior to the Scopes Monkey Trial in 1925, most Protestants believed in a recent creation, interpreting the days of Genesis, chapter one, as literal 24-hour days.

In the Scopes trial, Darrow (an evolutionist) humiliated Bryan (a creationist). The rout began when Darrow trapped Bryan on the length of the creation days and the age of the universe. From this time on, most creationists more or less "hid their heads in the sand" as evolution slowly took over public education. However, in the 1940's and 50's, many scientists and theologians, coming to grips with geology and astronomy evidence for an old earth, developed the Progressive (day age) Creationist position. The book, *Modern Science and Christian Faith* (1950) gave numerous evidences for an old creation. They cited the Grand Canyon and Specimen

Ridge in Yellowstone Park where in the face of a two thousand foot cliff cut by a river, there are a dozen successive layers of petrified trees—many fully grown. This indicates a long history for the earth. They also cited evidence from coal beds that were composed of carbon remains of pre-historic plants. The successive coal beds with intervening strata of various rock layers, suggested a tremendous time interval for the growth and carbonization of these forests and plants.

Then in the 1960's with a revival of Darwinism, new pioneers of creation such as Henry M. Morris, Duane T. Gish and Ken Ham began to turn the tide for Special Creation through their books, publications and debates at the major universities of America. In most cases, the evolutionists were defeated in the debates as new scientific evidence was presented for Special Creation. They spoke of ingenious design in the universe and nature, and the lack of transitional forms in the geological strata. Most evangelicals in the 1970's and 80's were strengthened in their belief in divine creation and also came to believe in a recent creation due to the impact of Henry W. Morris' book, The Genesis Flood, which relegated much of the geological strata to being a result of a recent global flood. But then came the defeat of the creationists with the Supreme Court ruling (1987) over the age of the universe.

Also, in the last ten to fifteen years, new scientific evidence began to mount for a beginning for the universe with a "Big Bang". With Cobe and Hubble satellites, more evidence for an old universe and ingenious design in the universe appeared. For the first time, many scientists began to doubt evolution and began considering the existence of God. Also, many "young earthers" became convinced of the possibility of the Big Bang and an old universe. This has generated a new group of Christians who believe in an old universe and earth while still holding to God's Special Creation and it leads us to these observations which I paraphrase from Dr. Hugh Ross:

- More than 99% of American scientists view the idea of a universe of 10,000 years as farfetched and unacceptable.

- Christians who hold to a recent creation date put off a large segment of secular society from accepting the Christian faith. They reason, "The Bible must be flawed if it states that the universe and earth are only a few thousand years old." Secular scientist considering the implausability of a recent creation, reject the Bible without seriously investigating.

- The universe and earth are available for research. There is abundant and consistent evidence from astronomy, physics, geology and paleontology that testify to an old earth. This evidence must be taken seriously.

- God's revelation is not limited exclusively to the Bible. The facts of nature may be likened to a sixty-seventh book of the Bible. Numerous Bible passages state that God reveals Himself faithfully through the voice of nature—Job 10:8-14, 12:7, 34:14-15, 35:10-12, 37:5-7, chapters 38-41; Psalm 8, 19:1-6, 50:6, 85:11, 97:6, 98:2-3, 104, 139; Proverbs 8:22-31; Ecclesiastes 3:11; Habakkuk 3:3; Acts 14:17, 17:23-31; Romans 1:18-25, 2:14-15, 10:16-18, Colossians 1:23.

- Because of the mounting evidence coming from the Hubble and Cobe satellites (as well as other evidences coming from physics and astronomy) for a vast and old universe, there has been a resurgence of the "appearance" of age and vastness of the universe argument (current scientific observations are only an *illusion* of age) among "young earthers". This runs counter to the scriptures.

"The heavens declare the glory of God and the skies proclaim the work of His hands" (Psalm 19:1-4).

- Hundreds of reliable scientific tools demonstrate that the creation (all but modern man) is old.

The following is taken from "Biblical Evidence for Long Creation Days" by Dr. Hugh Ross:

"In just the last several years the age of the universe itself, and hence a date for the events of Genesis 1:1, has been open to direct astronomical measurement. At least eight methods now exist for determining the date of the creation of the universe. The results of the application of these methods follow and reveal a level of consistency that permits the secure conclusion that the universe is roughly 20 billion years old. A description of the security of this conclusion comes from the California Institute of Technology's physicist and Nobel Laureate Murray Gell-Mann. In testifying before the Supreme Court, he said that it would be easier to believe that the world is flat, not round, than to believe the universe to be only 6,000 years old, not 20 billion."

Measuring Method	Age (billions of years)
general relativity	20 plus or minus 10
expansion of the universe	19.2 plus or minus 5.2
color-luminosity fitting	20 plus or minus 3
nucleochronology	20.4 plus or minus 3.4
microwave background radiation	20 plus or minus 5
mass density of the universe	20 plus or minus 10
light element abundances	21 plus or minus 4
anthropic principles	20 plus or minus 6
	mean age = 20 billion years + or - 3

- Acceptance of a young earth requires that we abandon essentially all of modern astronomy, much of modern physics and most of the earth sciences.

- In perhaps the most amazing scientific breakthrough of the century, we have gained the capacity to measure the size and age of the cosmos. Science has given our generation what no other generation has been able to see—a portrait depicting the physical event. The Creation Miracle recorded in Genesis 1:1 has been drawn in detail by the Cobe and Hubble satellites, as well as by telescopes in observatories.

- Considering the fossil record, the sequence of creation events in Genesis harmonizes with the record of astronomy, paleontology, geology and biology.

- In the 1987 Supreme Court ruling, the evolutionists defeated the young earth creationists. The creationists only presented evidences for a recent creation and never got into the main evidences against organic evolution (see Appendix A).

"How Long is a Day in the Bible?"

The word "day" in the original Hebrew is *yom*. It can be translated as a 24-hour day or as a period of time. As already related, Progressive Creationists (day-age theorists) interpret the days of Genesis as periods of time, not literal 24 hours as 24-hour Creationists do, "young earthers" as they are called. Progressive Creationists believe that the strata in the Earth's crust generally correspond to the days of Genesis chapter one and represent millions or billions of years. This position agrees with the latest discoveries in astronomy and physics as we have already seen and allows for the long geological ages—billions of years, not thousands, which corresponds with the latest scientific evidence.

To take the position that the earth is young requires a person to believe that all the scientific radiometric dating must be wrong, that the abundant and consistent evidence from astronomy, physics, geology and paleontology must be wrong, and that the 99% of all scientists who believe in an old universe must be wrong.

The geological strata in the earth's crust demonstrates explosions of fully-developed species with no known ancestors and then long ages with the extinction of animals, and then explosions of new species with more extinctions and so on. This agrees perfectly with the day-age theory of Special Creation and also with long geological ages, but does not support Evolution Theory.

The day-age theory also allows for the creation of the sun and the moon on the first day (light), not the fourth day as demanded by the position of "young earthers". Creationists who insist on a 24-hour day have trouble explaining the length of a day prior to the creation of the sun and the moon on the fourth day. How long were the first three days without the sun and what does it mean that the evening and morning ended each day? This interpretation makes the Bible contradict itself—what was causing the evening and the morning without the sun?

Also, if you interpret Genesis in the 24-hour-per-creation-day view, with each of the seven days being 24-hour days, you would have the origin of the universe about the same as the late Bishop Usher's calculations of about 4-5,000 B.C. which is not supported by the evidence. Special Creationists biblically push back the time of creation to about 15,000 B.C. stating that only the important genealogies of families stemming from the creation and Adam and Eve are recorded in Genesis which is probably true. But even this age doesn't make sense with our present-day knowledge of the universe. A universe with billions of suns and planets and "seemingly endless" space smacks of billions of years not thousands and, by the way, as the late Bible expositor and teacher, Dr. J. Vernon Mc Gee questioned, "What was God doing before 15,000 B.C. during all those billions of years?"

Throughout the Bible, *yom* is used many different ways. The Bible speaks of the "day (*yom*) of our Lord" as we today say "in Washington's day" or "in the day of Jefferson". This, of course, doesn't refer to a single 24-hour day but to the general time period when Washington or Jefferson lived. The Bible also says, "A day with the Lord is as a thousand years." The context shows this doesn't mean a literal thousand years but a long indefinite period of time. It also states **"as"** a thousand years, not **is** a thousand years, thus, unless the context demands otherwise, these days can be interpreted as thousands, millions or even billions of years. A billion year day for God who is of another, greater dimension than man makes more sense than our literal 24-hour day.

In his book, Truth in Religion, Dr. Mortimer J. Adler quotes St. Augustine's interpretation of Genesis one—an excellent definition of Progressive Creationism:

"According to Augustine's understanding of God as a purely spiritual being having eternal (i.e., nontemporal and immutable) existence, Genesis 1 cannot be interpreted as a succession of creative acts performed by God in six temporal days. In Augustine's view, the creation of all things was instantaneously complete. God created all things at once *in their causes*. The *actualization* of the *potentialities* invested in those *original causes* is a natural development in the whole span of time.

"The order of 'six days' is not a temporal order but an order of the graduations of being, from lower to higher. In thus interpreting Genesis 1 in light of twentieth-century knowledge, Augustine would be following his own two rules for (1) holding on to the truth of Sacred Scripture without wavering, but also (2) holding on to an interpretation of it only if that accords with everything else we now know."

Human beings are an excellent analogy of St. Augustine's interpretation of Genesis 1. At the moment of conception, human beings are created instantaneously complete. They are created all at once in their causes and the actualization and potentialities invested in the original causes is a natural development in the whole span of life. Beginning with conception, there is a graduation of being from undeveloped to maturity—from fetus to child to adult. This is what we see in the Creation Days of Genesis chapter one—the earth going from being "void" to completion.

Divine, Not Human Creation Days

"For a thousand years in your sight are like a day that has just gone by ... " (Psalm 90:4).

Considering the Bible as a whole, there are many scriptures and indicators that a literal reading of Genesis would seem to demand an ancient, rather than a recent creation day.

From the outset, the syntax of the specific creation days is a departure from the simple and ordinary, suggesting indefinite time periods. An incorrect rendering of the old King James Version of the Bible reads, "And the evening and the morning were the first day." A correct reading from the original Hebrew reads, "And there was evening and there was morning—one day" (NIV).

Another observation from this Hebrew reading is that the first day started in darkness and the subsequent days began with the fading of light from the day before as if signaling a kind of completion. For example, on the third day with a correct rendering of Genesis 1:13, a natural literal interpretation would lend itself to a long creation day. On that day, the land comes out of the sea (dry land appears and time is needed for the earth to cleanse itself of salt in preparation for the growth of vegetation). Then, vegetation appears, fruit plants and trees, and they bear fruit.

"And God saw that it was good, and there was evening and there was morning—the third day" (Genesis 1:9-13).

The following scriptures, when taken in context, suggest an indefinite period of time:

"After two days, He will revive us, on the third day, He will restore us ..." (Hosea 6:2).

Bible commentaries have always affirmed that Hosea 6:2 refers to a year, years, a thousand years, etc.

"The Lord will be exalted in that day ..." (Isaiah 2:11-12).

"As the heavens are higher than the earth, so are my ways higher than your ways and my thoughts than your thoughts" (Isaiah 55:9).

As God's ways are different than ours, perhaps His day, also, is different from ours. Dr. Hugh Ross in his book, "Creation and Time" (see Appendix B), says,

"God's 'work week' gives us a human-like picture we can grasp. This communication tool is common in the Bible. Scripture frequently speaks of God's hand, His eyes, His arm, even His wings. The context of each of these passages makes it obvious that none of these descriptions is meant to be taken concretely. Rather, each word presents a picture to help us understand spiritual reality about God and His relationship to us.... what I am suggesting here is ... a recognition of anthropomorphic usage that is clearly commonly used elsewhere in scripture to describe God and His relationship to His creation and His creatures. We need to recognize that the analog of our Sabbath to God's Sabbath does not demand seven 24-hour days. Age-long creation days fit the analogy just as well, if not better."

The late philosopher-theologian, Dr. Francis Shaeffer, in his book *Genesis in Space and Time* states:

"Before we move on there is a point we need to consider. This is the concept of day as related to creation, the answer must be held with some openness. In Genesis 5:2 we read: 'Male and Female, created He them; and blessed them, and called their name Adam, in the day when they were created.' As it is clear that Adam and Eve were not created simultaneously, 'day' in Genesis 5:2 does not mean a period of twenty-four hours. In other places in the Old Testament, the Hebrew word 'day' refers to an era, just as it often does in English. See, for example, Isaiah 2:11, 12, and 17 for such a usage."

We should note that the seventh day in Genesis is not closed as with the other six days. There is no verse saying, "The evening and the morning were the seventh day." Hebrews 4 and Psalm 95 relate that God's day of rest continues. Taking it to the present, that represents several thousand years. Given the parallels to the Creation account, the first six days were also very long periods of time. Jesus said, "I am the bread of life," "I am the door," etc. We know He didn't mean a wooden door with hinges or a loaf of bread; likewise Genesis also has spiritual applications. The Sabbath rest for the Jews is twenty-four hours, but in reality, the Sabbath rest is now thousands of years old.

The events of the sixth day cover more than 24 hours. Adam named all the animals and was told to have dominion over them (responsibility for managing all the plants, animals and resources). Could Adam have named hundreds of species of animals, including all the birds, as the Bible says, all in one day? On the sixth day, Eve was created after Adam. Upon seeing all the animals and exploring, he realized there was no partner for him in the garden. Common sense alone renders the sixth day as a long period of time.

Genesis 2:4 suggests a long time span, "These are the *'generations'* of the heavens and the earth when they were created in the 'day' of their making." Generations in the plural in Hebrew means multiple generations.

The abundant and consistent evidence from astronomy, physics, geology and paleontology testify to a universe, earth and life of long geological ages. Is God purposely fooling scientists with the appearance of age in all areas of science? Of course not, the Bible puts credence to the roots of nature. Both Old and New Testaments exhort the human race to test everything. All other religions ignore objective facts and say trust your feelings. The Mormons for example, say read the books of Mormon and look for the "burning of the bosom" to see if it is God's truth or not. The Bible, in every area of knowledge (social, historic, prophetic), exhorts, "Believe only that which passes the test."

We've already seen that all the latest scientific evidence points unmistakably to an ingenious designer, further confirming God's existence to the human race. We've also seen, through God's creation that He doesn't remove, hide or distort physical evidence. If this is axiomatic truth, then why would God deceive mankind with the appearance of age? Why would God deceive man in this one area? For example, are the rings on trees false records of a non-existent past? Did God make trees with annual rings for years that never existed? Is the age of stars an illusion? Is the size of the universe an illusion? Are the beams of light coming from planets billions of light years away an illusion? How did the beams of light reach us? We've watched star explosions that occurred billions of years ago, but if the universe wasn't created thousands of years ago, are we seeing light from stars that never existed?

A creation date of 10,000 years ago implies that much of the universe is an illusion, giving an "appearance of age". Scientists believe the universe is real and not an illusion. Thus, they could never accept a young universe creation. Also, fooling man with the appearance of age is contrary to God's nature. Throughout the Bible numerous scriptures encourage man to seek God's face through the "voice of nature" as well as through the Bible. Dr. Ross states, "For God to lie would violate His holiness."

Suffice it to say, when *yom* (day) is translated as a period of time instead of a literal 24-hour day, which it legitimately can be, all problems disappear. We'll see that there is remarkable agreement between science and the Bible as we progress through Genesis chapter one one day at a time.

Day I

> "In the beginning God created the heaven and the earth, the earth was without form and void and the darkness was on the face of the deep. ...Then God said, 'let there be light.' ...and God called the light day and the darkness He called night. And there was evening and there was morning, one day."

Dark, Diffuse Nebulae

The Bible states that the earth in its initial stage was in an unfinished chaotic condition and in darkness. This agrees with the theory held by scientists as to the origin of our solar system, called the dark, diffuse Nebulae theory. The basic tenants of the theory is that our solar system came from a cloud of primordial gases and matter. Because of gravitational pull, the cloud began to whirl, formed into a disc and the center of the disc (the nucleus) began to form into the sun as the outer pieces of matter began to form the satellites of the sun (planets). In time, the nucleus began to radiate as a star, but the first stage was still darkness. Scientists today believe that the first stage of our solar system was darkness and many state that Genesis 1:1 is a perfect description of the original state of our planet. Then God said, "Let there be light."

Day II

> "Then God said, 'Let there be an expanse in the midst of the waters, and let it separate the waters from the waters.' And God made the expanse, and separated the waters which were below the expanse from the waters which were above the expanse, and it was so. God called the expanse, sky. And there was evening and there was morning—the second day."

Scientists tell us that the earth in its initial stage was in a molten condition and all oceans were in the atmosphere; possibly, the massive cloud came down to the surface of the earth. Condensation took place but the water boiled, turned into steam, and went back into the cloud. Then, after millions of years (possibly) of cooling of the earth's surface and condensation, oceans began to form on the earth. In time then, a space (or expanse) would develop to separate the waters on the earth from the waters above the earth. In this stage of the earth's development, the earth was probably still in a state of darkness and not ready for life.

Day III

> "God said, 'Let the waters under heaven be gathered into one place, so that dry land may appear,' and it was so. God called the dry land earth, and the gathering of the waters, seas; and God saw that it was good. Then God said, 'Let the earth produce fresh growth, let there be on the earth plants bearing seed according to its kind.' And there was evening and there was morning—the third day."

The appearance of dry land again follows the proper sequence. Scientists say this was the time of the forming of continental shields and their graduation from the water. The earth cooled and shrank like a dried apple which forced the land out of the sea. Earthquakes and volcanoes characterized this period. This was also the time of the forming of mountain ranges. Next, plant life appeared on earth which again coincides with the findings of science. The geological strata in the earth's surface where life appears, algae and other plant forms are present.

Day IV

"Then God said, 'Let there be lights in the expanse of the heavens to separate the day from the night, and let them be for signs and for seasons, and for days and years; and let them be for lights in the expanse of the heavens to give light on the earth.' And it was so. ...And God made the two great lights. And there was evening and there was morning—the fourth day."

The Hebrew word for "create" in Genesis 1:1 is *bara* which means to create something entirely new out of nothing. This is the strongest word for create in the Hebrew language. The Hebrew word "made" used in the above portion (verse 16) referring to the luminaries or light is *asah* which can be interpreted "to fabricate or manufacture from something already there." It could also mean "made to function" or "made to appear", but this is not the word we find in Genesis 1:1. The Hebrew word *bara* is only used two more times—for the creation of mammals and finally for man.

Other verbs are used in describing God's creation event; for example, the divine imperative, "Let there be ...." Like *asah*, it can be interpreted "made to function", "made to appear" or "bringing forth", etc. Genesis one has examples of this usage:

"Let there be light" (verse 3),

"Let there be an expanse" (sky) (verse 6),

"Let the water under the sky be gathered and let the dry land appear ..." (verse 9),

"Let the land produce vegetation ... (verse 11).

Some translators in the past have translated them all as *bara*—creating something out of nothing, which would make the Genesis account contradict itself. The emphasis of chapter one is clearly on God's progressive ordering of a formless, empty world to its completion.

Evidently, the Bible is teaching that the entire universe (including the sun and moon) was created all at once, in a primordial state. Then on the fourth day, by continuous condensation, the cloud cover breaks or thins, and light becomes visible—now to be used "for signs and for seasons and for days and years".

We already saw the biblical dilemma of the special 24-hour creationist having the sun and moon created on the fourth day. How long were the three days before the sun was created ... and how could you have an evening and a morning without a sun, as stated on the first day ..., and what was causing day and night as stated in Genesis 1:2?

The faith of many college students is challenged by science professors who draw attention to the apparent contradiction that Genesis speaks of "morning and evening" (beginning with the first day) before the sun and moon are created on the fourth day. Coupled with materialism and evolution as taught in other departments of our colleges, the student's faith can be shaken or shattered completely. Many have spent years in doubt and unbelief before returning to the faith of their childhood, if they ever do return. This happened to me, but eventually I discovered the day-age theory and searched through apologetic materials which strengthened my faith once again.

Adhering to a 24-hour day creation theory produces another scientific dilemma concerning the plants being created before the sun. All the plants created on the third day would be destroyed because they would have frozen without the sun. Without the sun, the temperature would have been something like 360 degrees below zero. Everything would have been destroyed in a matter of minutes. Also, what was holding the earth in its orbit without the sun and moon? A literal 24-hour interpretation leads to contradictory, absurd, biblical and scientific conclusions.

Any open-minded, scholarly skeptic or scientist or even just plain "modern man" with a scientific frame of reference, just starting out to read the Bible, and wondering if the Bible could be the word of God, would immediately see the contradictions and conclude that the Genesis account of Creation was just another myth—the best myth, but nonetheless myth. They might even throw the entire Bible out, concluding that it is simply of human origin. Suffice it to say, with the day-age position, there are no problems as everything fits perfectly.

Science agrees with the book of Genesis that the earth proceeds from null and void to completion. Scientists believe that the earth in its beginnings was like a gigantic, tropical hothouse with an even temperature around the earth, because the cloud envelope completely surrounded the earth. They, for example, have found vegetation, wooly mammoths and dinosaurs near the North Pole. The luminaries were not seen or functioning on the earth until the fourth day when the cloud envelope thins to the extent of creating one temperature around the earth. In time, different temperature zones develop. Also, light and darkness— night and day—are a reality on earth, as the Bible says, "... to divide the day from the night and for signs, seasons, days and years." Possibly it took millions of years of condensation before the sun and moon appeared.

Day V

"God said, 'Let the waters teem with countless living creatures and let birds fly above the earth, across the expanse of heaven.' God then created the great sea monsters and all living creatures that move and swarm in the waters, according to their kind, and every kind of bird. And there was evening and there was morning—the fifth day."

Evidently, this is the age of the reptiles and the dinosaurs. Scientists tell us that in the Paleozoic era invertebrate life of all kinds—fish, amphibians, insects and reptiles appeared on the earth. The great dinosaurs that roamed the earth appear at the end of this period about 125 million years ago.

Day VI

"Then God said, 'Let the earth bring forth living creatures after their kind; cattle and creeping things and beasts of the earth after their kind,' and it was so. And God made the beasts of the earth after their kind; and everything that creeps on the ground after its kind; and God saw that it was good. *Then God said, 'Let us make man in our image, according to our likeness.'* And there was evening and there was morning—the sixth day."

The sixth day when mammals and man were created agrees with what science calls the Cenozoic era, the highest level of strata. The Hebrew word *bara* (to create out of nothing— Genesis 1:1) is again used. Mammals are created and last, humans are uniquely created—Adam and Eve.

The uniqueness of man is emphasized in the verse, "Let us make man in our image and according to our likeness." Man is the apex of God's creative acts. He is like God and thus is great. He is like God as he is an autonomous and free being, not a robot and he is above the animal world which is governed and controlled by instinct. Also, built into man (and not present in animals) is a disposition and a capacity to worship the Creator. In this initial stage, man, like God and the universe that He created, was good.

In the past, Christians were embarrassed by the apparent contradictions between the Genesis account of creation and science; but they don't have to be today. As science continues to unravel the mysteries of the universe, new light is constantly being shed on the scriptures, and God's word increasingly becomes vindicated; for example, scientists originally thought (about 50 years ago) that in the first stage of our solar system there was light. Today all agree that the initial stage was darkness, as related in Genesis.

The question arises as to how Moses could have broken from the irrational cosmology of his day. Remember, Moses as a prince of Egypt, was well educated in the bizarre, polytheistic cosmological myths of Egypt. How could he have known these things—the earth in its original state of darkness and in an unfinished chaotic condition, or about the development of the expanse between the waters, and then the earth's continents emerging out of the sea? Also, how did he know the proper sequence in the development of the universe, earth and man—inorganic matter, organic (plant life), conscious life (fish, reptiles, mammal, and man)? The answer the Bible gives is, "Holy men of God spoke as they were moved by the Holy Ghost." In other words, the creation story was not invented or developed by Moses but *revealed* to him; and the opening declaration (contrary to evolution) is, "In the beginning, God created the Heavens and the earth."

Dr. Ross, in his book *The Fingerprint of God*, gives some further significant insights concerning Genesis: He first relates that the scientific method was discovered in the Bible—probably during the Renaissance. Genesis chapter one remarkably gives the scientific method. First, a statement of the point of view or frame of reference, next the initial conditions, then a chronological account of the physical events and finally the conclusion of the matter—in a nutshell, the scientific method.

- The Origin of the Universe

"The Bible opens with this declaration: In the beginning God created the heavens and the earth. The Hebrew words for heavens and earth are *shamayin* and *erets*. Whenever these two words are joined together in Hebrew literature they refer to the entire physical universe. The Hebrew word for 'created', *bara*, refers always to divine activity. The word emphasizes the newness of the created object. It means to bring something entirely new, something previously nonexistent. Genesis 1:1 speaks of God's creating—originating—the fundamental constituents (all the space, time, matter, energy, galaxies, stars, planets, etc.) of the universe."

- Specific Point of View

"...the second verse of Genesis 1 places the point of view under the cloud cover, on the surface of the waters. It says, 'The Spirit of God was hovering over the surface of the waters.' The miracles described in the account take place in or under the earth's atmosphere, not in the broader scope of outer space."

- Initial Conditions

"Genesis 1:2 also states for us three initial conditions of planet earth:

It was dark upon the surface of the ocean;

The earth was formless, or disorganized;

The earth was void or empty.

"Since Genesis 1 focuses on the introduction of life upon the earth, formless and void (or disorganized and empty) are best interpreted in the context of life. That is, the Bible says that in its initial state, the earth was unfit to support life and was literally empty of life. We are told, too, that the earth's atmosphere (and/or interplanetary debris) blocked out the light that exists throughout the universe. Light could not pass through to the surface.

"The physics of star and planet formation verifies that the proto-earth indeed must have had an atmosphere (or debris cloud) opaque to light. Such studies also confirm the condition of the proto-earth made it entirely unfit for the support of life."

- **Order of Creation Events**

"With the point of view and initial conditions established, we can properly interpret the biblical chronology of events. What once seemed baffling or incorrect now becomes comprehensible and demonstrably accurate. It may be helpful to note, too, that six different Hebrew verbs are used for God's creative work. *Bara* appears in the manuscripts only twice more after Genesis 1:1, once for the creation of *nephesh*, or soulish animals—those creatures endowed with mind, will and emotions (namely, birds and mammals)—and again for the creation of Adam and Eve, or "spirit" beings—those creatures endowed with the capacity to respond to God himself.""

Order of Genesis 1 Creation Events

- Creation of the physical universe (space, time, matter, energy, galaxies, stars, planets, etc.)

- Transformation of the earth's atmosphere from opaque to translucent

- Formation of stable water cycle

- Establishment of continent(s) and ocean(s)

- Transformation of the atmosphere from translucent to transparent (Sun, Moon and stars became visible for the first time)

- Production of small sea animals

- Creation of sea mammals *(nephesh)*

- Creation of birds (possibly same time as in number 8) — more *nephesh*

- Making of land mammals (wild mammals, mammals that can be domesticated and rodents — still more *nephesh*)

- Creation of mankind (Adam and Eve)

Dr. Ross ably concludes that the Genesis account is "no coincidence". The events of Genesis had to be revealed by God to Moses. He stated:

"We must remember, first, that the recorder of the events, Moses, lived some 3,500 years ago, and he was writing not only for the people of his time and culture but for all people of all times and cultures. Use of the simplest possible terms was essential. Second, the apparent purpose of the account is to document various demonstrations of God's miraculous power in forming the earth and life upon it. With obvious necessity, the account is selective. Only the highlights, those events most important for achieving God's final goals, are included. As a result, dinosaurs, for example, receive no particular mention."

"The odds that Moses could have guessed the correct order even if he were given the events are one chance in roughly forty million. In addition, Moses scored three for three in describing the initial conditions. Of course, most amazing of all is the accuracy of his depiction of each creative event. Clearly, Moses must have been inspired by God to write as he did."

Sir Isaac Newton wrote,

"This most beautiful system of the sun, planets and comets, could only proceed from the counsel and dominion of an intelligent Being. This being governs all things, not as the soul of the world, but as Lord of all .... Atheism is so senseless. The motions of the planets require a Divine Arm to impress them. The true God is a living, intelligent and powerful being. His duration reaches from eternity to eternity; his presence from infinity to infinity."

Chapter 3

—The Evidence—

The Fossil Record

We have just seen the preponderance of evidence for a beginning to the universe and with the design in the universe (Earth-Sun system), the need of an all powerful, personal being of infinite wisdom. We have also seen that there is no contradiction between Genesis and science which supports creation, not evolution. Now let's see what the earth's geological strata reveal.

While evolutionists reluctantly accept a beginning to the universe and the evidences for ingenious design, they also admit that the only historical record of the evolution of life on earth is the geological strata (fossil record). Scientists agree that this has to be the final court of appeal, not only for the atheistic evolutionists, but for the theistic evolutionists as well. In other words, whether or not there is a God, evidence must support a gradual step-by-step transformation (from simple to the complex) of all plants and animals. For example, there should be at least *some* fossils with developing arms, legs, wings, eyes and other bones and organs such as fish fins changing into amphibian legs with feet and toes. In other words, there should be fossils with half scales, half feathers, half legs, half wings, half developed heart, half developed eye, etc.

Evolutionists again grudgingly admit that after one hundred years of research, and out of billions of fossils found (which fill our museums all over the world) not one certain transitional form or "in-between" creature has ever been found. If evolution were true, there should be millions of in-between creatures demonstrating how one creature slowly turned into another, but because forms appear suddenly, or abruptly, and fully developed in geological strata, scientists are desperately looking for a new method of evolution.

This revolutionary change of thought and the concession to creationists appeared in the *Los Angeles Times* (1978), in an article entitled, *New Evolutionary Evidence Causes Change of Thought*. The article states:

"Gatlinburg, TN — The search for 'missing links' between living creatures, such as humans and apes, is probably fruitless, a scientist says, because such creatures probably never existed as distinctive, transitional types.

"At a meeting of science writers here in the Smoky Mountains, Dr. Niles Eldredge of the American Museum of Natural History in New York City (an evolutionist) said that if the longstanding paleontological view of life was correct, one would expect to find such transitional forms.

"That school of thought, known as 'gradualism' or 'transformationalism', holds that all living things evolved from many branches on a tree.

"According to that theory, each species—from bluebirds to blue whales—evolved through a slow accumulation of small changes in its genetic make-up. Over vast periods of time, perhaps tens of millions to hundreds of millions of years, enough of these changes became incorporated into a given number of creatures to warrant their classification as a separate 'species'.

"...this pattern we were told to find over the last 120 years does not exist!"   **—Dr. Niles Eldredge**

"'If life had evolved into the wondrous profusion of creatures little by little, then there should be some fossiliferous record of those changes,' Eldredge said. That is, one would expect to find transitional creatures that were a little bit like what went before them and a little bit like what came after them.

"But no one has found any evidence of such in-between creatures. This was long chalked up to 'gaps' in fossil records; gaps that proponents of gradualism confidently expected to fill in someday when rock strata of the proper antiquity were eventually located.

"'But all of the fossil evidence to date has failed to turn up any such missing links,' Eldredge said, 'and there is a growing conviction among many scientists that these transitional forms never existed.' And if this is so, then the gradualist view of evolution is an inaccurate portrayal of how life developed."

Explosions of Evolution?

The most prominent "speculative" theory is called "Punctuated Equilibrium" which, in essence, says there were explosions of evolution. This theory, by the way, conspicuously smacks of creationism. The idea of "explosions" fits the creationists model of origins perfectly—the creation (or explosion) of the universe and the creation or "explosions" of life on earth. To the creationists, the evolutionists' model of explosions (Punctuated Equilibrium) translated another way sounds like "... an alligator lays an egg, out comes a canary."

Noted scientist, writer and Professor of Geology at Harvard University, Stephen Jay Gould, originated the theory of Punctuated Equilibria Evolution and was chosen "Man of the Year in Science" by *Discover* magazine and appeared on the cover of *Newsweek* magazine. At first, scientists thought they had a way out of the lack of transitional forms, but soon found out they hit a stone wall.

The theory states that when a certain species was ready to go extinct (down to the thousands or hundreds), miraculously, multiple favorable mutations would occur, creating a new species that could survive, followed by a new explosion of life. Thus, in the geological strata, since the fossils would be so few in the transformation period, they would leave no remains, but after the population explosion, fossils would again appear in the strata.

First of all, this is the reverse of what we have observed in nature. When species get down to small numbers, they simply go extinct unless they can be rescued. They don't all at once begin producing some new kind of species. In fact, speciation has never been observed. Also, in species there are always limits of variation. Man, by artificial selection has produced Great Danes and Chihuahuas, but that's as far as the gene pool permits. The theory was formed to get out of a dilemma but has no scientific basis. It's nothing but pure speculation.

Luther D. Sunderland in his book, *Darwin's Enigma*, sums up the present state of evolutionary scientists concerning the geological strata. He states,

> "The theory of punctuated equilibria is causing much turmoil among evolutionists. They know that there is no actual mechanism that would explain large rapid jumps from one species to another and yet they also know the fossil record doesn't support gradualism. They are left on the horns of a dilemma."

Evolutionists, while readily admitting that the fossil record has to be the only historical record of evolution are now beginning to admit that the fossils provide no real evidence for evolution.

"Naturalists must remember that the process of evolution is revealed only through fossil forms. A knowledge of paleontology is, therefore, a prerequisite; only paleontology can provide them with the evidence of evolution and reveal its course or mechanisms" —Dr. Pierre Grasse, a leading French zoologist (University of Paris and past President of the French Academy of Science).

"The absence of fossil evidence for the intermediary stages between major transitions in organic design, indeed our inability, even in our imaginations, to construct functional intermediates in many cases, has been a persistent and nagging problem..." —Dr. Stephen Jay Gould (Professor of Geology, Harvard University).

"In any case, no real evolutionist, whether gradualist or punctuationist, uses the fossil record as evidence in favor of the theory of evolution as opposed to special creation" —Dr. Mark Ridley (Professor of Zoology, Oxford University).

"Few paleontologists have, I think, ever supposed that fossils, by themselves, provide grounds for the conclusion that evolution has occurred...*the fossil record doesn't even provide any evidence in support of Darwinian theory...*" —Dr. David Kitts (Professor of Zoology, School of Geology and Geo-physics, University of Oklahoma).

The Cambrian Explosion

The lowest geological strata where life first appears is called the Cambrian period. In this strata are found abundant fossils of almost all the major groups of sea life including the most complex invertebrates, the nauctiloids, and the highly complex trilobites. Darwin called this fossil evidence "... perhaps the most obvious and serious objection to the theory of evolution." Why? In this lowest level where life first appears, there should be only simple, primitive forms that evolved from simple celled organisms, not highly complex invertebrates. Where are the missing links to these complex animals?

According to evolutionists, if life evolved from a single cell, it would have taken about 1.5 billion years to have arrived at the Cambrian level, but the fact is, there are no Precambrian fossils except some single celled types like bacteria and algae. The Precambrian layers should be the greater part of evolution, but no intermediate forms are found. In fact, **not a single,** indisputably multicellular fossil has been found anywhere in a rock supposedly older than Cambrian rocks. All these highly complex fossils appear suddenly and fully developed. Evolutionists today call it a mystery and refer to this period as the Cambrian "explosion".

High school and college textbooks usually support a few fossils that are (at the most) *possibly* ancestors of living groups such as the hominid Lucy, and the reptile archaeopteryx, but they rarely inform the public about the far greater mass of contrary evidence that appears in the Cambrian explosion. The overall fossil record is extremely disappointing to Darwinian expectations. Evidence for Macroevolution is conspicuously absent where the fossil evidence is most plentiful—among marine invertebrates.

These animals are plentiful because they are so frequently covered in sediment when they die, whereas land animals are exposed to scavengers and to the elements. Hence, it is here that we find the most complete record of the earth's fossils. In his book, Defeating Darwinism by Opening Minds (1997), Phillip E.

Johnson quotes Niles Eldredge, one of the world's leading experts on invertebrate fossils as saying:

> "No wonder paleontologists shied away from evolution for so long. It never seems to happen. Assiduous collecting up cliff faces yields zigzags, minor oscillations, and the very occasional slight accumulation of change—over millions of years, at a rate too slow to account for all the prodigious change that has occurred in evolutionary history."

There is no fossil history of a single-celled organism changing step by step into complex plants and animals. On the contrary, the major groups of animals all appear suddenly in the rocks of the Cambrian era—and no new groups appear thereafter. High school text books either fail to mention this fundamental fact of the fossil record, or refer to it so obliquely that students fail to get the implications.

> "One of the major unsolved problems of geology and evolution is the occurrence of diversified, multicellular marine invertebrates in Lower Cambrian rocks and their absence in rocks of greater age" —Dr. Daniel Axelrod (Professor of Geology at UCLA).

Professor George Gaylord Simpson world-famous paleontologist, has described the absence of pre-Cambrian fossils (other than alleged fossil micro-organisms) as "... the major mystery of the history of life".

The fossils not only appear suddenly and fully developed but they *remain unchanged* and, of course, many have become extinct. All this, of course, is crushing evidence **against** evolution because if you're researching where snails, octopuses, jellyfish, sponges, clams and fish came from, you have to go back to the beginning and sure enough, snails come from snails, octopuses come from octopuses and so on. In other words, there are no "snids" and "squails" and "squailobites." The Cambrian period is typical of the entire fossil record.

Throughout the remainder of the fossil record there is the regular absence of transitional forms demanded by the theory of evolution. There should be hundreds of thousands of missing links between invertebrates and vertebrates. According to evolutionists, it would have taken 100 million years for a fish to have evolved from an invertebrate, but there is absolutely no fossil evidence showing that this took place. Fish appear out of nowhere. Evolutionists claim that it took perhaps 50 million years for a fish to evolve into an amphibian, but again, **there are no transitional forms.**

The California State framework states:

> "Evolution is more than change, it is change with a direction. Through time, life has evolved from simple forms to the present array of organisms."

The framework quotes and reaffirms Charles Darwin's definition of evolution—"descent with modification". But does the fossil record really support Darwin's statement—"descent with modification" into the present array of organisms—or does it support that not only are there **no transitional forms** but also that **species don't change** at all or very little? This is the Micro-evolution which is observable. For example, the fossil fish Coelacanth (65 million B.C.) was once thought to be a transitional form between fish and amphibians—until recently. Why? Because fisherman have actually caught a couple of them, alive, in the last 50 years, and they have remained unchanged from their original discovery in the fossil record.

Stasis then, not the mutability of species, is what the historical record of the rocks reveals. We see the explosion of new species which remain unchanged and then extinction or survival such as sharks which are still with us today. Dr. Gould of Harvard related, in a conference at Hobart College (1980), a devastating statement against the theory of evolution (censored in textbooks). He states,

> "The fossil record is full of gaps and discontinuities, but they are all attributed to the notorious imperfection of the fossil record. The fossil record is imperfect, but I think that is not an adequate explanation...one thing it does show that cannot be attributed to its imperfection is that *most species don't change... They may get a little bigger or bumpier but they remain the same species and that's not due to imperfection and gaps but stasis. And yet this remarkable stasis has generally been ignored as no data. If they don't change, it's not evolution so you don't talk about it.*"

Dr. Duane T. Gish in his book, *Evolution: The Fossils Say No!* states,

> "In each level of the geological strata where life appears there is a sudden appearance of forms with no known ancestors. This is true between *every major plant and animal kind.* All higher categories of living things, such as complex invertebrates, fish, amphibians, reptiles, flying reptiles, birds, bats, primates and man, appear abruptly."

The Gaps

David B. Kitts, Ph.D. in Zoology (School of Geology and Geophysics, Department of the History of Science, University of Oklahoma, Norman, Oklahoma, USA), in *Paleontology and Evolutionary Theory*, says,

> "Despite the bright promise that paleontology provides a means of 'seeing' evolution, it has presented some nasty difficulties for evolutionists. The most notorious of which is the presence of 'gaps' in the fossil record. Evolution requires intermediate forms between species

and paleontology does not provide them. *The gaps must therefore be a contingent feature of the record.*"

Blue Green Algae — Pond Scum

It is the position of evolutionary scientists that all life forms have evolved from blue-green algae or "pond scum", but one of the latest discoveries in Paleobiology demonstrates that blue-green algae hasn't changed at all in its two-billion-year-plus history. This is a severe challenge to Darwinian as well as Punctuated Equilibrium Evolution. In an article in *Facts and Faith* (summer 1994), "Pond Scum Defies Evolution," Dr. Ross states,

> "Biologists and paleontologists have long acknowledged the existence—and thus the problem—of certain species in which little or no change has occurred through the ages. Examples include crocodiles and horseshoe crabs. Hundred-million year old fossils of both are identical in form to crocodiles and horseshoe crabs of today.

> "More disturbing, however, has been the discovery of fossils of some blue-green unicellular life forms with dates of one billion years that appear identical to blue-green microbes alive today. When such findings first came to light several years ago, the response of many researchers was to toss aside this discovery as an exception to the rule.

> "But the finding can no longer be dismissed. A total of 3,000 fossils of blue-green unicellulars have been found with dates falling between 0.5 and 2.5 billion years. Among these 3,000 fossils, about 300 species are represented. Of these 300 species, some 90 have modern counterparts, and the rest have apparently (and expectedly) gone extinct. *These 90 exhibit no change in their sizes, shapes and structures. Even the way they assemble themselves into colonies is identical. In other*

words, in 2.5 billion years, no evolution has taken place at all."

The Plants

Chester A. Arnold (Professor of Botany and Curator of Fossil Plants, University of Michigan) says,

"The facts derived from a study of fossil plants are of paramount importance for the bearing they have had on the broader subjects of phylogeny and evolution. It has long been hoped that extinct plants will ultimately reveal some of the stages through which existing groups have passed during the course of their development, but it must be freely admitted that this aspiration has been fulfilled to a very slight extent, even though paleo-botanical research has been in progress for more than one hundred years. *As yet we have not been able to trace the phylogenetic history of a single group of modern plants from its beginning to the present.*"

The Fishes

"The geological record has so far provided no evidence as to the origin of the fishes" —J.R. Norman (British Museum of Natural History, London).

The Amphibians

These words come from Barbara J. Stahl (St. Anselm's College, USA) in *Vertebrate History: Problems in Evolution:*

"...none of the known fishes is thought to be directly ancestral to the earliest land vertebrates. Most of them lived after the first amphibians appeared, and those that came before show no evidence of developing the stout limbs and ribs that characterized the primitive tetrapods....

"Since the fossil material provides no evidence of other aspects of the transformation from fish to tetrapod, paleontologists have had to speculate how legs and aerial breathing evolved...."

The Birds

We read from W.E. Swinton (British Museum of Natural History, London), *The Origin of Birds:*

"The [evolutionary] origin of birds is largely a matter of deduction. There is no fossil evidence of the stages through which the remarkable change from reptile to bird was achieved."

The Reptile is supposed to have evolved into the bird. Archeopteryx is supposed to be a transitional form, but it is clearly a bird. Dr. E.C. Olson in *The Evolution of Life Biology and Comparative Physiology of Birds*, an evolutionist's book, says:

"The origin of birds is largely a matter of deduction. *There are no fossils of the stages through which the remarkable change from reptile to bird was achieved.*"

The Mammals

"The [evolutionary] transition to the first mammal, which probably happened in just one or, at most, two lineages, is still an enigma" —Roger Lewin, *Bones of Mammals: Ancestors Fleshed Out.*

"Because of the nature of the fossil evidence, paleontologists have been forced to reconstruct the first two-thirds of mammalian history in great part on the basis of *tooth morphology*" —Barbara J. Stahl.

The Primates (Monkeys and Apes)

"In spite of recent findings, the time and place of origin and order of Primates remains shrouded in mystery" —Elwyn L. Simons (Department of Geology and Geophysics, Yale University, USA, and co-editor of Nuclear Physics), *The Origin and Radiation of the Primates.*

"...the transition from insectivore to primate is not documented by fossils. The basis of knowledge about the transition is by inference from living forms" —A. J. Kelso (Professor of Physical Anthropology, University of Colorado), *Origin and Evolution of the Primates.*

What About Fossil Man?

The California State framework (grades three through six) relates that man emerged through the ape line and through the hominids (near-men). It states,

"Just as humans are mammals, they are also primates, and they retain characteristics of other primates seen in the hands, eyes, brains and genetic and biochemical systems. Within the primates, humans are classified with the other anthropoid apes because they lack tails and have an unusual erect or semi-erect stance and semi-brachiating forelimbs. Anatomical, genetic, and biochemical data indicate that chimpanzees and gorillas are the closest living apes to humans. The first hominids (animals on the evolutionary line from the other apes to living humans) appeared over two million years ago; human evolution since then has been marked by important changes, including upright posture, larger brains, tool making, speech, art and other cultural aspects."

Textbooks and magazines today still present a graded series of the evolution of man (from tree shrews to Cro-Magnon Man) but knowledgeable scientists know of the contradictions. The most prominent of the graded scales include Australopithecines (South African ape), Homo-Erectus (Java and Peking man) and Neanderthal Man. This scale has been presented in sequence (3 million B.C. to the present) as the evolution of modern man; however, the scale has proven to be fallacious—especially because of recent discoveries. The different varieties of Australopithecines (Zinjanthropus, Africanus, a. Robustus, Lucy, etc.) are now known to be extinct apes (not near man, nor half ape and half man) and **not** in the ancestral line of man.

Anyone who has gone to school in America in the 1950's and 1960's has undoubtedly seen the face of Pithecanthropus Erectus, Java Man. The artist's conception had him looking half ape and half man with a philosophical stare of the beginning of intelligence. He's now **known** to have been a gibbon, although he and the Peking Man are still found in some textbooks. Dr. Robert Jastrow on Lucy—"The brain was not large in absolute size; it was a third the size of a human brain." *New Scientist* states that "Lucy" had a skull very much like a chimpanzee. Dr. Duane T. Gish states,

> "All of these animals (Australopithecus) possessed small brains, the cranial capacity averaging 500 c.c. or less, which is in the range of a gorilla, and about one–third of that for man. These animals thus unquestionably had the brains of apes, regardless of what else can be said about them."

Dr. Solly Lord Zuckerman, the famous British anatomist and scientist who is regarded as having done more research on the Australopithecines than any other scientist, creationist or evolutionist, stated in his book, *Beyond the Ivory Tower*,

"If man evolved from ape-like creatures, he did so without leaving a trace of that evolution in the fossil record."

For 15 years, Lord Zuckerman and his research team studied all of the fossil fragments of Australopithecus alongside bones of hundreds of monkeys, apes and humans. He concluded that Australopithecus was an ape, in no way related to the origin of man.

"Amid the bewildering array of early fossil hominids, is there one whose morphology marks it as man's hominid ancestor? If the factor of genetic variability is considered, the answer appears to be no" —Robert B. Eckhardt, Ph.D. *Human Genetics and Anthropology* (Professor of Anthropology, Pennsylvania State University, USA).

Evidence Too Fragmentary!

Will Durant, claimed by many as the most knowledgeable historian in the area of ancient civilizations, made a statement to the effect that our knowledge of what really happened in ancient times (with written records) is "at best an educated guess". No doubt, we do have quantity as well as quality (the Bible as example) information of ancient times, but we are missing most of the history of this time period. In many areas we are guessing. If we are guessing—trying to piece together what happened in ancient times, then how much credence can we give the history of prehistoric times? Consider the following quotes:

"Lucy's skull was so incomplete that most of it was 'imagination made of plaster of paris'" —Richard Leakey, Weekend Australian, May 7-8, 1983.

"Not being a paleontologist, I don't want to pour too much scorn, but if you were to spend your life picking up bones and finding little fragments of heads and little fragments of jaws, there's a very strong desire to exaggerate the importance of those fragments" —Dr. Greg Kirby, Flinders University.

"The fossils that decorate our family tree are so scarce that there are still more scientists than specimens. The remarkable fact is that all the physical evidence we have for human evolution can still be placed with room to spare inside a single coffin" —Dr. Lyall Watson, *Science Digest*, May, 1982.

"The family trees which adorn our textbooks are based on inference — not the evidence of fossils" —Prof. Stephen Jay Gould, *Natural History*, 1977, Vol. 86, p.13.

The above quotes tell the real story of the so-called History of Man. The graded series presented in text books and such magazines as *National Geographic* are based on the flimsiest of evidence and could never be used as scientific evidence. All knowledgeable scientists know that there is no real paleontological evidence for the evolution of man. As with the theory of Punctuated Equilibrium, all theories of man's evolutionary origin are based on nothing more than pure speculation.

"And God created man in His own image..."

Although the Genesis account of man's creation is brief and simple, it in no way contradicts the findings of science. In fact it makes sense. For example, the latest scientific findings corroborate the biblical position that all humans came from a single source, not many sources as many scientists formerly thought.

"The anatomy of persons of all races is the same; they all have the same protein structure and all the same ancestors" —Anthropologist Dr. George Glowatzki.

"All the peoples of the earth are a single family and have a common origin" —Anthropologist Ruth Benedict and George Welfish.

"Science now corroborates what most great religions have long been preaching: Human beings of all races are...descended from the same first man" —Science Writer Amaram Scheimfeld.

"All varieties of man belong to the same species and have the same remote ancestry. This is a conclusion to which all the relevant evidence of comparative anatomy, paleontology, serology and genetics points. On genetic grounds alone it is virtually impossible to conceive of the varieties of man having originated separately" —Anthropologist M.F. Ashley Montagu.

"All of us, if we went back far enough, hundreds of generations, would arrive at the same place...the evidence of science (is) that present men derive from a common stock" —Educational, scientific and cultural organization of the United Nations.

In the headlines of the *Los Angeles Times* (April 15, 1995), an article entitled, *Is Concept of Race a Relic?* has thrown another wrench into evolutionary philosophy. The article related that the biological sciences that classified the races into Caucasoid, Mongoloid, Negroid, etc. (which are included in our science textbooks) has now been discredited. In other words, races are not different physiologically. All races are the same. This categorizing of races was used in the past by evolutionists to demonstrate that some races were superior—evolved higher than others. But all this has now been disproven, which you can now add to the many other evidences discrediting organic evolution.

Another headline of the *Los Angeles Times* (May 26, 1995), entitled, *Genetic Study Says All Men Have a Common Ancestor,* has thrown yet another monkeywrench into evolutionary theory. Not only are all humans physiologically the same, coming from an original couple (only having outward, physical differences because of geography, climate, breeding, etc.), man's origin has

now proven to be very recent—thousands, not millions of years
ago.

An article from Facts and Faith by Hugh Ross and Sam
Conner (First Quarter, 1998) entitled, "Eve's Secret to Growing
Younger", confirms the recent origin of mankind:

> "A new discovery about a genetic phenomenon called
> 'heteroplasmy' revises the date for our oldest female
> ancestor, Eve.   This latest discovery recalibrates the
> earliest date down to one much closer to the rough
> biblical date of 12,000 to 60,000 years ago. Mitochon-
> drial DNA (mDNA) can be used as an evolutionary clock
> because it passes from one generation to the next through
> the mother only."

Isn't it interesting how the latest scientific findings are getting
closer and closer to the Genesis account of creation? What about
all of the above hominids—man's so-called ancestors of one or
two million years ago? They're not even in the picture for they
had all become extinct about one-half to one million years before
mankind arrived on the scene.

"And Adam named all the animals"

Biblical scholars agree (tracing the genealogies of families in
the Bible back to Adam) that the creative event of Mankind was
between 8 and 20 thousand years ago. The exact date is unknown
because there are missing genealogies. Undoubtedly only the
important ones were given. Also, the Hebrew word for *father* can
be translated as father, grandfather or great grandfather, adding
more antiquity. The approximate date is agreed upon and it agrees
with what archaeology and history scholars believe about the time
that civilization began.

We say man began to be civilized when he left written records and developed organized economic, political and religious systems. This all happened about 5 to 10 thousand years ago with the Sumerians, Babylonians, Assyrians, Hittites, Chaldeans, Egyptians and finally the Hebrews. The Bible records the historical sources of all these ancient civilizations.

Scientists admit again to the mystery of another explosion. The explosion of all the above civilizations at once from prehistoric times. Scientists are amazed at the new "thinking man" making contributions at this time such as the calendar, medicine, dentistry, arithmetic, geometry, surveying, sun dials, sail boats, bow and arrows, chariots, etc. With the civilization explosion came the knowledge explosion.

Adam and Eve, and their appearance, brought a new kind of species—a reflective, creative species, much different from prehistoric times. The so-called hominids and Australopithecus had long gone extinct 500,000 to 1,000,000 years before.

According to the Bible, Adam and Eve were unique, having been created in the image of God. "Adam" means spirit creature and was a creature endowed with body, soul **and spirit.** Mankind was unique, not only because he was a thinking being, but he had a built in consciousness of God and a moral code written on his heart. Archaeology confirms the fact that organized religion also came about at this time.

Dr. Ross, in his book, *The Fingerprint of God,* summarizes the agreement between the Bible and science. He states:

"Clearly, as man's story unfolds through subsequent chapters, one discovers that what makes him different is a quality called 'spirit'. Man is unique among all species of life. By 'spirit', the Bible means aware of God and capable of forming a relationship with Him. Evidence of man's spiritual dimension would include divine worship, shown by religious relics, altars and temples. From the

Bible's perspective, painting, burial of dead, or use of tools would not qualify as conclusive evidence of the spirit. Moreover, non-spirit beings such as lower birds, elephants and chimpanzees are observed to engage in these activities.

"...evidence for religious relics and altars dates back only 8,000 to 24,000 years. Thus, the secular anthropological date for the first spirit creatures is in complete agreement with the biblical date."

Summary of the Fossil Record

By way of review, we've seen that the fossil record does not support a gradual evolution of all things, but just the opposite — it shows the sudden appearance of complex species that don't change, then extinction and then explosions of new species. We also saw that Punctuated Equilibrium offers no plausible explanation for the lack of missing links and no cognitive scientific evidence that it ever occurs. We did see that the six days of special creation, as given in the Bible, generally agrees with the geological strata of explosions of different kinds of life (plants, sea creatures, reptiles, mammals, man) and the biblical account agrees with the findings of archaeologists and anthropologists as to beginning of intelligent civilizations and cultures.

Now, let's look at some more quotes from eminent scientists, including Darwin himself on the lack of fossil evidence:

Newsweek, November 3, 1980 reporting on a meeting of the world's leading evolutionists at a Chicago conference made the following statements and quotes:

"The missing link between man and the apes is merely the most glamorous of a whole hierarchy of phantom creatures. In the fossil record, missing links are the rule.... The more scientists have searched for the transitional forms between species, the more they have been frustrated."

Dr. Colin Patterson, a senior paleontologist and editor of a prestigious journal at the British Museum of Natural History and now an agnostic, wrote that he didn't know of any real evidence of evolutionary transitions either among living or fossilized organisms. When asked why he didn't put one single photograph of a transitional fossil in his book *Evolution* (which was written for the British Museum of Natural History) he replied,

"If I knew of any, *fossil or living*, I would have certainly included them."

Dr. Philip E. Johnson summarizes the dilemma of evolutionists in their search for transitional forms and relates how the Bighorn Basin in Wyoming has a continuous record of fossil deposits for about five million years and yet no transitional forms. He states,

"It isn't merely that grand-scale Darwinism can't be confirmed. The evidence is positively **against** the theory. For example, if Darwinism is true then the bat, monkey, pig, seal and whale all evolved in gradual adaptive stages from a primitive rodent-like predecessor. This hypothetical common ancestor must have been connected to its diverse descendants by long linking chains of transitional intermediaries, which in turn put out innumerable side branches. The intermediate links would have to be adaptively superior to their predecessors, and be in the process of developing the complex integrated organs required for aquatic life, flight and so on. Fossil evidence that anything of the sort happened is thoroughly missing, and in addition it is extremely difficult to imagine how the hypothetical intermediate steps could have been adaptive.

"One can't make problems of this magnitude go away simply by announcing that there must be gaps in the fossil record. According to Steven Stanley, the Bighorn Basin in Wyoming contains a continuous local record of fossil deposits for about five million years during an early period in the age of mammals. Because this record is so complete, paleontologists assumed that certain population of the basin could be linked together to illustrate continuous evolution. *What they discovered was that species that were once thought to have turned into others turn out to overlap in time with their alleged descendants, and 'the fossil record does not convincingly document a single transition from one species to another.'"*

What is the conclusion, then, of the most eminent scientists on the fossil record, which is the only evidence for the history of origins? There is *no evidence for the evolutionary descent of man*. Things have actually gotten worse for the evolutionists since Darwin, for animals that were once thought to be transitional forms and that were in our old science and social studies text books are no longer accepted as bonafide transitional forms. One, for example, was archaeopteryx who was first thought to be the ancestor of all birds (a reptile with feathers), it is now accepted as a true bird that probably flew. Also, modern birds have been found in the same geological strata. Thus, archaeopteryx could not have been the forerunner of birds since birds were already in existence.

"Archaeopteryx has simply become a patsy for wishful thinking" —Dr. Patterson.

Another recent development concerns the Cambrian explosion of 530 million years ago. Evolutionists had held out hope that they could stretch this period by about 50 million years to give more time for the Precambrian worm-like organisms to evolve into all the complex phyla of the Cambrian period. Instead, with new discoveries in Siberia and Canada, the Cambrian period has shrunk to the range of 0 to 10 million years—an instant in geological time.

Dr. Hugh Ross in *Facts and Faith* (Winter 1993,1994) states,

> "[Scientists] were able to date the beginning of the
> Tommotian geologic era at 530 million years ago and the
> end of the next, the Atdabanian, geologic era at 525
> million years ago. The burst of diverse animal phyla
> took place during these two eras. Dating uncertainties
> could stretch the explosion over ten million years at most
> or shrink it to zero years.

> "When these ecological and genetic speed limits are
> compared to the 0-to-10-million-year span of the
> Cambrian explosion, the possibility (with respect to time
> alone) for naturalism becomes absurdly remote, and the
> plausibility of supernaturalism substantially increases."

Finally, the hypothetical evolutionary scenario, according to
current biochemical studies of the DNA "molecular clock" relates
that the supposed common ancestor to both apes and humans
would have existed five to eight million years ago. This supposed
last ancestor, common to both apes and man has never been found;
in fact the American Scientific Affiliation states,

> "There are no known fossil hominids of any kind found
> in this time period!"

In spite of all the new scientific evidence surfacing and
discrediting organic evolution and fossil man, because of our
educational system and media, even some evangelical Christians
are being sucked into theistic evolution. Dave Hunt in his book, *A
Cup of Trembling*, states,

> "In spite of the impotence of science where it really
> matters and the confession of that fact by the world's
> greatest scientists, religious people continue to bow to
> this sacred cow and thereby try to gain a certain
> credibility. In order to be 'scientific', a hybrid belief is
> becoming popular among Christians: that God allowed
> evolution to proceed, then stepped in to transform an
> apelike [sic] creature into Adam when it had evolved

high enough. But evolution **is a fraud.** And the Bible
says that the moment God breathed life into the form He
molded from dust, it was a man, Adam (Genesis 2:7), so
he couldn't have existed in a previous form."

No Transitional Forms, Species Well Defined — No Evolution!

What is the situation today since Darwin published his book,
Origin of Species, in 1859? After over one hundred years of
scientific research with the expectation of discovering millions of
transitional forms, the opposite has happened. **All** scientists agree
today that the gaps have grown bigger. Evolutionists and
creationists both ask the same two questions Charles Darwin asked
after he presented his theory of evolution—Darwin said,

> "...Why, if species have descended from other species by
> fine graduation, do we not everywhere see innumerable
> transitional forms? Why is all nature not in confusion
> instead of the species being, as we see them, well
> defined? ... but, as by this theory innumerable forms
> must have existed, why do we not find them embedded in
> countless numbers in the crust of the earth?"

Chapter 4

—The Evidence—

The Origin of Life

Having conceded a beginning to the universe, the need for a primal mover and no evidence of a history of evolution (the lack of "Missing Links" and the fact that species don't change), evolutionists are equally baffled on how the first single, self-reproducing cell came about. Their original theory (still taught in most educational institutions) was that things proceeded from the simple to the complex—that life emerged spontaneously from lifeless matter. This was called spontaneous generation. In other words, out of the young earth's primordial sea came simple dead molecules (inorganic matter) which in time turned into complex molecules and finally into the first living, self-reproducing single cells (organic matter). Given millions or billions of years, all life came about. This is called the "molecule-to-man" theory of evolution.

The problem from the outset is that spontaneous generation has been scientifically disproved. The law of Biogenetics states that *life comes from pre-existing life.* It also dictates that life only produces its own kind and type. Dr. George Wald (late Professor of Biology, Harvard University) in *The Origin of Life,* states,

"We tell this story [talking about Pasteur's disproof of spontaneous generation of life] to beginning students of biology as though it represents a triumph of reason over mysticism. In fact it is very nearly the opposite. The reasonable view was to believe in spontaneous generation; the only alternative, to believe in a single, primary act of supernatural creation. There is no third position. For this reason many scientists a century ago chose to regard the belief in spontaneous generation as a 'philosophical necessity'. It is a symptom of the philosophical poverty of our time that this necessity is no longer appreciated. *Most modern biologists, having reviewed with satisfaction the downfall of the spontaneous generation hypothesis, yet unwilling to accept the alternative belief in special creation, are left with nothing.*"

Spontaneous generation not only has been disproved by the law of bio-genesis, it does not stand up to the second law of thermodynamics. This law states that *everything goes from order to disorder* (like an unkept room or backyard). In other words, spontaneous **dissolution** not spontaneous **generation** is nature's law.

Dr. Duane T. Gish in his Critique, *Speculations and Experiments Related to Theories on the Origin of Life,* quotes Dr. Wald on the problem of dissolution.

"In the vast majority of the processes in which we are interested the point of equilibrium lies far over toward the side of dissolution. That is to say, spontaneous dissolution is much more probable, and hence proceeds much more rapidly, than spontaneous synthesis. After discussing how organisms accomplish the feat of synthesizing organic substances in spite of this tendency towards dissolution, Wald says, '*What we are asked here is to synthesize organic molecules without such a machine. I believe this to be the most stubborn problem that confronts us—the weakest link at present in our argument.'"*

Dr. Gish states,

"Thus, from predictions based on thermodynamic consideration, the known results of polymerization studies, and the investigations of sequences found in naturally occurring proteins, *it can be said that no ordering process based merely on chemical and physical laws could have been operating on the primitive earth.* Imagine, however, the vast quantity of any particular molecule that would have been required to give rise to a significant concentration in the primeval oceans. Hundreds of different kinds of complex molecules would have had to arise in huge quantities in order to give rise to the first living thing. If known physical and chemical laws are valid, this possibility must be considered nil. *The probability of the origin of life through a purely materialistic process is thus reduced to zero.*"

In considering the time necessary for the ability to reproduce to evolve, Dr. Gish states:

"*The accretionary process necessary to reach the self-replicating state would have required geological ages. Dissolution, on the other hand, would have required only minutes, days, weeks or a few months at the very most.* This fact, dissolution without reproduction, presents an insurmountable barrier to the mechanistic, evolutionary origin of life. It is therefore concluded, for this and many other reasons, that *an evolutionary origin of life is impossible.*"

The problem becomes even more complicated in that a single self-reproducing cell with its newly discovered DNA code is, according to many scientists, more complex than the entire city of New York with its network of subways. The genetic code in the nucleus of the cells is the most complex and effective code in nature which demands an ingenious, intelligent design and designer as a dress demands a pattern and pattern maker and a building demands a blueprint and a blueprint maker.

Did all this come about by random, accidental chance and also contrary to the second law of thermodynamics—or is there more evidence for an ingenious, intelligent designer? When we observe cameras, computers and automobiles, we logically acknowledge an intelligent human designer. Why, then, do we illogically conclude that such marvels of nature, as the single cell, the human eye or the brain are the result of blind, accidental evolution? George Gallup, the American statistician stated,

> "I could prove God statistically. Take the human body alone—the chance that all the functions of the individual would just happen is a statistical monstrosity."

The Enigma of Life's Origin

The California State Framework on natural science states.

> "Chemical evolution refers to the assembly of more complex organic molecules from simpler ones, given appropriate materials, environmental conditions, and input energy. These complex molecules are part of biotic compounds."

Naturally Emergent Life Theory

Is life a naturally emergent property of matter that given correct conditions could spawn life on earth as well as all over the universe, as inferred by the state framework? This atheistic theory was originated by Friedrich Engels in his philosophy of Dialectical Materialism which Communism incorporated. Engels said, "Life is the mode of existence of protein bodies." This Dialectical Materialism dogma is still held in the Western world as it was in the 'party line' of the former Soviet Union.

Is it fact or blind faith, now taught as fact,

and is it in violation of the U.S. constitution?

Dr. Yockey is the world's foremost authority on information theory in molecular biology. Dr. Yockey is an agnostic who states in his book that he believes that anyone after reading his book would not be able to draw the conclusion that life could spontaneously arise on this planet. An article taken from *Facts and Faith* (Fall 1993) comments on his recently published book, *Information Theory and Molecular Biology* and states,

> "Woefully, the dialectical materialist doctrine of the spontaneous origin of life from a primeval soup has been *incorporated not only into NASA's policies but also into high school and college textbooks nationwide (world-wide, for that matter).*

> "Despite the nonexistence of any trace of this soup, to oppose such teaching has been virtually impossible, for the argument has always been that 'we are teaching science, and this is what science says.'

> "The recently published book, *Information Theory and Molecular Biology* by Hubert Yockey, shows that science says no such thing. *The genetic message, recorded in DNA, that distinguishes living matter from non-living is measurable but non-material. Our schools are teaching not science but rather the dialectical materialistic and atheistic faith—a scientifically fraudulent faith—that life is 'a naturally emergent property of matter.'*

> "Were the courts in this country truly open and objective, a case could be made that the government's teaching of Engels' ideology, and specifically of life from prote-noids, *constitutes establishment of religion and thus violates the establishment clause of the First Amendment.*

If justice prevailed, the government's standard model would be hanged on a hangman's gallows."

Recent Attempts to Salvage Materialism

Is life a naturally emergent property of matter as evolutionists stubbornly propound? Neo-Darwinism is based on materialism which holds that matter is all there is. Thus, in evolutionary terminology, philosophical reductionism means that everything can be reduced to matter. Even our minds can be reduced to their material base (chemicals), thus, life's origin comes from non-living matter, not God.

But we have seen (Hubert Yockey, Information Theory and Molecular biology) that the genetic message recorded in DNA which distinguishes living matter from non-living is measurable, but non-material. There are two recent books which attempt to resolve the dilemma of matter and information being separate entities and the question of the origin of information.

The first is a work by George C. Williams who is best known for pioneering the "gene selection" version of Darwinism and the second is by Richard Dawkins who is possibly the most popular evolutionary biologist in the world. Dawkins popularized Williams' gene selection in his book, The Selfish Gene. However, in a 1994 interview, Williams seems to have second thoughts about reductionism. He stated:

"Evolutionary biologists have failed to realize that they work with two more or less incommensurable domains: that of information and that of matter .... These two domains can never be brought together in any kind of sense usually implied by the term 'reductionism' .... The gene is a package of information, not an object .... In biology, when you're talking about things like genes and genotypes and gene pools, you're talking about information, not physical objective reality."

Williams elaborates on how Dawkins had been misled (as were other materialists) in their presupposition that matter is all that there is and he relates that Dawkins is forced into this position in order to escape a "first cause" for information. This fact is extremely important for if highly complex information is independent of matter, it demands an intelligent source.

The Death of Materialism

The following analogy illustrates the nagging, perplexing problem Dawkins, and numerous evolutionists, had with this problem concerning information. Highly complex information can be contained in a computer or on paper, in a book. The information is not part of the book or the computer, but is altogether different in kind. The book and computer (both of them are matter) can be destroyed, but the ideas (information) can live on and be reproduced by the author. In scientific language, information is not DNA but is encoded in DNA.

It is also true that information written in DNA is not the product of DNA. The question is, "Where did the information come from? Who is the author?" Dawkins admits this materialist's conundrum. He candidly adknowledges that random happenings (like shuffling letters in a barrel) could never produce a book or even a phrase such as "In the beginning God ...." In other words, matter could never produce information. In acknowledging this fact, Dawkins concedes the defeat of materialistic reductionism and inadvertently admits the need of an intelligent source (God). In his latest book, Climbing Mount Improbably (1996), he vividly elaborates on his quandry:

> "Physics books may be complicated, but ... the objects and phenomena that a physics book describes are simpler than a single cell in the body of its author. And the author consists of trillions of those cells, many of them different from each other, organized with intricate

architecture and precision-engineering into a working machine capable of writing a book .... Each nucleus ... contains a digitally coded database larger, in formation content, than all 30 volumes of the Encyclopedia Britannica put together. And this figure is for *each* cell, not all the cells of the body put together."

No Evidence for a Pre-biotic Soup

Michael Denton (Ph.D. in Molecular Biology, former evolutionist now agnostic) in his book, *Evolution: A Theory in Crisis* (1986), demonstrates not only the impossibility of the origin and development of life from non-life but also the lack of evidence to support it. Concerning the so called "pre-biotic soup," he states,

"Accordingly, the first cell was supposed to have risen following a long period of pre-cellular evolution. The process is presumed to have begun with a primitive self replicating molecule that slowly accumulated beneficial mutations that enabled it to reproduce more efficiently. After eons of time, it evolved into a more complex self-replicating object acquiring a cell membrane, metabolic functions, and eventually all the complex biochemical machinery of the cell.

"The first stage on the road of life was presumed to be the buildup, by purely chemical synthetic processes occurring on the surface of the globe, of the basic organic compounds necessary for the formation of the first cell. It was supposed to have accumulated in the primeval oceans, creating a nutrient broth, the so called pre-biotic soup. After eons of time macro-molecules evolved and were endowed with the ability of self-reproduction—in time the first simple cell.

"The existence of a pre-biotic soup was crucial to the whole scheme. If this is true, there should have existed for many millions of years, a rich mixture of organic compounds trapped in sedimentary rocks. *Yet rocks of great (earliest) antiquity have been examined the last two decades and none of them have any trace of a pre-biotic soup with organic compounds.*"

No Evidence for a Reducing (Oxygen-free) Atmosphere

Another dilemma for the evolutionary scientist is that the latest scientific findings do not support a reducing (oxygen-free) atmosphere. The presence of oxygen would have destroyed all organic compounds. In other words, if oxygen were present when the first organic compounds or bacterial cells were about to evolve, they would have been destroyed, making evolution impossible.

Dr. H. E. Urey of the National Academy of Science (1982) relates that the precipitation of limestone in great quantities presents a difficulty for the hypothesis of a long period during which a reducing atmosphere was present. After mentioning that most of the great iron bodies were laid down in the late Precambrian Age or were extensively eroded during this time, he states that iron ore of the Vermilion range of Minnesota is much earlier (Keewatin) and, thus, oxidation of ferrous iron to ferric oxide took place early in the earth's history. Later in this same paper, he states that the presence of highly oxidized iron justifies a strong presumption of an oxidizing atmosphere. These observations, based on facts drawn from geological data rather than assumptions based on cosmogonical theories, provide evidence that the earth may have had an oxidizing atmosphere over most, if not all, of its history.

Dr. Sunderland in his book, *Darwin's Enigma,* states,

"The April 1984 issue of *Scientific American* reported on an international conference of the Precambrian Paleobiology Research Group which reviewed the latest thinking on the Precambrian atmosphere. Although it concluded that there wasn't a lot of oxygen present, the report said, 'It was not however, oxygen free; the bands [oxidized iron] represent a large sink for the reactive oxygen.' It said that oxidized iron bands appear at about the same time as the first bacterial cells. Also, at about the same time that the first life appeared, carbon dioxide was present, perhaps even abundant. Actually, the report said that the earliest rusted iron bands were 3.8 billion years old and the oldest fossils of cells were 3.5 billion years old. *So, according to this group of Precambrian specialists, there is evidence of free oxygen at least 300 million years before there were living cells.*"

Molecular Transitional Forms?

Dr. Michael Denton (expert in the area of molecular biology) adds another dilemma for the evolutionists of the impossibility of the evolution of the single cell in that the *simplest* of all living cells is complex beyond our comprehension and (as with the geological strata) the final clincher is that there is no evidence of a gradual evolution (*no transitional forms*). He states,

> "Is there a break from life to inorganic life? The existence of a definite discontinuity was only finally established after the revolutionary discoveries of molecular biology in the early 1950's. Until then it was still hoped possible that science would reveal intermediates between chemistry and the cell. Instead of revealing a multitude of transitional forms, molecular biology has served only to emphasize the enormity of the gap. We now know not only of the existence of a break but *it represents the most dramatic and fundamental of all the Discontinuities of Nature.*
>
> "Molecular biology has shown that even the simplest of all living systems (Bacterial Cells) are exceedingly complex objects. The tiniest living cell has a micro–miniaturized factory containing thousands of exquisitely

designed pieces of intricate molecular machinery, made up altogether of one hundred thousand million atoms, far more complicated than any machine built by man, and is absolutely without parallel in the non-living world. *The meaning of the genetic code is virtually identical in all living cells, therefore no living cell can be thought of as being primitive or ancestral with respect to any other system. Nor is there the slightest empirical hint of an evolutionary sequence among all the incredibly diverse cells on earth.*"

Last Ditch Effort?

Life Evolved in the Bottom of the Ocean?

We first had Darwin's "peaceful warm pond" then the tops of the oceans or the seas and now the latest speculation theorizes the bottom of the oceans in a "hot pressure cooker". Scientists have discovered organisms living in oceanic hot springs. They are speculating that life evolved early in the earth's history (while it was being bombarded by the largest asteroids) at the bottom of the ocean in chimney-like structures set atop cracks of underwater geysers. This new "hot vent" hypothesis developed, of course, because of the multiple problems mentioned before, such as the wrong kind of atmosphere and the bombardment of asteroids. Even though these scientists know that this new theory is nothing but a hypothesis, the Miller experiment and theory that lightning struck the primordial sea, thus starting life, is no longer accepted.

The front cover of *Time* Magazine, October 11, 1993 had the feature article, "How Did Life Begin?" The article related all of the above and that the Scripps Research Institute in La Jolla, California was making startling new discoveries, experimenting with synthetic RNA in a thimble size test tube. They're hoping the RNA will solve the mystery of how life began.

There is a wide recognition developing with scientists not only of the impossibility of life evolving in the primitive ocean, but that traditional mechanistic models of the self assembling by molecules is also hopelessly flawed. They've hit a stone wall concerning chemicals responsible for life chemistry, such as DNA (molecule that holds master blueprints) and RNA (molecule which carries DNA information necessary to form proteins). Proteins, DNA and RNA cannot function by themselves and for life to originate, all three molecules had to emerge spontaneously and simultaneously from inorganic compounds. Researchers agree that the chance appearance of these incredibly complex molecules exactly at the same time is impossible—thus the new hope concerning RNA.

Scientists have discovered that one kind of RNA can act as an enzyme and can also function like a protein. Scientists then speculate that a primitive RNA molecule functioning as a protein and as DNA evolved in a primeval soup. Of course, as we already saw, there's no evidence of a pre-biotic soup. They then speculated that they solved the riddle of the self assembling of molecules, however, they've hit other stone walls. An article by Dr. Hugh Ross and Dr. Walter Bradley in *Facts and Faith* (Winter 1992/1993) entitled "Theories on Life Origin Take New Directions" comments on the new impossible barriers for a purely naturalistic origin of life. It states,

> "The discoveries reported this past summer showed yet more protein-like capabilities of certain RNA molecules. Researchers Noller, Hoffarth and Zimniak presented evidence that a certain RNA molecule could stimulate two amino acids to join together with a peptide bond (the kind of chemical bond formed in proteins). The team of Piccirillii, McConnell, Azug, Noller and Cech observed another RNA molecule both making and breaking the bonds that join amino acids to RNA.

"Though these capabilities plus the ones observed earlier add up to only a tiny fraction of all the functions proteins perform, several origin-of-life theorists are proposing that no proteins at all were necessary for the first life forms.

"These new findings may *seem* to make 'easier' the origination of life by strictly natural processes, but that is not necessarily the case. Even if a single primordial molecule could perform all the functions of modern DNA, RNA and proteins, such a molecule would have to be no less complex in its information content (i.e., its built-in 'knowledge' of what to do) than the sum of modern DNA, RNA and proteins. In other words, the task of assembling such an incredibly versatile molecule is no easier than that of assembling the three different kinds of molecules. The information content of the three is simply concentrated into one enormously complex molecule. Even Leslie Orgel, a leading proponent of an RNA origin of life, admits, 'You have to get an awful lot of things right and nothing wrong.'

"Another catch in these arguments is the false notion that RNA is easier to assemble than proteins or DNA. For twenty years researchers and texts taught that RNA had been synthesized in a lab under pre-biotic conditions. This myth, however, was exploded by Robert Shapiro at a meeting of the International Society for the Study of the Origin of Life held at the University of California at Berkeley in 1986. Some 300 of the top origin-of-life researchers from around the world were present.

"Shapiro traced all the references to RNA synthesis back to one paper—one ambiguous paper published in 1967. At the same meeting, he went on to demonstrate that the synthesis of RNA under pre-biotic conditions is essentially impossible. No one at the meeting challenged the soundness of his conclusion. Shapiro then published his case against RNA synthesis in the journal, *Origins of*

Life and Evolution of the Biosphere, a case that remains unchallenged to this day."

Dr. Ross and Dr. Bradley conclude,

"In some ways, the quest for a naturalistic theory for the origin of life reminds us of the 200-year effort to defend a crumbling non-theistic model for the origin of the universe. Eventually, the weight of accumulating evidence turned the tide in favor of God. What's amazing about the origin-of-life debate is that an overwhelming accumulation of evidence for God's involvement already exists, but the most vocal theorists persist in shutting God out of the picture."

What's the conclusion to the riddle of the origin of life? The latest scientific breakthroughs have now rendered a naturalistic, evolutionary explanation as impossible. The renowned Professor of Chemistry at New York University, Robert Shapiro, in his book, *Origins: A Skeptics Guide to the Origins of Life on Planet Earth*, explored seven ways to make evolution work. Shapiro, thought to be one of the foremost chemists in the world, concluded that all current theories of the mechanisms for the origin of life simply don't work. The book ends in despair as he states,

"No natural explanation for the origin of life exists."

Dr. Hugh Ross, in a hand-out entitled, "Evolution/Origin of Life" gives the following basic argument that virtually refutes organic evolution. He states,

"Compared to the inorganic systems comprising the universe, biological systems are enormously complex. The genome (complete set of chromosomes necessary for reproduction) of an E. Coli bacterium has the equivalent of about two million nucleotides. The human genome contains about six billion nucleotides. Moreover, unlike inorganic systems, the sequence in which the individual components (nucleotides) are assembled is critical for the survival of biological systems. Additional complications include the following:

- Only amino acids with left-handed configurations can be used in protein synthesis.

- Each amino acid must be activated by a specific enzyme.

- Multiple special enzymes (themselves enormously complex, sequence-critical molecules) are required to bind messenger RNA to ribosomes before protein synthesis can begin or end.

- Most mutations apparently are not spontaneous (i.e., random), yet certain adaptive "evolutionary" processes would require a multiplicity of spontaneous mutations.

"A more quantitative approach for demonstrating the impossibility of life developing by natural process was calculated by molecular biologist, Harold Morowitz. If one were to take the simplest living cell and break every chemical bond within it, the odds that the cells would reassemble under ideal natural conditions (the best possible chemical environment) would be one chance in $10^{100,000,000,000}$ (one with **a hundred billion zeros** following). Such calculations have been made by researchers, both theists and non-theists, in a variety of disciplines. A vigorous treatment has recently been done by Hubert Yockey, a leading authority in informational theory in molecular biology."

Microbiologist Michael Denton said,

"If we were to magnify a cell a thousand million times, what we would then see would be an object of unparalleled complexity and adaptive design."

Sir John Eckles, Noble Laureate in neural physiology said, "The odds against intelligent life evolving are about 400,000 trillion, trillion, trillion to one." He said that it was fantastically improbable although he believed it happened. He stated that it will never happen again on any planet or solar system.

A.K. Morrison, the brilliant scientist, stated that,

> "For life to have evolved it would demand so many billions of minute involved circumstances that must appear absolutely, simultaneously in the same infinitesimal moment for any kind of life to appear that it becomes beyond belief and possibility."

What's the conclusion? Simply that it's now known that life could **only** have come about by a supernatural act of God. Genesis 1 of the Bible reads,

> "... and the spirit of God moved on the surface of the waters ... and God said,
>
> - 'Let the earth sprout vegetation ....
>
> - Let the waters team with swarms of living creatures and let the birds fly above the earth ...
>
> - let the earth bring forth living creatures after their kind, cattle and creeping things and beasts of the earth after their kind.'
>
> - And God created man in his own image ... male and female he created them .... And God blessed them; and God said to them, 'Be fruitful and multiply.'"

Chapter 5

—The Evidence—

Homology

Even though we see ingenious intelligent design in the universe, the earth-sun system, the single cell and the geological strata as evidence for Special Creation and an ingenious architect, evolutionists have been attempting to demonstrate evolution in the area of homology (close similarity of species). They say that homology supports descent from a common ancestor. Isaac Asimov (1981) states, "Our ability to classify plants and animals on a groups-within-groups hierarchical basis virtually forces scientists to treat evolution as a 'fact.'"

When comparing apes and humans as to their skeletal, muscular, nervous, digestive and cardiovascular systems, there *is* great similarity. Also, certain bones in the human arm, the forelimb of dog, a bat's wing and a penguin's flipper is a demonstration of homology in that they all share a similarity in their basic structural pattern. Many scientists hold that the most logical explanation of this is evolution.

Creationists hold that similarity does not prove relationships between nor descendants among groups, but rather that there was a common plan in the mind of God—the works of one God would be expected to be similar. In fact, creationists look at the similarity, symmetry, purpose and interdependence in nature as a logical argument **for** an intelligent designer. Actually, on the basis of the classification system alone (looking at the sequential hierarchy scale of animals from the most simple to the most complex), it may *look* like one animal turned into the next, but this is not real proof. Just because something looks like something doesn't prove anything; a closer analysis must be made. The scientific method must be applied. Because of the latest findings, many evolutionists are now reluctantly accepting the fact that anatomical homology does not support descent from a common ancestor and that "convergence", once thought to be a freak occurrence, has become the general rule.

Convergence is a clear contradiction of the theory of evolution since evolutionary theory says that all life has evolved from the simple to the complex in animals. This would include all living systems of the body (skeletal, muscular, eyes, blood, etc.). Consequently, if evolution were true, animals that are more closely related (more recently descended from a common ancestor) would consistently have more traits in common than those that are more distantly related; however, this is not the case. Dissimilarities are also the rule.

As we proceed, we shall see that new findings are demonstrating that convergence (which demonstrates only relationship in design, not evolution) is the characteristic pattern of all life. For example, an invertebrate octopus' eye which should be lower on the evolutionary scale than vertebrates and humans (if evolution were true) is actually highly complex and in many ways essentially the same as the human eye. Both the octopus and the squid eye as well as the vertebrate eye are complete, complex and totally distinct from one another right from their first appearance in the fossil sequence.

Some evolutionists might say at this point, "Well, maybe the octopus' and squids' eye evolved during the Cambrian period." First of all, something as extremely complex as an octopus' eye would have taken eons of time, and would not likely appear until the time of the vertebrates, as evolutionists admittedly assert. Moreover, as we just saw, the Cambrian period has now shrunk to a range of 0-10 million years—an instant in geological time. If it is highly unlikely that worm-like organisms evolved into all the complex phyla during this period, how much more unlikely is it that the octopus' eye could have evolved then? Evolutionists call such examples as the octopus' eye "convergent evolution" which really means we have another example of similarity in structure that cannot be explained as evolutionary descent from a common ancestor. Creationists invite the question: "What's the most logical inference—descent from a common ancestor or creation by a common designer?" Michael Land (1979), biologist and evolutionist at Sussex University, speaks like a creationist when he states, "The vertebrate eye shares design features, not evolution, with the eye of the cephalopod Molluscs, such as the octopus."

How About Sexual Homology?

Evolutionists of the past, using crude conjectures, had presented a sequence scale of evolution of man such as the *Life* series which has now been discarded. In the graded scale, they gave elaborate explanations of how man evolved, but one question that always baffled them was how females evolved. Who evolved into whom? Which came first? (Something like the chicken and the egg controversy.) The problem for evolutionists is that there is no homology when comparing female and male reproductive organs. The famous British evolutionist, Sir Gavin de Beer (eminent British Embryologist and former director of British Museum of Natural History), in his Oxford Biology Reader, *Homology, An Unsolved Problem*, states:

"One problem concerns corresponding parts between male and female reproductive systems, something biology students are taught to call 'sexual homology'.

De Beer wants to use 'homology' only for evolutionary relationship. He tells us, in effect, *not to use that term for similarities in the basic plan of male and female anatomy. We can't even imagine, he argues, that females evolved into males, or vice versa, or that human beings evolved from an animal that had only one sex.*"

What About the Biogenetic "Law?"

The State Framework on Natural Science states,

"Scientists compare the gradual differentiation of embryonic stages from nearly identical beginnings. To establish relationships, they identify unique characteristics of development, such as going through the metamorphosis of a butterfly or the veliger stage of a larval mollusk.... These observations constitute some of the evidence that evolution has occurred."

In 1866, Earnst Haeckel advanced the so-called Biogenetic Law. It is also known as the Recapitulation Theory. The basic premise of the law is, "Ontogeny recapitulates phylogeny" which means that the development of the embryo (ontogeny) is supposed to retrace the imagined evolutionary development (phylogeny) of the organism.

Haeckel made wood carvings which indicated that the embryos of a fish, tortoise, horse, pig, monkey and man had similar appearances at various embryonic stages and claimed that his discoveries validated the theory that all life had come from a common ancestor—hence the "so called" Biogenetic "Law". Charles Darwin, disillusioned over the lack of fossil evidence said the law was second to none in importance and believed it was the best evidence for the common ancestry of all life.

It was later found that Haeckel had forged some of the drawings of embryos to make them appear in accord with his theory and used the same sketches to represent several different animals. For his forgery, he was convicted by a German Court. His book was brought to the attention of the public in 1911 in no less a book than *The Encyclopedia Britannica*:

> "Haeckel was the originator of the dictum that ontogeny recapitulates phylogeny. It has since proved to be false."

> "The biogenetic law—embryologic recapitulation—I think, was debunked back in the 1920's by embryologists. I don't see embryology as any different than any other kind of comparative morphology" —Dr. David N. Raup (Chicago Museum of Natural History).

> "Years and years of embryological research was essentially wasted because people, convinced of the theory of evolution and that embryos recapitulated their evolutionary ancestry, spent much of their time in embryological research trying to develop phylogenies based on the data of embryology. As I mentioned earlier, embryologists have abandoned the theory of embryological recapitulation. *They don't believe it. They know it is not true...it produced bad research rather than the good research that should have been done*" —Ashley Montagu (world famous anthropologist) in a debate with Dr. Duane Gish (Biochemistry U.C. Berkeley) at Princeton University (1980).

> "The theory of recapitulation was destroyed in 1922 by Professor Walter Gasbang in a famous paper, since then no respectable biologist has ever used the theory of re-capitulation, because it was utterly unsound, created by a Nazi–like preacher named Haeckel" —Dr. Montagu

> "Ladies and gentlemen, I have traveled all over the world. I have debated and lectured on many, many major university campuses, and there is *hardly a single university campus that I appear on that some student does not tell me that he is taught the theory of*

embryological recapitulation right there at that university. I've had many evolutionists argue the evidence for evolution from embryological recapitulation. Unfortunately, as Dr. Montagu has said, *it is a thoroughly discredited theory but it is still taught in most biology books and in most universities and schools as evidence for evolution"* —Dr. Gish.

"Well, ladies and gentlemen, that only goes to show that many so-called educational institutions, called universities, are not educational institutions at all or universities; *they are institutes for mis-education"* —Dr. Montagu.

Dr. Luther Sunderland ably sums up the discrediting of "ontogeny recapitulates phylogeny". He states,

"Why do modern embryologists not believe in embryological recapitulation? First, when scientists studied the embryological development of various animals and got beyond the *superficial appearance level,* they soon discovered that no higher embryo develops along the same route as is assumed for common ancestry evolution.

"The most popular evidence offered to support recapitulation is the presence of so-called 'gill slits' in the embryos of fish, mammals and human beings at a certain stage of development. This is supposed to show that man and other mammals came from an ancestral fish. It is true that the embryos of these animals have a series of folds in the tissue of the neck region. In the fish embryo the gills develop in this region, but in mammals they never form slits and are never part of the respiratory system. These folds transform into other organs having no connection with respiration, which in mammals is accomplished though the placenta. If they are never slits and are never gills, they could hardly be honestly called 'gill slits'.

"Since the human embryo has been photographed at every stage of development, *it is now known to be specifically human at every stage.*

"Even though knowledgeable embryologists have abandoned the discredited theory of embryological recapitulation, it is likely to retain its place in school and university textbooks for many years. In April 1984, it was still being taught in Ivy League colleges where this author lectured. *Yesterday's myths die hard, especially when they so nicely help to perpetuate a particular favored philosophical belief system.*"

We conclude then, that scientific research has completely discredited the so-called "Biogenetic Law". No genuine scientists or science teachers any longer use this line of argument in support of evolution. Man and animals are similar as to their muscular, skeletal, nervous and digestive systems as well as in their embryonic development. We would expect to see this—the works of one God would be expected to be the same. Commonality qualifies as evidence for a common creator. Doing away with "crude conjecturing" (the antithesis of pure science), the growing process of the human embryo is what we would expect to see as organs and systems develop from simple to complex.

How About Molecule Homology?

Some evolutionists, admitting their frustration in looking for evolution in large structures, began looking for homology in molecules. Again, they experienced the same exasperating results. Their attempt in the last twenty years has been to demonstrate the sequential evolution of proteins in the different species. The following are examples of their results, taken from the book, *What is Creation Science?* by Dr. Parker and Dr. Henry M. Morris:

- *Hemoglobin*—protein that carries oxygen in the red blood cells

Two evolutionists, Dickerson and Geis (1969), made a significant contribution in describing the three-dimensional structure of proteins and claimed that they could demonstrate the relationship between species and the evolution of proteins. However, they came up with the following contradictions and contradictory statements.

> "Hemoglobins pose a puzzling problem. Hemoglobins occur sporadically among the invertebrate phyla (the animals without backbones) in no obvious pattern" —Dickerson.

> "I would suggest that Hemoglobin does occur in a creationist mosaic. We find hemoglobin in nearly all vertebrates, but we also find it in some annelids (the earth worm group), some echinoderms (the starfish group), some mollusks (the clam group), some anthropods (the insect group), and even in some bacteria! *In all these cases, we find the same kind of molecule — complete and fully functional* —Dr. Parker.

> "It is hard to see a common line of descent snaking in so unsystematic a way through so many different phyla..." —Dickerson.

If evolution were true, we ought to be able to trace how hemoglobin evolved. But we can't. As far as creationists are concerned, *hemoglobin occurs, complete and fully functional, where it is appropriate in creation.*

- *Lysozyme* — protein that attacks bacteria

The same seems to be true for a fascinating protein called lysozyme. By comparing lysozyme and lactalbumin, Dickerson was hoping to "pin down with great precision" where human beings branched off from the mammal line. The results are surprising. In this test, it turned out that humans are more closely related to the *chicken* than to any living mammal tested! Every evolutionist knows this can't be true. And things haven't gotten better with the passing years. Ayala (1978) and Kimura (1979) show turtles more closely related to birds than to rattlesnakes (their fellow reptiles); humans and monkeys less related to placental mammals than the marsupial kangaroos are; and humans and fish closer than humans and amphibians. As Vincent Demoulin (1979) put it, "The composite evolutionary tree encompasses all the weaknesses of the individual trees." That is, adding all the evidence to look for some consistent picture makes matters even worse for the case to prove the theory of evolution.

The Failure of Homology

What are the results in the study of homology (anatomical, sexual, molecular)? They are the same as the search in the geological strata for transitional forms. Evolutionists have come up with a big zero. Such research further disproves the theory of descent from a common ancestor. All the evidence evolutionists can hang onto is the same as the classification of plants and animals and their similarity in that "... it *looks* like one evolved into another". Closer analysis through the scientific method proves otherwise.

The following is an excerpt from an address given by Colin Patterson of the British Museum to leading evolutionists at the American Museum of Natural History (1981). Dr. Patterson, by the way, is now an anti-evolutionist. Patterson first lamented that his topic, creation and evolution, had been forced on him and then he acknowledged that he has recently been entertaining non-evolutionary ideas. Why? Because, he said, after twenty years of research in evolution, he asked himself to name just one thing about evolution he knew for sure—and **he could not come up with anything.** When he asked other leading evolutionists, the only thing anyone could say was that "... *convergence is everywhere!*" Finally, Patterson said with dismay, he was faced to conclude that "Evolution is an 'anti-theory' that generates 'anti–knowledge'—a concept full of explanatory vocabulary that actually explains nothing and that even generates a false impression of what the facts are."

Evolutionists have been leveling these same accusations at creationists for decades, Patterson said, but now we have to admit that they apply to evolution as well. His chief example? Molecular taxonomy, using similarities among molecules to try to establish evolutionary lines of descent.

Evolutionists "know" (for example) that organisms which are closely related (more recently descended from a common ancestor) have more traits in common than those which are more distantly related. *But this knowledge turns out to be "anti-knowledge"* and the theory of evolution that suggested it is falsified by the data in hand. Patterson said that he finally awoke after having been duped into taking evolution as revealed truth all of his life, to find that evolutionary theory makes bad systematics (the science of classification).

Cladistics — New Classification System of Taxonomy

The evolutionary classification system of taxonomy according to Michael Denton and other scientists, is being replaced by a new school of taxonomy which supports typology, not evolution, and is known as cladistics. Michael Denton states,

> "Perhaps the most influential of the new schools of taxonomy is now widely known as Cladistics. Cladistics tend to generate classification schemes from which most of the intermediate or ancestral groups traditionally cited by evolutionary biology as 'evidence' are absent or revealed to have no objective basis. *As a rule, Cladistic*

procedures tend to depict nature in striking non-sequential terms. Cladistics aim only to discover the pattern of nature as it actually is. Cladisticism takes no account at all of any evolutionary claim regarding the genealogy or the derivation of any particular species or group.

"The hierarchic schemes correspond beautifully with the topological model of nature and the relationship between evolution and hierarchical systems is curiously ambiguous.

"Nature betrays no hint of natural evolutionary sequential arrangements, revealing species to be related as sisters or cousins but never as ancestors or descendants as required by evolution. The form of the tree makes explicit the pre-evolutionary view that is discontinuity and the absence of sequence which is the most characteristic feature of the order of nature. *The hierarchic pattern is nothing like the straight forward witness for organic evolution. If it suggests any model of nature it is typology not evolution."*

Michael Denton further confirms the emergence of typology and Cladistics that is replacing the evolutionary model. He states,

"Typology is re-emerging in the thinking of zoologists and taxonomists today."

"In a way, I think we are merely discovering pre-evolutionary systematics or if not, **rediscovering it,** fleshing it out" —Colin Patterson (Senior Paleontologist, British Museum of Natural History, London) quotes Dr. Gareth Nelson, in his book, *Systematics and Biogeography* (1981).

Colin Patterson, now a leading exponent of the new science of Cladistics, in a recent interview on the British Broadcasting Corporation program stated,

"I mean the stories, the narratives about evolution change over time—how the dinosaurs became extinct, how the mammals evolved, whether man came from molecules. These seem to me to be little more than story-telling. And this is the result of thinking about Cladistics because as it turns out, as it seems to me, all one can learn about the history of Life is learned from systematics, from groupings one finds in Nature. The rest of it is story-telling of one sort or another. We have access to the tips of a tree, but the tree itself is theory and people who pretend to know about the tree and to describe what went on with it, how the branches came off and the twigs came off are, I think, telling stories."

The evolutionary community was viewing Cladism with a growing sense of unease. *It could cause an intellectual revolution which could destroy the evolutionary model.* Dr. Keith Thompson of Yale University states,

"To the Darwinian evolution model has been added a new *Cladistic anti-thesis* which says that the search for ancestors is a 'fools errand'; it's hard to accept because it runs counter to all we have been taught."

Many biologists (in the 1980's) were saying that no species could be considered ancestor to another.

"This marks a watershed in evolutionary thought"
—Beverly Halstead.

Chapter 6

—The Evidence—

The Impossibility of Evolution

As the knowledge explosion continues to expose the mysteries of ingenious intelligent design, many scientists are beginning to question even the **possibility** of evolution. The following are examples of the reasons many scientists are questioning this theory:

The Molecular Level

It has been discovered that the simplest cell contains almost a trillion bits of data in its genes at the molecular level. Carl Sagan in *Cosmos* relates that this is the equivalent to the total number of letters in all the books in the world's largest library. He also related that there are as many atoms in one molecule of DNA as there are stars in a galaxy, and in a single-cell amoebae there is the equivalent of 80 volumes each 500 pages long, each page filled with information. In other words, each cell is a miniature factory and contained in the nucleus (headquarters of the cell) is all the information on how to reproduce itself.

The question is, if there is no God, where did this enormous amount of information come from and what kind of impersonal laws directed the formation of these cells? Evolutionary theory in essence is saying, "Nobody and nothing = everything" and, "Chance and time = everything."

Dr. Henry M. Morris (a creationist, author of the book, *The Genesis Flood*), speaking of the origin of the first cell, says,

> "What primeval DNA molecule had no previous DNA molecule to go by? Could mindless darting particles plan the systematic structure of the elements that they were to form and later get together and program the genetic code which would direct the formation of the most complex living system of all time and even enter into the replication process?"

Dr. Morris' statement is something like saying, "If you were to take your watch apart and put it in your pocket and jiggle it around, in time (if you waited long enough), you would finally hear the first tick" Keep in mind that a single cell is **infinitely more complex** than a watch, also, all this is supposed to happen **against** the relentless second law of thermodynamics (entropy) which is:

- deterioration of energy in a working system,

- progressive disorder in a structured system and

- loss of information in a programmed system.

Evolution postulates just the opposite, that everything goes from randomness to complexity, from disorder to order. Entropy demonstrates that everything is going in just the opposite direction. Evolution, then, is based on speculation with no scientific evidence, while entropy is a well-documented concept in science. In the recent Shapiro vs. Bradley debate on the origin of life, Bradley stated that putting everything together for the formation of the single cell by natural causes was like trying to straighten up a closet by throwing a stick of dynamite into it.

Fred Hoyle, (Professor of Astronomy at Cambridge University) famous British mathematician and astronomer, wrote that it is absurd to think that life evolved from dead molecules to single cells by accident. It is mathematically impossible, saying this would be the equivalent of a tornado going through a junk yard and 'accidentally' creating a Boeing 707. Evolutionists counter by saying that given enough time, anything is possible. That's about the same as saying that if you gave fifty apes enough wire and metal and millions or billions of years, they would eventually produce a B1 Bomber.

"The probability of life originating by accident is comparable to the probability of the unabridged dictionary resulting from an explosion in a print shop" —Professor Edward Conklin, noted biologist.

Dr. Hugh Ross in his tape, "Evolution versus Creation", gives other vivid illustrations, making clear the impossibility of random happenings for the self assembly of an organism. He relates that the crudest possible entity—a simple virus—is ingeniously complex. It has 600 protein molecules and the problem of having these molecules come together to produce the organism is insurmountable. To self assemble, they need enzymes—the right enzymes—in the right place at the right time. The amino acids needed must be all left-handed. Ross further relates that the chance of a random assembly is less than one in $10^{15,000,000,000}$ (10 to the 15 billionth). To picture this, take a Bible and fill it with zeroes. You would need 3,000 of these Bibles. Another illustration given by Dr. Ross for the impossibility of the origin of life by natural processes would be like putting letters of many different alphabets from different languages into a barrel and then through some kind of random sifting and shuffling process, coming out with the plays of Shakespeare or a textbook on science.

Did Life Originate on Mars?

In an article, entitled *New Developments in Martian Meteorite* in *Facts and Faith* (fourth quarter 1996), Dr. Hugh Ross (from new evidences and research) documented the high improbability of the atheistic, naturalistic, emergent life theory, especially concerning planet Mars.

This theory that life is a property of matter, in layman's language, means that life spontaneously generates, given the combination of a little liquid water and a few essential elements. In other words, as evolutionists have dogmatically asserted, "Given the right conditions, formulation of life is the inevitable consequence of chemical processes on any planet."

One exciting breakthrough which is "throwing a monkey wrench into the machinery" of the evolution of life on this planet, is the shrinkage of the geological ages. Scientists are now admitting the "Big Bang in Biology"—the instantaneous origin of life equaling the "Cambrian Explosion". Recently, *Time* magazine featured a cover story article entitled *Biology's Big Bang*. With prejudice, the article first demeaned the Bible but admitted that the Cambrian Period, instead of being more than 50 million years long, had shrunk to less than 5 million years. The article elaborated on the factual evidence of lifeforms evolving in a "geological instant" from wormlike forms to all the major animal groups—skeleton, legs, antennas, etc., but gave no explanation for this lethal anti-evolutionary evidence.

Dr. Ross relates that because of the evolutionist's present dilemma of short geologic ages, many are now being forced to conclude that life must have come from outer space and it was probably from the planet Mars. Dr. Ross quotes Cornel Astronomer Joseph Burns to this effect: "If you want to believe life originated on just one planet and transferred elsewhere, the transfer would have to be from Mars to Earth."

Scientists admit, however, that Mars simply doesn't meet the critical conditions necessary for the origin of life. Consequently, they're being forced to speculate that life must have come from planets outside our solar system. Dr. Ross states,

> "Because Mars falls far short of ideal as a life-origin site, scientists are dragging up Fred Hoyle's bizarre 'panspermia' proposition (from the late 1970's) that life originated 'out there' somewhere in the cosmos and came to our solar system, more particularly (in the new scenario) to Mars, carried on star-generated 'wind'.

> "What is the appeal of this panspermia hypothesis? It cannot be scientific plausibility. Here are just a few of its difficulties: Such interstellar space travel would require more intense light than the sun's to push the microbes, but such light's ultraviolet rays would kill bare organisms in just a few days. If the microbes were encased in dust grains, their survival could be assured; however, the extra mass of this dust grain shield would necessitate stars as bright as red supergiants to propel them through space. And yet, as I explain in *The Creator and the Cosmos*, life cannot possibly have ever survived on planets orbiting supergiant stars.

> "For these reasons alone, without even addressing the virtually impossible odds of finding a planet anywhere in the observable universe with precise features for life support, panspermia should (in the scientific sense of 'should') be a dead hypothesis. My hunch as to why scientists resist pulling the plug finds support in Christopher McKay's profound 'confession'. McKay, co-author of the ALH84001 (mars meteorite) study, aware that life arose on Earth in a geologic instant (less than five million years), admits we face a narrow choice,

'Either life on Earth began whole... or it began somewhere else.'"

Present Processes

The final acid test is what do we see now? Dr. Ross states,

"Do we see viruses popping out of nothing, by assembling amino acids? We have billions of tons of the stuff! Are we seeing new bacterium being formed, coming together by chance? We are not seeing that—we've been observing this planet for thousands of years —why do we expect such extrapolation?"

Dr. Henry M. Morris in Impact, July 1990, in an article entitled "The Logic of Biblical Creation" comments on present processes. He states,

"By definition, evolution should still be occurring now, since it is to be explained by present processes.... If there is anything certain in this world, however, it is that there is *no evidence whatever* that evolution is occurring today —that is, true vertical evolution, from some simpler kind to a more complex kind. No one has ever observed a star evolve from hydrogen, life evolving from chemicals, a higher species evolve from a lower species, a man from an ape or anything else of this sort. Not only has no one ever observed true evolution in action, no one knows how evolution works, or even how it might work. Since no one has ever seen it happen (despite thousands of experiments that have tried to produce it), and no one yet has come up with a workable mechanism to explain it, it would seem that it has been falsified, at least as far as the present world is concerned."

In the geological strata, the fossils record extinctions but also speciation—God creates new species to replace those that went extinct. A good question is, "Where are the new species today, to replace those that are going extinct?" Also, "Why has the creation of new species ceased?"

Dr. Ross, in a paper entitled "The Shell Game of Evolution and Creation", ably sums up the origin of life debate and gives the biblical reason for no new life, or even new species of animals coming into existence. He first quotes biologists, Paul and Anne Ehrlich. He states,

> "'The production of a new animal species in nature has yet to be documented...[it is] so slow that it has not even been possible to detect an increase in the amount of differentiation.'
>
> "At the same time, as the Ehrlichs also point out, we are witnessing an extinction rate of about one species per hour. Even if the human activity factors are removed, one is still left with an extinction rate of at least one species every year. Yet, the fossil record reveals millennia of both a high extinction rate and a high speciation rate. *The Bible offers a solution to the enigma. We are now in God's seventh day (the present era), He rested.*"

The Human Brain

Besides the universe of outer space and the universe found within the single cell in the molecular world, another universe which evolutionists have great difficulty in explaining (as to its origin and nature) is the human brain. This organ composed of 10 to 15 billion highly differentiated but profoundly interlocked cells is a baffling mystery as well as an unbridgeable gap between Homo Sapiens and the animal world.

Dr. Richard Restak, a neurologist and author of *The Brain: The Last Frontier*, states,

"The functioning of the brain has been variously linked to the working of a telephone switch board, a railway system, a computer. None of these models has proven entirely adequate. So far as we know, the brain is unlike any other structure in the universe, and perhaps only the vast universe itself presents conceptual problems of equal complexity.... *If the workings of the brain remain elusive, even that has its uses. It reminds us that human beings are a race apart.*"

Sir Charles Sherrington, a Nobel Prize winning neurophysiologist, referred to the brain as an "enchanted loom" that weaves a dissolving pattern, always a meaningful pattern though never an enduring one; a shifting harmony of sub-patterns . Scientists today are baffled over these subpatterns, as Dr. Restak states,

"How are they formed? What is the guiding principle by which billions of neurons can be orchestrated to produce a symphony or a sonnet, a poem or a play, a pet scanner or a paradigm, a trianon or a trance? We do not, of course, know."

Dr. Mark Looy, in an article in *Impact* entitled "I Think, Therefore There Is a Supreme Thinker", comments on the complexity of the human brain. He states,

"The adult brain—weighing only about three pounds and averaging about 1400 cubic centimeters—contains about ten billion (10^{10}) neurons. The neuron (or nerve cell) is the basic unit of the brain. Each contains branching fibers, called dendrites, and each neuron is in dendritic contact with as many as 10,000 other neurons. Amazingly, the total number of neuron interconnections (also called 'bits') is approximately 100 trillion (10^{15}), and if the dendritic connections were laid end to end, they would circle the earth more than four times."

In the same article, Isaac Asimov is quoted as stating,

"In Man is a three-pound brain which, as far as we know, is the most complex and orderly arrangement of matter in the universe."

Michael Denton in his book, *Evolution: A Theory in Crisis*, has offered the following descriptive observation and analogy regarding the brain's 10^{15} connections:

"Numbers in the order of 10^{15} are of course completely beyond comprehension. Imagine an area about half the size of the USA (one million square miles) covered in a forest of trees containing ten thousand trees per square mile. If each tree contained ten thousand leaves, the total number of leaves in the forest would be 10^{15}, equivalent to the number of connections in the human brain."

Physicist Dr. Don De Young and Richard Bliss in an article in *Impact* (February 1990) entitled "Thinking About the Brain", ably sum up the complexity of an evolutionary origin:

"But there is one particular aspect of design which is so powerful, so convincing, that it almost seems unfair to challenge evolution with it. The reference is to our brain, the greatest concentration of chemo-neurological order and complexity in the physical universe. It is a video camera and library, a computer and communication center, all in one. And the more the brain is used, the better it becomes! A detailed picture of the human brain is slowly emerging, the origin of which seems entirely beyond comprehension from a naturalistic point of view. We see remarkable purpose and interdependence within the brain—every part works for the benefit of the whole.

"In addition, every single neuronal cell within the brain contains a trillion atoms. This is like a microscopic universe within each cell, complete with order, purpose, and interdependence of components."

The Mind Versus the Brain

Many scientists today are beginning to concede the absurdity of the idea that mankind's brain is only some kind of sophisticated physiological chemical computer machine and some admit that because of the brain's uniqueness, there is an unbridgeable gap between animal and man. Within this context, they admit their quandary over the "mind" versus the "brain" concept. Why do humans, unlike animals, reflect on the universe and upon themselves? Why do humans use expressive language and where, in the human brain is the "I"? Dr. Richard M. Restak in an essay in the magazine, *The Wilson Quarterly*, entitled "The Brain", writes,

> "What brain events correspond with conscious experience? For instance, what is going on in my brain when, in a restaurant, I order a chocolate soufflé? How does it differ from events that would accompany my choosing an apple pie a la mode instead? Implicit in such questions is the assumption that there must exist correlations between my choices and the events going on in my brain. But what are they?

> "The answer immediately introduces two levels of discourse masquerading as only one. To choose a chocolate soufflé will be meaningful to the waiter *and involve innumerable variables that can never be reduced to an explanation at the level of a chemical slipping across a synapse.* Why am I in the restaurant in the first place? What does my ordering of a highly caloric dessert imply about my attitude toward obesity?

> "To ask such a question is immediately to participate in a long-standing debate regarding the place of language in human motivation. To some researchers, human language is only a more sophisticated version of all the kinds of communication seen in lower primates.

Attempts to teach chimps to speak have, on occasion, been declared successful, yet, invariably, *the 'language' has been revealed as only a clever form of imitation or, in the words of Sir Edmund Leach, 'a series of circus tricks.'*

"To conclude, a detailed study of the brain is not ever going to shed much light on why I choose a chocolate soufflé over pie a la mode. *As Leach put it, the capacity to make choices, which is linked to language, 'represents a major discontinuity with the rest of nature.' Our biology may constrain our behavior, but it does not dictate it.*"

Is the Mind Nothing but the Brain?

The above quote by Dr. Restak illustrates the dilemma of scientists holding on to their non-theistic, materialistic, evolutionary-based views of reality. New scientific findings attest to an ingenious creation by a Creator of unsearchable, infinite wisdom and majesty, as revealed in the Bible. The Bible also provides an answer to the scientist's quandary over the "mind versus the brain" concept, by revealing that an individual person is housed in the human body and brain. The apostle Peter relates in II Peter 1:13,14,

"I live in the tent of this body...I know that I will soon put it aside, as our Lord Jesus Christ has made clear to me."

Paul also writes, "... absent from body, present with the Lord" (II Corinthians 5:8).

Many scientists and psychologists agree with the biblical position. Sir John Eccles, author of *The Self and Its Brain, The Human Mystery*, and *The Human Psyche* (1980), concludes after years of brain research, "There is an ontologically distinct soul or mind that gives rise to or initiates visual perception, memory or emotional responses." Daniel N. Robinson, Professor of Psychology at Georgetown University states,

> "The question, 'Can the brain understand itself?' should be recast in the form, 'Can the lung understand itself?' if the silliness of radical materialism is to be disclosed. The optic nerve does not 'see' anything; *we* see, and we do so using the machinery of the (visual) nervous system. This no more confers experience on the nervous system than a handshake confers friendliness on the hand."

Is the mind nothing but the brain, as the evolutionist is forced to believe, or is there a person housed in the body using the ingenious mechanism of the brain? Are humans only different in "degree" from animals because of a larger or more complex brain; or are humans different in "kind" by special creation? From what we now know about the brain, the Bible has been vindicated. Man is **not** just a mass of nucleated protoplasm with electricity going through him, but a creature with a soul created in the image of God.

As with the single cell and the human brain, the examples of ingenious design in nature are uncountable, demonstrating the impossibility of evolution. A very important book, *The Creation Explanation*, provides many other examples. The authors, Kelley Seagraves and Robert Kofahl, state that they believe the *most* powerful evidence for creation over evolution is to be found in specific evidences of intelligent, purposeful design. The following are paraphrased examples of the latest scientific findings which defy an evolutionary explanation.

• Bird Navigators

The navigational abilities of birds remain largely a mystery to science. One example is the navigation of a species of warbler summers in Germany. After the young are raised, and at the close of the season, the parent birds depart for the headwaters of the Nile in Africa, leaving the young birds behind for they are not yet ready for the long flight. A few weeks later the young birds take off and fly to Africa traveling thousands of miles without a guide over a path they have never seen, to join their parents. How do they accomplish this? German scientists proved that they navigate by the stars. These birds are hatched from the egg with this ability and with the pre-programmed navigational and flight instructions already in their little bird brains.

Evolutionary science has absolutely no explanation as to how bird and animal navigational capabilities could have evolved. The simple, reasonable explanation is that these creatures were designed this way by the Creator.

- **Spider Aquanauts**

Most spiders do not like water. They are dry land creatures. But Argyroneta lives under the water! These clever creatures live in little silken diving bells a foot or so under the surface of ponds and streams in Europe. At the surface they capture bubbles of air, which cling to the hairs of their abdomens, and they fill their diving bells with bubbles brought down from the top. The female Argyroneta lays her eggs in her diving bell, and the little spiderlets begin their life there beneath the surface. When they are ready to begin an independent life, they dart out into the water sheathed in a silvery bubble of air borrowed from their mother's diving-bell home. We challenge evolutionary science to come up with a rational explanation for the origin of Argyroneta.

- **Cyanide is Good for the Millipede**

The millipede species, Apheloria Corrugata, is a very clever chemist. On both sides of each segment of its body where a pair of legs attach, subsurface glands produce a liquid containing a chemical compound, mandelonitrile. When the millipede is attacked by ants or other enemies, it mixes the mandelonitrile with a catalyst, causing it to decompose to form benzaldehyde, a mild irritant, and hydrogen cyanide gas. Hydrogen cyanide is the deadly poison used in the gas chamber to execute criminals. There the millipede sits, happily basking in a cloud of lethal fumes while his attackers flee in all directions. When the coast is clear, he crawls off, for some unknown reason totally unaffected by his own deadly poison.

* **The Cowboy Fungus**

Another example of intelligent and purposeful design in living creatures is that of the predatory molds. There are many species of soil molds which capture and feed upon the tiny, exceedingly numerous nematode worms which inhabit the soil. Some of these molds grow sticky knobs with which they entrap the worms. But the star predatory mold species is *Arthrobotrys dactyloides* which lassos its prey like a cowboy lassos steers. Only when nematodes are present in the soil does this mold grow tiny loops. Within one-tenth of a second, the loop cells swell and the loop clamps shut on the worm, strangling it. The worm is then digested at leisure.

The above are examples of design for which there is no evolutionary explanation. These things point unmistakably to an infinitely wise and powerful Designer and Creator.

Will a Rifle Work with Any of Its Parts Missing?

Another unanswerable question to the evolutionist is, "How does an organism function or survive in the evolutionary process, with any of its parts missing?" For example, scientists have discovered a one-celled bacteria, used for digestion in the stomach, called E. Coli, the smallest known organism. E. Coli has little hairs called cilia which propel it around. Right where the hair intercepts the wall is a very complex motor of 32 nodes. The motor induces a flow of proteins in the nodes which produces electricity, allowing the tiny one-celled organism to turn around and move. If any part of the intricate motor isn't there, it does not work and the organism isn't able to move. *In other words, creation not evolution, is the only answer — all parts had to come into being at once or the organism wouldn't survive.*

Another example from nature is Brachinus, the Bombardier Beetle. This beetle was a puzzle for many years as to how it warded off its enemies until recently, when a German scientist, Professor Schildnecht, unraveled the mystery. On close microscopic analysis, Brachinus was shown to possess in its tail, two swivel tubes which could be aimed like flexible guns in the tail of a bomber. In its body, it has two glands producing a liquid mixture, two connected storage chambers and two combustion chambers. The stored liquid is of the same chemical substances used in rockets which, when put together in a test tube, will cause an explosion. When an enemy approaches, the beetle immediately transfers the liquid to the combustion chambers, where a reaction takes place—and for some unknown reason, it doesn't blow up the beetle. The resulting products are fired boiling hot at the enemy (212 degrees F). Spiders, ants and even toads are repelled by Brachinus' chemical warfare. Scientists admit to their quandary over how such an insect could have evolved.

"To suppose that the eye could have been formed by natural selection seems, I freely confess, absurd in the highest degree" —Charles Darwin, Origin of Species.

Evolutionists believe that species developed by slow adaptations. The changes take place over millions of years, and each intermediate stage or mutation confers a selective advantage upon the organism. The question is, what selective adaptation would be advantageous to Brachinus—one fourth, one half, two thirds, to completion? Did Brachinus drag its tail around for millions of years until one day it evolved far enough to work?

Remember, Brachinus' tail gun, like a rifle, won't work if **any part** of it is missing.

The same is true of the evolution of the eyes. Did animals and human stumble around for million of years with bumps or holes in their heads until some kind of adaptive advantage made their eyes work? The conclusion is obvious—the latest scientific findings have turned into nightmares for scientists who had hoped for and were confident that through the advances of science, answers to mankind's evolutionary origin would finally be resolved. They have hit a fog bank or in fact, a stone wall.

Could Mutations Cause Evolution?

Many scientists now admit that the random mutations that are supposed to be the cause of evolution by producing changes in the genetic structure, are 99.9% mistakes and harmful and can't account for the evolution of life. They represent losses, not gains to the genetic structure. For example, scientists have done many different experiments on fruit flies causing mutations on the genetic structure of the fly. The results in the offspring of the fly (while trying to turn a fly into a mosquito) produced only deformities such as flies with one wing, no wings, one leg, curled wings, wavy wings, red eyes, etc. Some scientists are looking for new "miracle laws", again sounding more like creationists.

"Some contemporary biologists, as soon as they observe a mutation, talk about evolution. They are implicitly supporting the following syllogism: mutations are the only evolutionary variations, all living beings undergo mutations, therefore all living beings evolve. This logical scheme is, however, unacceptable: first, because its major premise is neither obvious nor general; second, because its conclusion does not agree with the facts. *No matter how numerous they may be, mutations do not produce any kind of evolution.*

"We add that it would be all too easy to object that mutations have no evolutionary effect because they are eliminated by natural selection. Lethal mutations (the worst kind) are effectively eliminated, but others persist as alleles. The human species provides a great many examples of this, e.g., the color of the eye, the shape of the auricle, dermatoglyphics, the color and texture of the hair, the pigmentation of the skin. Mutants are present within every population, from bacteria to man. There can be no doubt about it. But for the evolutionist, the essential truth lies elsewhere: in the fact that mutations do not coincide with evolution" —Pierre-Paul Grasse (University of Paris and past–President, French Academic des Science) in *Evolution of Living Organisms*, Academic Press, New York, 1977, p. 88.

Dr. Scott M. Huse in his book, *The Collapse of Evolution* (1980), states concerning mutations,

"Incidentally, mutations do not account for the giraffe's long neck either. The slight differences in neck lengths are now known to be caused by differences in food; or by variation in the genes that control neck length. Mutations are not only harmful, but they are also very rare. They occur once in about every ten million duplications of a DNA molecule! Furthermore, mutations are random, not directional. Thus, mutations are unpredictable and do not follow any ordered design or plan, as would certainly be expected if the concept of organic evolution is to have any hope at all. Consequently, random mutations cannot account for organized directional evolution; they lack the all-important capacity for intelligent design."

What About Natural Selection?

Evolutionary textbooks regularly present the English Peppered Moth (Biston Betularia) as the most famous and sometimes as the greatest proof of natural selection under conditions of environmental change. The argument goes, that before the industrial revolution both light and dark moths were present. Soon, the light colored trees darkened, leaving the light colored moths vulnerable to birds, and in time dark colored moths prevailed. The problem here is that the moth is still the same species of moth, there's no real evolutionary change. The change is trivial. There's an enormous difference between color change of different kinds of fruit flies in Hawaii and the evolution of an organ like the brain, or an animal like an elephant or a bee.

Evolutionist L. Harrison Matthews, concerning the English Peppered Moth states,

> "The experiments show the effects of predation on the survival of the dark and of the normal forms of the Peppered Moth in a clean environment and in one polluted by smoke. The experiments beautifully demonstrate natural selection—or survival of the fittest—in action. But they do not show evolution in progress, for however the populations may alter in their content of light, intermediate or dark forms, all the moths remain from beginning to end Biston Berularia."

Dr. Philip E. Johnson, concerning one of the latest alleged evidences for natural selection, states,

> "Currently, the Darwinists are trumpeting some research on guppies as providing the elusive proof. The breeding practices of guppy populations vary according to the kind of predators they face. When predators attack adults, guppies tend to produce more offspring earlier in life, and when predators attack primarily juveniles the adults tend to bear their offspring later in life.
>
> "Variability like this does not show guppies on the way toward turning into something else. On the contrary, it shows flexibility within limits. Like peppered moths, guppies avoid extinction by retaining the genetic capacity

for back-and-forth modification as circumstances change. Nonetheless, reports of the guppy observations are being presented to the public as proof of 'evolution'. The misunderstanding is not the fault of journalists, but of a science that is working too hard to support a creaky paradigm."

In his book, *Defeating Darwinism*, Philip Johnson comments on the recently published book, *The Beak of the Finch*, by Jonathan Weiner which describes new studies on the Galapagos Islands that supposedly confirm Darwin's original work. He states,

"Studies show that the average size of finch beaks on a particular island varies from year to year in response to environmental changes. However, anyone who has even the slightest acquaintance with the evolution-creation controversy would know that such minor variation is readily accepted by even the strictest biblical creationists. The evolution-creation controversy is not about minor variations but about how things like birds come into existence in the first place."

Carl Sagan of *Cosmos* illustrated natural selection with a dandelion. He states, "At first look, it gives the impression or sensation of design—that something or someone must have created it." He then showed his pocket watch, saying, "A watch implies a watchmaker, but I will show you a better way and much more convincing—natural selection." He then goes on to demonstrate artificial (man-made) selection showing how farmers through selective interbreeding create different types of cattle. The problem is, of course, a cow remains a cow, there's no real evolution. Carl Sagan seems to ignore the need for a pre-existent human intelligence in order to produce these variations.

Dr. Sunderland in his book, *Darwin's Enigma*, quotes Dr. William Fix on the failure of natural selection and how the general public is not being informed of the true status of evolution theory.

"In *The Bone Peddlers*, William Fix, after documenting how the various assumed ancestors of man had been discredited, then went on to enumerate the difficulties with other aspects of evolution, such as the lack of transitional fossils and the vacuous nature of natural selection.   He pointed out that many prominent evolutionists like Ernst Mayr and George Gaylord Simpson had admitted that Darwin really did not solve the question of how the different species originated. He questioned '... how in *Cosmos* (1980) Carl Sagan can invoke natural selection as if this were an uncontested immutable law of nature' *when it was pure speculation with no positive evidence that it was ever responsible for creating anything new.*"

He agreed with Norman Macbeth that the public was not being informed about the status of evolution theory: "More than one responsible person has voiced concern that *the real facts about Darwinism and evolution are simply not reaching the public.*"

Design Demands a Designer

"The recognition of design in nature is no ephemeral scientific conclusion based upon the researchers of a decade or two in the history of science—a conclusion which might at any time be reversed were a few new facts to come to light. Rather it is a conclusion so certain that if it should one day transpire that it was a gigantic mistake, man would have every ground for doubting whether valid conclusions of any kind can be reached by thinking" — *Scientific American.*

Hume Refuted — Paley Vindicated

The teleological argument (watch-to-watchmaker) has always been a valid argument for the existence of a supreme being, and now in modern times with the latest scientific findings, the argument is conclusive. Chuck Missler in *Personal Update* (July 1996) in an article entitled, *The Divine Watchmaker? — The Accidental Watch,* illustrates the truth of Bishop Paley's watch-to-watchmaker argument for the existence of God and divine creation. He states,

> "If I told you that this watch on my wrist was designed by a team of engineers, skillfully crafted by a team of highly trained technicians, sent to a jobber and from there to the store where my wife bought it as a gift for me, would you believe me?
>
> "Well, let me tell you what *really* happened: Millions and millions of years ago there were atoms freely floating through the universe. Cosmic winds drew them together, clustering them into various materials: silicon, crystals, metals and other various parts. Through the random effects of chance—over millions of years, of course—these various elements were thrown together into this interesting device that now adorns my wrist.... and it has been keeping pretty good time ever since!
>
> "Ridiculous, isn't it? The notion that this complex little device 'happened' by the caprice of chance alone is, of course, absurd. It is obviously the object of careful, skillful design.
>
> "Strange. We reject the notion that this watch happened by accident; yet it is vastly simpler than the wrist upon which it resides.
>
> "The watch is a simple 'open loop' design. The wrist is a 'closed loop' servo system, which is vastly more sophisticated. It adjusts to ambient conditions, fights off invaders—even repairs itself—and involves design elements we are only just now beginning to understand! Why is it that we require a designer to explain the origin of the watch, yet are willing to ascribe the biological systems which it adorns to chance?"

Bishop Paley

This rhetorical example was first suggested by Bishop William Paley in 1818. He pointed out that the watch with its gears, springs and other mechanisms could never rise by the actions of random chance alone.

He was rebutted, however, by David Hume, who countered:

"Living systems only have the appearance of machines. Unless it can be proven that living systems are indeed machines at the molecular level, then Paley's watch-maker argument is irrelevant."

Modern science, however, has clearly refuted Hume and totally vindicated Paley. Modern microbiology has revealed that even the simplest organisms are complex machines beyond our imagining. Sir Fred Hoyle summed it clearly:

"The speculation of *The Origin of the Species* turned out to be wrong. It is ironic that the scientific facts throw Darwin out, but leave Paley ... the ultimate winner."

Michael Denton in 1986 pointed out:

"Although the tiniest bacterial cells are incredibly small, each is in effect a veritable micro-miniaturized factory containing thousands of exquisitely designed pieces of intricate molecular machinery, made up of 100 billion atoms, far more complicated than any machine built by man and absolutely without parallel in the non-living world.

"How strange that we ascribe the evident genius in *their* design to the caprice of accident or chance.

"The ancient cultures worshipped idols and false gods. Modern society has invented the most insulting 'god' of all: randomness. We've chosen to declare a master designer unnecessary and non-existent. How humiliating!"

The book, *Darwin's Black Box — The Biochemical Challenge to Evolution* (1996), by Michael J. Behe, provides by use of the most sophisticated electronic microscopes, numerous examples of irreducible complexity at the molecular level—the "bottom line". Dr. Behe, Associate Professor of Biochemistry at Lehigh University and formerly a convinced neo-Darwinist, now persuasively argues that biochemical "machines" could not have been produced by gradual evolution, but must have been designed by God or some other higher intelligence. The renowned chemist, Robert Shapiro, stated,

> "*Darwin's Black Box* should be on the essential reading list of all those who are interested in the question of where we came from, as it presents the most thorough and clever presentation of the design argument that I have seen."

Peter Van Inwegen, Professor of Philosophy at Notre Dame University, states, "If Darwinians respond to this important book by ignoring it, misrepresenting it, or ridiculing it, that will be evidence in favor of the widespread suspicion that Darwinism today functions more as an **ideology** than as a **scientific theory**."

The following ten brief excerpts are taken from Dr. Behe's book, *Darwin's Black Box:*

- "A watch is *not* a black box. We can take the back off and see how it works. From Darwin, in the last half of the 19th and up until the middle of the 20th century, the molecular level was a black box. But now, with the great scientific advances in biochemistry, the last black box of the source of life has been opened.

- "Modern science has learned that, ultimately, life is a molecular phenomenon: All organisms are made of molecules that act as the nuts and bolts, gears and pulleys of biological systems. Therefore the science of biochemistry which studies those molecules, has as its mission the exploration of the very foundation of life.

- "It was once expected that the basis of life would be exceedingly simple. That expectation has been smashed. Vision, motion and other biological functions have proven to be no less sophisticated than television cameras and automobiles.... the elegance and complexity of biological systems at the molecular level have paralyzed science's attempt to explain their origins.

- "The cumulative results show with piercing clarity that life is based on *machines*—machines made of molecules! Molecular machines haul cargo from one place in the cell to another along 'highways' made of other molecules, while still others act as cables, ropes and pulleys to hold the cell in shape. Machines turn cellular switches on and off, sometimes killing the cell or causing it to grow. Solar-powered machines capture the energy of photons and store it in chemicals. Electrical machines allow current to flow through nerves. Manufacturing machines build other molecular machines, as well as themselves. Cells swim using machines, copy themselves with machinery, ingest food with machinery. In short, highly sophisticated molecular machines control every cellular process. Thus the details of life are finely calibrated, and the machinery of life enormously complex.

- "Can all of life be fit into Darwin's theory of evolution? If you search the scientific literature on evolution, and if you focus your search on the question of how molecular machines—the basis of life—developed, you find an eerie and complete silence.

- "What type of biological system could not be formed by 'numerous, successive, slight modifications?' Well, for starters, a system that is irreducibly complex. By *irreducibly complex* I mean a single system composed of several well-matched, interacting parts that contribute to the basic function, wherein the removal of any one of the parts causes the system to effectively cease functioning. Any precursor to an irreducibly complex system that is missing a part is by definition nonfunctional.... Since natural selection can only choose systems that are already working, a biological system cannot be produced gradually. It would have to arise as an integrated unit, in one fell swoop, for natural selection to have anything to act on."

- "Some bacteria boast a marvelous swimming device, the flagellum, which has no counterpart in more complex cells. In 1973 it was discovered that some bacteria swim by rotating their flagella. So the bacterial flagellum acts as a rotary propeller—in contrast to the cilium, which acts more like an oar.

"The rotary nature of the bacterial flagellar motor was a startling, unexpected discovery. Because the bacterial flagellum is necessarily composed of at least three parts—a paddle, a rotor and a motor [rod (drive shaft), studs, rotor, bushings, universal joint, filament (propeller)]—it is irreducibly complex. Gradual evolution of the flagellum, like the cilium, therefore faces mammoth hurdles.

"Even though we are told that all biology must be seen through the lens of evolution, no scientist has *ever* published a model to account for the gradual evolution of this extraordinary molecular machine."

- "Molecular evolution is not based on scientific authority. There are assertions that such evolution occurred, but absolutely none are supported by pertinent experiments or calculations.

"...In the face of the enormous complexity that modern biochemistry has uncovered in the cell, the scientific community is paralyzed. No one at Harvard University, no one at the National Institutes of Health, no member of the National Academy of Sciences, no Nobel prize winner—no one at all can give a detailed account of how the cilium, or vision, or blood clotting, or any complex biochemical process might have developed in a Darwinian fashion. But we are here. Plants and animals are here. The complex systems are here. All these things got here somehow: if not in a Darwinian fashion, then how?

"Clearly, if something was not put together gradually, then it must have been put together quickly or even suddenly. If adding individual pieces does not continuously improve the function of a system, then multiple pieces have to be added together."

- "There is an elephant in a roomful of scientists who are trying to explain the development of life. The elephant is labeled 'intelligent design'. To a person who does not feel obliged to restrict his search to unintelligent causes, the straightforward conclusion is that biochemical systems were designed. They were designed not by the laws of nature, not by chance and necessity; rather they were *planned*. Life on earth at its most funda-mental level, in its most critical components, is the product of intelligent activity."

- The knowledge we now have of life at the molecular level has been stitched together from innumerable experiments in which proteins were purified, genes cloned, electron micrographs taken, cells cultured, structures determined, sequences compared, parameters varied, and controls done. Papers were published, results checked, reviews written, blind alleys searched and new leads fleshed out.

"The result of these cumulative efforts to investigate the cell —to investigate life at the molecular level—is a loud, clear, piercing cry of *'design!'* The result is so unambiguous and so significant that it must be ranked as one of the greatest achievements in the history of science. The discovery rivals those of Newton and Einstein, Lavoisier and Schrödinger, Pasteur and Darwin. The observation of the intelligent design of life is as momentous as the observation that the earth goes around the sun .... But no bottles have been uncorked, no hands slapped. Instead, a curious, embarrassed silence surrounds the stark complexity of the cell.

"Why does the scientific community not greedily embrace its startling discovery? Why is the observation of design handled with intellectual gloves? The dilemma is that while one side ... is labeled intelligent design, the other side might be labeled God."

The teleological argument (watch-to-watch maker) has **always** been a valid argument for the existence of a supreme being, and now in modern times, with the latest scientific findings the argument is conclusive — unless (as someone has said) we are all insane! Michael Denton (expert in molecular biology) ably sums up the argument from design, which any thinking person, must ultimately realize means the demise of evolution. He stated,

"We would never infer in the case of a machine, such as a watch, that its design was due to natural processes such as the wind and rain; rather, we would be obliged to postulate a watchmaker. *Living things are similar to machines, exhibiting the same sort of adaptive complexity and we must, therefore, infer by analogy that their design is also the result of intelligent activity.*

"Is it really credible that random processes could have constructed a reality, the smallest element of which—a functional protein or gene—is complex beyond our own creative capabilities, a reality which is the very antitheses of chance, which excels in every sense anything produced by the intelligence of man?"

Michael Denton concludes,

"Considering its historic significance and the social and moral transformation it caused in western thought, one might have hoped that Darwinian theory was capable of a complete, comprehensive and entirely plausible explanation for all biological phenomena—that it is neither fully plausible, nor comprehensive, is deeply troubling. *One might have expected that a theory of such cardinal importance, a theory that literally changed the world, would have been something more than metaphysics, something more than a myth.*"

"*Ultimately the Darwinian theory of evolution is no more nor less than the great cosmogonic myth of the twentieth century.*"

Michael Denton, a former evolutionist, put it quite succinctly. Webster defines a myth this way: "A commonly held, accepted belief not supported by the evidence." The tragedy is that evolution is still the foundation and frame of reference for the western world. This lie has had a devastating effect in essentially every area of human endeavor.

Chapter 7

Evolution's Effect on American Society

- If the theory of evolution fails to explain the data that is coming to light, then why do scientists desperately hold onto their positions?

- Also (considering the importance of origins to a person's philosophy of life), is it possible that the primary reason for our country falling apart at her moral seams is that America has been bombarded with evolutionary thought for the last fifty years?

Both of these crucial questions must be faced openly and honestly. Science literally means knowledge, or truth. Many scientists today who once taught their university students that the bottom line on origins had finally been figured out are now confessing that they were wrong. They are forced to admit their indefensible position by the explosion of scientific knowledge in the last ten to fifteen years. New information runs absolutely counter to evolutionary orthodoxy and they have come to a realization that evolutionists often "bend" the evidence to support their theories—deceptions are common. Public school students are still being taught the science of fifty years ago and false assertions are still being made; e.g., life has almost been produced in a test tube. People are not being told that transitional forms are still imaginary and are only assumed to have existed by evolutionists.

Because of the lack of substantiating evidence for evolution, many knowledgeable scientists are leaving the evolution camp. They have rightly come to the same conclusion as Philip E. Johnson (*Defeating Darwinism*) that "evolution is simply a belief system - an ideology that goes far beyond scientific evidence."

Why do so many scientists still hold to the theory of evolution, when the evidence is pointing toward creation? First of all, there is an information gap. Many scientists are not aware of the latest breakthroughs in cosmology, geology, paleontology and biology. Science teachers are following traditional lines of their peers which in many cases is the science of fifty years ago. The second reason is that most scientists are materialists, and look only for naturalistic explanations of the data. Thus, they approach the question of origins with two assumptions—number one, there is no God, and number two, miracles are impossible. They conclude that if this is true, then the only way all things could have come about is by evolution. When confronted with the evidences for creation, many reply, "We don't discuss myth" or, "That position is irrational and unacceptable" or, "This is a religious question that has nothing to do with science." Is this an honest approach for arriving at the truth? Is it possible that such a close-minded attitude has resulted in an educational system that is really teaching that $2 + 2 = 5$?

As already mentioned, many former evolutionists are becoming creationists. Others are agnostic (they say we cannot know) and many are expressing serious doubts. Some are admitting their reluctance to change because evolution is really their religion, in a sense. Prominent scientist, F. Appleton (an evolutionist) stated in a weekend magazine:

> "We admit there are gaping holes in the evidence for evolution.... Even for an advanced scientist, there is a point where explanations become threadbare and you have to admit you really don't know.... Yes evolution is

only a theory. Believing in evolution, then is an act of faith."

Fred Hoyle, on the origin of life:

"The likelihood of the formation of life from inanimate matter is one to a number of 40,000 noughts (zeroes) after it.... It is big enough to bury Darwin and the whole theory of evolution .... If the beginnings of life were not random, they must therefore have been the product of purposeful intelligence."

Larry Azar, evolutionist and philosopher states concerning transitional fossils:

"I can understand the inherent difficulty in attempting to discover intermediate forms. My problem concerns the *methodology* of science: if an evolutionist accepts gaps as a prerequisite for his theory, is he not arguing from a lack of evidence? Is he not really like the man of religious faith who says: 'I believe, even though there is no evidence?'"

"The fact that a theory so vague, so insufficiently verifiable, and so far from the criteria otherwise applied in 'hard' science has become a dogma can only be explained on sociological grounds" —Ludwig von Bertalanffy, Ph.D. Professor of Biology.

"A growing number of respectable scientists are defecting from the evolutionist camp ... moreover, for the most part these 'experts' have abandoned Darwinism, not only on the basis of religious faith or biblical persuasions, but on strictly scientific grounds, and in some instances, regretfully" —Wolfgang Smith, Ph.D. physicist and mathematician.

The following is a summary and excerpt from an article by British physicist, H. S. Lipson (1980) (Professor of Physics, University of Manchester U.K.). Lipson first expressed his interest in life's origin and his feelings—quite apart from any preference for creation—thus:

> "In fact, evolution became in a sense a scientific religion; almost all scientists have accepted it and many are prepared to 'bend' their observations to fit with it."

And wondering how well evolution has stood up to scientific testing, Lipson continues:

> "To my mind, the theory (evolution) does not stand up at all. I think, however, that we must go further than this and admit that the only acceptable explanation is creation. I know that this (creation) is anathema to physicists, as indeed it is to me ..., but we must not reject a theory that we do not like if the experimental evidence supports it."

> "There are only two possible explanations as to how life arose: Spontaneous generation arising to evolution or a supernatural creative act of God ... there is no other possibility. Spontaneous generation was scientifically disproved 120 years ago by Louis Pasteur and others, but that just leaves us with only one other possibility ... that life came as a supernatural act of creation by God, but *I can't accept that philosophically because I do not want to believe in God. Therefore I **choose** to believe in that which I know is scientifically impossible, spontaneous generation leading to evolution"* —Dr. George Wall, Professor Emeritus of Biology at Harvard, Nobel prize winner in Biology in 1971.

Are America's Students Victims of a Sectarian Doctrine?

> "Einstein's theory of relativity, or Heinsenberg's of statistical prediction, could hardly have had any effect on anybody's personal beliefs. The Copernican revolution and Newton's world view required some revision of traditional belief. *None of these theories, however,*

raised as many new questions concerning religion and ethics as did Darwin's theory of evolution through natural selection" — Ernst Mayr.

America, now more than ever, needs to be informed of the true status of evolution and needs true answers to origins—that all evidence points to special creation and a creator. The crisis in America today, as the recent government-financed *Carnegie Report on Education* has related, is *spiritual*. The Carnegie Report written by Charles Silberman (a leading secular educator and researcher) cost three million dollars. The title was *Crisis in the Classroom*. The report, which was thought to be a secular report, recommending new techniques and strategies, related rather that students have lost their compass or map of what life is all about. In other words, students today are simply spiritually lost. The report states,

> "The crisis (in the classroom) is real involving as it does the basic question of meaning and purpose, the meaning and purpose of life itself. It may well be a religious or spiritual crisis of the depth and magnitude that has no parallel since the Reformation."

Today we face the worst social problems in our history. Where we used to lead the world in nearly every virtuous arena, we now lead the world in violent crimes, divorce, drugs, teenage pregnancies and social diseases. The American family, which is the backbone of our culture, is in danger of collapsing. Divorces have doubled over the last twenty years and one out of three households are now single-parent families. There are one million teenage pregnancies each year and 4,000 abortions **each day.** Suicide is the number one killer of teenagers and drug abuse and rape is rampant.

While there are many culprits, the bottom line is that our culture has swallowed a false world view through indoctrination of the so-called "intelligentsia" of the scientific and academic community, which has resulted in the secularization of our government, institutions and media, and has also taken control of our educational system by Supreme Court and legislative actions. The result is textbooks only presenting evolution and our educational system (elementary, junior high, high school and college), teachers simply teaching what they were taught, have indoctrinated students into evolutionary thought. They are not only teaching evolution as fact, but have "homogenized" it with secular humanistic philosophy and are teaching it as the official "religion" of the nation. This mechanistic world view has been readily accepted because the whole package has been presented as science. Dr. Duane T. Gish (Biochemistry, U.C. Berkeley) in his book, *Evolution: The Fossils Say No!* states,

> "No doubt a large majority of the scientific community embraces the mechanistic materialistic philosophy of Simpson, Huxley and Monod. Many of these men are highly intelligent, and they have woven the fabric of evolution theory in an ingenious fashion. They have then combined this evolution theory with humanistic philosophy and have clothed the whole with the term, 'science'. The product, a non-theistic religion with evolutionary philosophy as its creed under the guise of 'science' is being taught in most public schools, colleges, and universities in the United States. *It has become our unofficial state-sanctioned religion.*"

It is imperative that Americans realize that the average student in the classroom as well as the average person "on the street" in America takes seriously what the leadership of this country holds to and is expounding. The average person literally "follows their leaders" (especially our educational system), and our leadership (by and large) is following the implications of evolution—the philosophy of materialism with its by-product of atheistic naturalism and cultural relativism.

Students (even those who are brought up in Christian homes sometimes) rationalize, "Maybe evolution is true; Maybe there isn't a God. If there isn't, why am I following Christian rules on ethics, morals, sex and marriage. Why can't I do what I want to do?"

Philip E. Johnson in his book, *Defeating Darwinism*, elaborates on changing American culture which began with the rejection of God in the 60's. He states,

"The change took hold in the late 1960's, as the new religious assumptions that had been gradually gaining ground began to have practical effects. When God's existence is no longer a *fact* but a subjective *belief* (and a highly controversial belief at that), God's moral authority disappears. It is no coincidence, therefore, that a drastic change in the nature of marriage immediatly followed the change in the ruling philosophy. Both the legal restrictions on divorce and the social stigma evaporated practically overnight. Marriage ceased being a sacred covenant involving God and the community as well as husband and wife. It became an ordinary contract that could be ended by either party practically at will. What used to be called illegitimacy became respectable as single parenting, and the traditional two-parent houshold even began to seem ridiculous, a pathetic attempt to emulate an *Ozzie and Harriet* dream family that had never existed in reality.

"With the divorce revolution came the sexual revolution, as the death of God and the availability of contraceptives seemed to make chastity obsolete. Hard on the heels of the sexual revolution came the feminist revolution, with a radical wing that explicitly rejected the traditional family model that had previously been regarded as the backbone of society. Feminism demanded an unrestricted right to abortion, which the Supreme Court duly read into the constitution and imposed on a reluctant nation. Homosexual liberation came next, and homosexual activists quickly gained 'victim' status and consequent support for their cause from the media. The Supreme Court again fell compliantly in line with the cultural trend, managing to find in the Constitution a principle that laws based on 'animosity' toward homosexuality are unconstitutional. The moral and legal reversal was unstoppable once the crucial change in the established religious philosophy had been made."

When Did It All Begin?

In 1947, the Warren Court (without legal or historical precedent) began the undertaking of the systematic secularization of America "to bring society into compliance with the first amendment," beginning with education. Declaring that the state must be neutral in religious affairs, it began the "de-Christianization" of education, but instead of neutrality, something more radical was afoot. After expelling Bible instruction, prayer, the posting of the Ten Commandments, Christmas and Easter celebrations, the vacuum was not intended to be unfulfilled but would be replaced by a new creed and philosophy—evolutionary-based, secular humanism. Evolutionists in our science classrooms did not settle for equal time in perpetuating their philosophy but proceeded to eject from public schools all competing theories of origins. Even today, efforts to subject Darwin's theory to the same critical scrutiny the evolutionists turned on biblical theory is rejected with passion.

While most working scientists today realize the bankrupt state of Darwinian evolution, it is still taught as the main theme in science throughout a student's public school and college experience with devastating philosophical and moral results. **Our students are victims of a planned sectarian doctrine.**

Most high school students in science and social studies classes have never even heard of Creation Science but have only been exposed to evolution and humanistic philosophy. Dr. Jim Hitchcock, in his book, *What is Secular Humanism?* states,

"Humanism is hardly the benign, tolerant force it pretends to be. Indeed, it is highly intolerant. It has a keen sense of being locked into continuous philosophical and social struggle with religious belief, in which the ultimate stakes are nothing less than the moral foundations of society."

The Collapse of Meaning and Morality

Secular humanists do not believe that man's body, mind and soul were supernaturally created but that they are products of evolution. Humanists are, at best, agnostic and atheistic in practice with their position that "man is the measure of all things". In effect, they have led man to reject God and place himself at the center of the universe with the egotistical assumption that "man is sufficient unto himself". This is the exact frame of reference the Nazis demonstrated in World War II. They believed they were the "Master Race" and free of any moral responsibility toward God. In our own country, with dysfunctional as well as broken homes where there is no teaching about God and morality, we are creating the same kind of rebellious youth. The 'skin heads' today in America, are an example of kids growing up with the same kind of egotistical mental attitude of the Nazis, thinking of themselves as the ultimate power with no rules of morality to follow.

The humanist philosophy, in teaching that all life has come into existence through natural materialistic chance processes, leads to the conclusion that man is a natural phenomenon like plants and animals. It logically follows then, that life is without moral direction and intelligent purposes. This relativistic philosophy has already filtered through all levels of our culture and has caused the erosion of moral absolutes.

Ken Ham and Paul Taylor, in their excellent book, *The Genesis Solution*, give the basic world view of secular humanists. It states,

"This life is the only one you're going to get, so enjoy it while you can. Do what makes you happy.

"Why worry about trying to figure out what is right and wrong if there is no ultimate, eternal meaning to life anyway?

"We have a right to make our own rules and guidelines about living in this world. Why not do whatever you can get away with?

"There is no reason to feel guilty about anything done with our sexual drive. There is nothing morally wrong with homosexuality, fornication or adultery.

"There are no moral absolutes.

"Because we are just animals anyway, what's wrong with aborting unwanted babies? Abortion is a great thing for women. Why should they have to suffer distressing consequences for their little mistakes and accidents?

"You have a right to decide how to live, and you have a right to put your own interests first. Never forget old Number One."

The magazine, *Insight* (May 11, 1987) has on it's front cover a picture of a little-known professor from Chicago University by the name of Alan Bloom because as they commented, "His book, *The Closing of the American Mind*, is the most penetrating analysis of the United States that has appeared in many years." *In his book, Bloom relates that the intellectual and moral crises in the United States are one. He argues that malignant Relativism is destroying the ideas of moral truth, wisdom and greatness.* He sees it throughout our society and most pervasive in our learning institutions where learning to think has given way to learning a skill. The following are excerpts from their article:

> "The United States is sinking into a kind of moral illiteracy, the result of decades of thought and discussion devoted to the proposition that morality is a matter of personal choice. *Today's youth are dedicated not to learning or to serving their fellow man but to the exercise and fulfillment of their passions. Hedonism, promiscuity, the refusal or inability to distinguish between forms of behavior—these characterize the best and brightest among today's youth.* Today's students, Bloom says, are 'nice' but incapable of seeing a thought through from its beginning to its conclusion.
>
> *"Differences of opinion once raised the questions of which ideas are true and good, which false and evil. Now those questions have been banished and our minds have been closed. Not only do students now tend to lack a knowledge of their own tradition; they often have no standpoint from which to appreciate any other tradition, or even have a sense of tradition.*
>
> "He describes the effects of close mindedness on today's student. 'They have,' he says sorrowfully, '*impoverished souls.*'"

The moral standards of our high schools are a prime example of the acceptance and resulting effects of evolutionary based humanistic moral relativism. Students are rarely exposed to the Ten Commandments and Bible teachings on sex and family. These moral instructions have been replaced by sex education and values clarification courses that in many cases teach all consentual sexual relations in or outside of marriage merely represent varied 'lifestyles'. The current epidemic of aids, rapes, child molestation and other social problems is the result of this line of reasoning.

History has also shown that following religious apostasy, comes secularization and materialism, then moral decay with the collapse of the family and the final outcome is the fall of the civilization. Americans today are viewing the future with a great sense of uneasiness and most agree that America is literally 'hemorrhaging' in practically every arena.

The Soviet Union ought to be our lesson on how *not* to run a country, yet it seems as though we are creating the same kind of secular humanist society that did them in. Former Assistant Chief of Police of Los Angeles,Bob Vernon, in a speech related that a few years ago, just before the Soviet Union collapsed, a committee of Russians came to Los Angeles to examine the so-called model police department. As second in command, police officer Vernon had the responsibility of interviewing the Russian officials. He stated that one of the Russian leaders stood up with passion, conviction and a tinge of anger and through an interpreter stated,

> "Why is it that you Americans are going the way of the Soviet Union? Why are you moving in that direction of taking out God and changing to humanism and socialism? Can't you see that is where we have been? It does not work!"

Why doesn't it work? *The Wilson Quarterly* (Woodrow Wilson International Center for scholars—Smithsonian Institution Building, Autumn 1991) in an article on the collapse of socialism related that secular humanist-based socialism has failed in the 20th century because it did not provide an answer for the meaning and purpose of human existence and provided no foundation for morality.

Dr. Irving Kristol, in *Commentary* (August 1991), states,

> "We have, in recent years, observed two major events that represent turning points in the history of the 20th century. The first is the death of socialism, both as an ideal and a political program.... The second is the collapse of secular humanism—the religious basis of socialism.

"If one looks back at the intellectual history of this century, one sees the rationalist religion of secular humanism gradually losing its credibility *even as it marches triumphantly through the institutions of our society–through the schools, the courts, the churches, the media.* The loss of credibility flows from two fundamental flaws in secular humanism.

"First, the philosophical rationalism of secular humanism can, at best, provide us with a statement of the necessary assumptions of a moral code, but it cannot deliver any such code itself..."

"For a long time now, the Western world has been leading a kind of schizophrenic existence, with a prevailing moral code inherited from the Judeo-Christian tradition and a set of secular-humanist beliefs about the nature and destiny of man to which that code is logically irrelevant. *Inevitably, belief in the moral code has become more and more attenuated over time, as we have found ourselves baffled by the Nietzschean challenge; if God is really dead, by what authority do we say any particular practice is prohibited or permitted?*

"A second flaw in secular humanism is even more fundamental.... If there is one indisputable fact about the human condition it is that no community can survive if it is persuaded—or even if it suspects—*that its members are leading meaningless lives in a meaningless universe.*"

The Collapse of the American Family

Some Americans (especially those of high morals and commitment) would reply, "Evolution and secular humanism hasn't affected me one way or the other. I don't care if evolution or creation is true, my value system wouldn't change either way."

I would agree that there are many people (possibly non-religious, even evolutionists) that are still helping to hold this country together but I believe if they would look back far enough in their families, they will see that they are products of the Judeo-Christian heritage. A good question to ask is, "Will your children go by your moral and ethical principles and their children, and their children, etc., or somewhere down the line will the hypocrisy of it all hit them when they realize that their parents are obeying the Judeo-Christian commandants without believing they were commanded?"

The American family *is* collapsing and so are the morals of Americans and that's because America by and large has given up God and has accepted a philosophical system that has been proven false as well as impotent. This country was once largely Christian and put the family first but now the residual is running thinner and thinner even in religious families and even in churches as secular humanist-based moral relativism threatens to destroy our country.

A very important book, *The Declining Well-Being of American Adolescents* by two Harvard sociologists, Peter Uhlenbery and David Eggebeen (published Winter 1986), documents the fact that peripheral programs will not save American youth. The article demonstrates what we're doing now in our schools simply isn't working because parents are becoming less and less concerned about their families and many are leaving their homes "to find their own place—to do their own thing". The problem is philosophical and moral; only a strong traditional family structure supplies the needs of youth. The following is a synopsis of the book taken from the *Wilson Quarterly*, summer 1986:

> "Pointing to 'leading indicators' of child welfare, social scientists and Washington policymakers predicted great progress for America's youth during the 1960's and 1970's. Indeed, the proportion of white 16 and 17 year olds living in homes with poverty or large families of

poorly educated parents—all factors believed to crimp a teenager's prospects—dropped from 68 percent in 1960 to 37 percent in 1980. Meanwhile, expenditures per pupil in the nation's high schools nearly doubled; in 1980 dollars, the average swelled from $1,248 to $2,491. All told, 20 federal agencies now administer some 260 programs designed to benefit young Americans. Despite such striking improvements, write Uhlenberg and Eggebeen, both Harvard sociologists, the well-being of America's youth (not just minority youths) has actually shown a 'marked deterioration' over the last quarter century. Fewer high school students now make it through to graduation; and many that do can't read. Between 1970 and 1980, the percentage of (white) 18-year-olds holding high school diplomas declined by five percent. *Worse, since 1960 the rates of juvenile crime and delinquency, unmarried (white) teenage pregnancy and youth mortality from homicides and suicides have all more than doubled.*

"What went wrong? The authors blame a breakdown in family ties, specifically a weakening of the bonds between parent and child. From 1960 to 1980, the proportion of children under 18 years of age who experienced their parents' divorce increased by 140 percent. During the same period, the proportion of mothers in the labor force with children under 18 years of age rose from 28 percent to 57 percent; no evidence exists that fathers are filling the gap in parental supervision. *Citing a 1981 study by pollster Daniel Yankelovic, the authors observe that parents are clearly putting their own 'self-fulfillment' ahead of their commitment to sacrificing personal pursuits for their children's welfare. Until parenthood once again takes higher priority, no amount of government effort will improve the lot of the nation's youth.*"

The *Los Angeles Times Magazine*, of the *Los Angeles Times* Newspaper (June 14, 1992), confirms the continuing trend of the '*me*' generation—the "I-love-me, I-have-a-duty-to-myself-to-perform" generation. The "you-only-go-around-once-in-life, so-get-all-the-gusto-you-can" generation. The "self-fulfillment generation". The article is entitled, *The Invisible Dad*, with the subtitle, *Life without Father*, and relates the fact that more and more American men are disconnecting from family life as society suffers the consequences. The following are excerpts from the article, further documenting that the primary problem in America is moral and spiritual, not race and income, and that peripheral programs alone such as high self-esteem programs or the restructuring of education are nothing more than "putting Band-Aids on cancer". The article states,

> "Consider two of our nation's most serious problems—crime and teenage pregnancy. Studies show that the most reliable prediction of these behaviors is not income, nor race. It is family structure: Pregnant girls and criminal boys tend to come from fatherless families. An astonishing 70% of imprisoned U.S. minors have spent at least part of their lives without fathers. Gangs feed on fatherless sons. Father Greg Boyle of Dolores Mission Church in East Los Angeles once listed the names of the first 100 gang members that came to mind and then jotted a family history next to each. All but five were no longer living with their biological fathers—if they ever had.

> "Many researchers now single out fathers as providing a form of childrearing distinct from that of mothers—and just as essential to a child's development. Whether they are roughhousing with a 5-year-old or scaring the 'bejesus' out of a delinquent teen, fathers bring a different style of parenting, says Kyle Pruett, psychiatry professor at the Yale Child Study Center and author of 'The Nurturing Father'.

> "Without men around as role models, adolescent boys create their own rites of passage: perhaps getting a girl pregnant or dealing drugs or murdering a rival.

"Throughout history, men have been torn from their families by war, disease and death. But in '90s America, men are choosing to disconnect from family life on a massive scale, and at far higher rates than other industrialized countries. 'Men are drifting away from family life,' says Blankenhorn. 'We are in danger of becoming a fatherless society.'

"All across America tonight, one–third of the nation's children will go to bed without their biological fathers in the next room. And most of them won't see their fathers the next day either."

Many secular humanists are admitting to the failure of their philosophical system as the moral collapse continues and the American family continues to disintegrate. Dr. Robert Maynard Hutchens, recent president of the University of Chicago, amply illustrates the despair and pessimistic world view held in common by many humanists.

"We do not know where we are going, or why we have almost given up the attempt to find out. We are in despair because the keys which were to open the gates of heaven have led us into a larger but more oppressive prison house. We thought these keys were science and the free intelligence of men. *They have failed us. We have long since cast off God—to what can we appeal?*"

This is an accurate description of America today—not only our scientists and the academic community have thrust God out of the sphere of our activity, but the general populace, for the most part, are secularized. It is a legitimate question to ask, "Will God judge America?" The Bible clearly teaches that God is no respecter of people or nations. He judges sin wherever He finds it. It is also clear that "... whatsoever a man soweth, that shall he also reap." God has not changed His mind about that principle, either. Perhaps those among us who remain faithful to God and His principles have been enough to stem the tide of God's wrath against sin up to now, but for how long will God be patient with us? His laws of eternal justice are still true. Past fallen empires are mute testimony to the fact that after unbelief and degradation comes judgment and collapse.

In our present generation, we have seen how Germany was destroyed when they gave up on God, saying, "God is dead" and followed Adolf Hitler. We saw Russia become atheistic and follow Lenin into economic collapse and national despair. Is America next?

Billy Graham, in his book *Storm Warning* published in 1992, said, "Without a sudden and massive worldwide revival of God's people and a return to the morality and values set down in the Word of God, earth is already under the condemnation of God and its judgment will be swift, unavoidable and total."

In II Chronicles 7:14, God spoke to His Chosen People, Israel, and offered His prescription for recovery. I believe this same formula will work for America today. He said,

"If my people which are called by My name will humble themselves and pray and seek My face and turn from their wicked ways, then I will hear from heaven and will forgive their sins and heal their land."

Chapter 8

Evolution's Effect on the World

Knowledgeable students of history are well aware of the detrimental effect of evolutionary-based secular humanist philosophy on the world, as well as on our own past and present. In summary, consider the track record of this erroneous foundational philosophy.

- **Russian and Chinese Communism**

Aleksandr Solzhenitsyn, famous author and Nobel prize winner, documented in his books the criminal and decadent experience of human life under communism. He estimated that 66 million people were executed (and many more tortured and imprisoned) in Russia and about 30 million in China. That's a total of 96 million murders which can be traced back to Darwin's "natural selection" and "survival of the fittest" ideas. Karl Marx (atheist, materialist and founder of Communism and the man who almost dedicated his book, *Das Kapital*, to Darwin) wrote to Engels in 1860 and stated, "Darwin's book (*Origin of Species*) serves me as a basis of natural science for my theory of 'class struggle' in history."

- **Nazi Germany**

Adolph Hitler accepted the teaching of the German philosopher, Nietzsche (1844-1900), who wrote that because of the advances of modern science and because evolution was a fact of science, the Christian myth would have to be eliminated in Germany. Nietzsche coined the phrase, "God is Dead" and related that although life now has no meaning, Germany must be brave and create the "German Superman". Hitler, following Nietzsche and Darwin, believed that evolution was the law of nature and he also believed that the German people had evolved the highest and were "the master race". He applied Darwin's principles of "natural selection" and "survival of the fittest" in order to "... clean out and purify" his people (currently called "ethnic cleansing"). Hitler thus justified the liquidation of the old, the sick, the blind and disabled as well as six million Jews and a host of other so-called sub-human races. In his book, *Evolution and Ethics*, Sir Arthur Keith (former Scottish Anthropologist) stated,

> "The German Fuehrer (Hitler), as I have consistently maintained is an evolutionist; he has consciously sought to make the practice of Germany conform to the theory of evolution.

> "Such conduct is highly immoral as measured by every scale of ethics, yet Germany justifies it; it is consonant (in agreement) with tribal or evolutionary morality. Germany has reverted to the tribal past, and is demonstrating to the world in their naked ferocity, the methods of evolution."

The "skin head" movement (also called the white supremacy movement or the fourth Reich skin heads) is in reality Adolf Hitler's Nazism comeback. Historians used to ask, "How did such a movement ever happen in Germany, the land of Luther and Bach?" Well it's reviving today in America and in Europe. How could it happen? Ask any skin head and they'll tell you the foundation of their movement is the same as it was for Hitler's Germany—social Darwinism. They believe as the Nazis did that the white race is the race that has evolved to the highest degree and is destined to rule the world.

They plan to do as Hitler did and to apply the "evolutionary laws of natural selection" eventually having a race war and then seeking domination of the world. They're egotistical and vocal and, like the earlier Nazis of Germany, they will use any means to accomplish their ends (murder, cruelty, etc.). This movement is a vivid illustration of the application of the theory of evolution.

- **The United States**

In our own country, in the day of the Carnegies and Rockefellers, there was an application of social Darwinism as the rich exploited the poor immigrants in factories with long hours, low pay and terrible working conditions. Their claim was that their sub-human workers were lower on the evolutionary scale and they should be content with their state.

The United States also participated in the Age of Imperialism (1870-1914), and many accepted the so-called evolutionary world pattern and the belief that it was the "duty" of advanced nations to get colonies (exploit people and their raw materials) to speed up the evolution of man.

- **Racism, Nationalism, Imperialism and the World Wars**

Evolution was the modern day basis of racism, nationalism, imperialism, militarism and war. Historical theorists agree that World War I was caused mainly by extreme nationalism which had its basis in racism which in turn had its basis in evolution. Prior to World War I, Darwinism was prominent in the minds of the world leaders who taught racial supremacy and the survival of the fittest (often the strongest and most brutal). A recent review of the book, *Outcasts From Evolution: Scientific Attitudes of Racial Inferiority* by John S. Haller, Jr. (1859–1900), states:

"This is an extremely important book, documenting as it does what has long been suspected: the ingrained, firm and almost unanimous racism of North American men of science during the nineteenth (and into the twentieth) century....

"What was new in the Victorian period was Darwinism.... Before 1859, many scientists had questioned whether blacks were of the same species as whites. After 1859, the evolutionary scheme raised additional questions."

The book, *The Genesis Solution*, gives further insights as to the evolution-racism connection. It states,

"Many white settlers in Australia believed the aborigines were primitive sub-humans and thus incapable of under-standing the white man's technology and ways. And so they were thought to be a threat. This is one of the reasons why some settlers in the state of Tasmania shot every aborigine they could find, with little remorse.

"Europeans believed similar racist concepts about the blacks of Africa and the Mongolian (or Mongoloid) races. Non-whites were thought to be less evolved. According to evolutionist Stephen J. Gould, this is one of the reasons why the term *mongoloid* was later applied to certain mentally defective people. Such misguided ideas were just another one of many sad results of teaching Evolution as undeniable fact in our public-education system."

With militarism and the arms race, war, killing and destruction became an expression of diplomacy. War has even been called the logical extension of a nation's foreign policy. Nationalism characterized by an extreme perverted love or allegiance for your own place, culture and country and prejudice against other races and cultures was responsible for the murdering of the flower of youth of a score of nations in World Wars I and II. These wars were actually defended as a means of eliminating the weak and perpetuating the strong (survival of the fittest). World War II was Hitler's and the Nazi Party's war of racial superiority having brainwashed the German people into believing that the Aryan race had evolved the highest.

The track record of Communism and evolutionary-based secular humanist philosophy, continues to the present. Followers of this philosophy placed no value on human life for, if there is no God, then there are no moral absolutes. This provides a rationale for events such as in Vietnam, when the government fell, there was a blood bath and frantic boat people attempted to escape. In Cambodia, there was genocide as two million people were put to death by the atheist communists.

- **Modern Psychology**

Sigmund Freud (after reading Darwin's *The Descent of Man* stated, "Man is no different or better than the animals.... I stand in no awe whatever of the almighty." Freud believed that man was an evolved animal and was driven by two basic instincts: survival and reproduction. His diagnosis was that all man's hang-ups could be traced to sex. His therapy for these mental hang-ups—take away all religious and social restrictions on sex. According to author John Weldon,

> "Freud purposely replaced God with evolution and guilt became an offense against the inner law of man's conscience rather than the result of violating God's moral law."

Was Freud right? Has man lost his hang-ups? Consider the results of his therapy (besides our overcrowded mental institutions): promiscuity, teenage pregnancies, an epidemic of sexually transmitted diseases, pornography and the sexual abuse of women and children. Conclusion—the evolutionary view of psychology has failed!

- **Modern Medicine**

In discussing evolution in various scientific fields, including medicine, some people would reply, "If we get rid of evolution, what will be its substitute in science?" The California State framework on natural science relates, "Evolution is one of the major unifying themes in science."

First of all, if its false, couldn't it be leading scientific progress astray? For example, in the 1950's and 60's in the "heyday" of evolution, it was believed that the body contained over a hundred different organs that were "left over" from man's evolutionary development. Scientists claimed that these "vestigial remains" were no longer necessary for man's survival. The so-called vestigial organs included the tonsils, adenoids, appendix, pituitary and thyroid glands. Consequently in operating, the thinking was, "While we're operating, we might as well take out this or that useless organ."

Today, doctors realize they were misled by evolutionary theory, and that organs like the tonsils, adenoids and appendix are necessary for fighting disease, thus they are no longer taken out except when absolutely necessary.

- **Medical   Philosophy   on   Abortion   and Euthanasia**

Dr. Carole K. Tharp from Northwestern University Medical School, and her husband Dr. Gary Alm of the Chicago Medical School, feel that the *wide acceptance of the theory of evolution among doctors has caused a lower regard for the sanctity of life*. They expressed this concern in a letter to the Chicago Tribune:

> "Evolution gives the philosophical foundation needed for one segment of society to eliminate another under the guise of natural selection, and with this philosophy, that segment considered unfit steadily increases.

> "Evolution was all we ever heard in college and medical school. I do believe that it has laid the groundwork for the acceptance of abortion. I think the stage is totally set for another Holocaust because doctors will not face the problem. They will believe anything if it is printed in

the right medical journals or presented at the right meetings."

The book, *The Genesis Solution,* gives significant insights of the "abortion-evolution" connection. It states,

"Although few Christians realize it, the increasing acceptance of abortion has gone hand in hand with the increasing popularity of evolutionary theory. Abortion has been promoted by Evolutionism in at least three ways:

1. *Evolutionism has taught that humans are just animals,* one of many other creatures living on an insignificant speck of a planet in a vast universe.

2. *Evolutionism has removed the moral basis for obeying the Ten Commandments.* If there is no God—at least not the personal God of the Bible—"thou shalt not kill" and other such divine commands are just arbitrary rules written by the ancient Israelites. Thus people claim an absolute right to do what they want to with their own body, including the contents of their body.

3. *Evolutionism once taught that human embryos are not human beings.* Many people still believe the erroneous evolutionary view once widely taught in schools. Tragically, one can occasionally still find this theory being taught or implied in schools and universities. This has enabled the abortion clinics in a major way.

- **Scientific progress**

Evolutionary theory has devastatingly influenced, not only education, but nearly every other field of knowledge and endeavor. The doctrine of organic evolution has been accepted by biologists, geologists, chemists and physicists, by anthropologists, psychologists, educators, philosophers, sociologists and even by historians, political scientists and linguists.

In scientific research, if a researcher approaches his problems with a biased view that evolution is true, he often overlooks helpful conclusions because they contradict his pre-conceived ideas of evolution. The following are quotes from eminent scientists who are now anti-evolutionists or simply non-evolutionists.

"One of the reasons I started taking this anti-evolutionary view, or let's call it a non-evolutionary view, was that last year I had a sudden realization that for over twenty years I had thought I was working on evolution in some way. One morning I woke up and it struck me that I had been working on this stuff for twenty years and there was not one thing I knew about it. That's quite a shock to learn that one can be so misled so long. Either there was something wrong with me, or there was something wrong with evolutionary theory. Naturally, I know there is nothing wrong with me, so for the last few weeks I've tried putting a simple question to various people and groups of people.

"Question is: Can you tell me anything you know about evolution, any one thing, any one thing that is true? I tried that question on the geology staff at the field Museum of Natural History, and the only answer I got was silence. I tried it on the members of the Evolutionary Morphology Seminar in the University of Chicago, a very prestigious body of evolutionists, and all I got there was silence for a long time and eventually one person said, '*I do know one thing—it ought not to be taught in high school*'" —Dr. Colin Patterson (Senior Paleontologist of the British Museum of Natural History, London) during his keynote address at the American Museum of Natural History, New York City, November 5, 1981.

"There was little doubt that the star intellectual turn of last week's British Association for the Advancement of Science meeting in Salford was Dr. John Durant, a youthful lecturer from University College Swansea.

Giving the Darwin lecture to one of the biggest audiences of the week, Durant put forward an audacious theory — *that Darwin's evolutionary explanation of the origins of man has been transformed into a modern myth, to the detriment of science and social progress....*

"Durant concludes that the secular myths of evolution have had 'a damaging effect on scientific research,' leading to 'distortion, to needless controversy, and to the gross misuse of science'" —Dr. John Durant (University College Swansea, Wales), as quoted in *How Evolution Became a Scientific Myth.*

"Evolutionism is a fairy tale for grown–ups. This theory has helped nothing in the progress of science. *It is useless*" —Prof. Louis Bounoure (former President of the Biological Society of Strasbourg and Director of the Strasbourg Zoological Museum, later Director of Research at the French National Center of Scientific Research).

The noted Swedish botanist and geneticist, Dr. Herbert Nilsson (former director of the Swedish Museum of Natural History also former evolutionist turned agnostic) ably sums up the evidence against the fallacious philosophy of evolution and for those "diehards", the futility of further scientific research to substantiate this bogus theory. He related prior to this quote that *he was making this statement so that scientists in the future would rethink and reorient their research in another direction.* He states,

"My attempts to demonstrate evolution by experiment carried on for more than forty years, have completely failed.... I should hardly be accused of having started from a preconceived anti-evolutionary standpoint.... It may be firmly maintained that it is not even possible to make a caricature out of paleo-biological facts. The fossil material is now so complete that it has been possible to construct new classes, and the lack of transitional series cannot be explained due to the scarcity of material. Deficiencies are real. They will never be filled. The idea of a evolution rests on pure belief."

Chapter 9

Creation Science Belongs in the Classroom

According to the U.S. Constitution and the tradition of freedom in our country, all knowledge in our public schools is to be passed on without bias following the principles of academic freedom. But the point in fact is, in contrast to the reputed neutrality of science, science education has become a vehicle for a metaphysical perspective—a religious point of view.

The presentation of evolution and secular humanistic philosophy as fact is sectarianism and no different than a Communist, Mormon, Catholic or Baptist indoctrinating his or her students into their religion. While the educational establishment is quick to reprimand these teachers for indoctrinating students, they seem to be blind to teachers presenting evolutionary philosophy as fact. This also amounts to the governmental establishment of a religious point of view, prohibited by the first amendment. Duane T. Gish has stated it plainly,

> "Evolution-based secular humanist philosophy has become our unofficial state sanctioned religion."

This same principle of sectarianism applies to teachers and textbooks that, by omission, fail to expose students to evidences **for** Special Creation as well as evidences **against** the theory of Evolution. This also applies to Social Studies teachers and textbooks that fail to expose students to the Judeo-Christian heritage of our country. By omission, teachers are giving signals to their students that such matters are not true and are of no importance.

Our educational system needs a major transformation with a true application of "academic freedom" and the "free exchange of ideas". A new openness, as well as new textbooks are needed in which both evolution and creation are equally presented, allowing the students to examine the evidences and come to their own conclusions. Of course, if this were to happen, it would be a monumental, revolution in California's and in America's public education systems. This is because, as Philip E. Johnson in his book, *Darwinism on Trial*, states,

> "Evolution has been the universally accepted paradigm in the scientific and academic community and as the accepted, reigning paradigm, the thinking has been, 'It can't be discredited, only improved.'"

He further relates that the scientific community has tremendous political clout because most people think, "Well, scientists are the ones who sent rockets to the moon, so they must be right on evolution also."

Of course, most people are ignorant about the many scientists who are now leaving the evolutionary camp or who are now expressing serious doubts about evolution. Maybe as more information comes out, this revolution will take place and the reigning evolution paradigm will be dismantled.

Why Creation Science is Excluded From Our Public Schools

Dr. Philip Johnson, in his booklet, *Evolution as Dogma* and the subtitle *The Establishment of Naturalism,* gets to the heart of how Creation Science is excluded from the classroom. He relates that "Darwinists" and the National Academy of Sciences, by establishing the belief that science is synonymous with naturalism or that science should be exclusively defined as naturalism, have been successful in excluding creation science from the classroom. In other words, by stereotyping creation science as being religious in nature, it has been taken out of the science curriculum and our students are only getting one point of view, without criticism— atheistic evolution. The following are excerpts from *Evolution as Dogma — The Establishment of Naturalism*:

> "The theory in question is a theory of naturalistic evolution, which means that it absolutely rules out any miraculous or supernatural intervention at any point.

> "Victory in the creation-evolution dispute therefore belongs to the party with the cultural authority to establish the ground rules that govern the discourse. *If creation is admitted as a serious possibility, Darwinism cannot win, and if it is excluded a priori Darwinism cannot lose. In science as in other fields, you can't beat something with nothing, and so the Darwinist paradigm remains in place.*

> "In the U.S. Supreme Court's decision of 1987, the Science Academy's brief went on to cite evidence for evolution, but evidence was unnecessary. Creationists are disqualified from making a positive case because science, by definition, is based upon naturalism. *The rules of science also disqualify any purely negative argumentation designed to dilute the persuasiveness of the theory of evolution. Creationism is thus out of court —and out of the classroom—before any consideration of evidence.*

> *"With creationist explanations disqualified at the outset, it follows that the evidence will always support the naturalistic alternative."*

> *"Because the claims of Darwinism are presented to the public as 'science', most people are under the impression that they are supported by direct evidence such as*

experiments and fossil record studies. This impression is seriously misleading. Scientists cannot observe complex biological structures being created by random mutations and selection in a laboratory or elsewhere. The fossil record, as we have seen, is so unhelpful that the important steps in evolution must be assumed to have occurred within its 'gaps'. Darwinists believe that the mutation-selection mechanism accomplishes wonders of creativity not because the wonders can be demonstrated, but because they cannot think of a more plausible explanation that does not involve an unacceptable *creator*, i.e., a being or force outside the world of nature.

"Methods used by evolutionists to establish evolution as fact:

- They identify science with naturalism which means they insist as a matter of first principle that no consideration whatever be given to the possibility that mind or spirit preceded matter.

- They can impose a rule of procedure that disqualifies purely negative argument, so that a theory which obtains some modest degree of empirical support can become immune to disproof until and unless supplanted by a better naturalistic theory.

- They take advantage of the prestige that science enjoys in an age of technology, by asserting that anyone who disputes Darwinism must be an enemy of science, and hence of rationality itself."

The 1987 U.S. Supreme Court Ruling

From the above information given by Johnson which is a clarion description of the thinking on the high school and college level, it would seem like the creationists are in an impossible dilemma. However, all this can change when we see what the U.S. Supreme Court really ruled regarding creation science in 1987.

The headlines of the *Los Angeles Times* (June 20,1987), in reporting on the U.S. Supreme Court decision concerning the battle between evolutionists and creationists, made the following false statement, "Creation Science banned in Schools". The popular press—TV, radio, *Time* magazine, *U.S. News and World Report* and other media never made the correction and made similar misleading or false reports even though, as with the *L.A. Times,* correct reporting was within the content of the articles. But as they say, "Covers sell books." Thus this misleading statement became the frame of reference concerning creation science. In other words, the damage was done.

What the U.S. Supreme Court did say is that the states could not demand the teaching of creation science, but added and encouraged a variety of different theories and criticism of any theory of origins including the theory of evolution as long as it is based on established scientific facts. The following is a short summary of the U.S. Supreme Court decision.

U.S. Supreme Court Ruling on the Louisiana Balanced Treatment Act (June 19, 1987)

"It is equally clear that requiring schools to teach creation science with evolution does not advance academic freedom. The Act does not grant teachers a flexibility that they did not already possess to supplant the present science curriculum with the presentation of theories besides evolution, about the origin of life. Indeed, the Court of Appeals found that no law prohibited Louisiana public school teachers from teaching any scientific theory (765 F.2d, at 2157). As the president of the Louisiana Science Teachers Association testified, '(A)ny scientific concept that's based on established fact can be included in our curriculum already, and no legislation allowing this is necessary' (2 App. E616). The Act provides Louisiana school teachers with no new authority (p.8.).

"Teaching a variety of scientific theories about the origins of humankind to school children might be validly done with the clear secular intent of enhancing the effectiveness of science education." (p.14.)

As the above excerpts state, the U.S. Supreme Court did declare that the 1981 Louisiana law that demanded the teaching of creation science was unconstitutional because it did not advance academic freedom. The Court went on to relate, however, that *the Louisiana Act did not grant teachers a flexibility that they did not already possess, which is to supplant the present science curriculum with the presentation of theories besides the theory of evolution, as long as it is based on scientific fact. Thus, any theory (or criticisms of any theory such as evolution) does not violate the constitution and is encouraged by the U.S. Supreme Court for the effectiveness of science instruction. This, of course, presents a golden opportunity for science and social studies teachers to present current arguments against evolution and for special creation.*

The question is, "If the Supreme Court has given the freedom to present alternative points of view—as long as they are based on scientific fact—why are our public school students receiving only one, non-theistic viewpoint of organic evolution, and why are criticisms of this theory generally discouraged or not presented?"

A statement from the California State Framework of Science regarding Creation Science framework will suffice:

"Teachers should be aware that the theory of evolution has been tested and refined for over a hundred years and that the majority of criticisms that find their way into popularly circulated publications have not been validated scientifically; usually, the criticisms have been evaluated and reflected by the scientific community.   Teachers should consider the validity of such criticisms carefully before accepting them or deciding whether they are worth consideration. *The particular case of "creation science" (or "scientific creationism") has been thoroughly studied by the leading scientific societies and rejected as not qualifying as a scientific explanation."*

The above quote clearly demonstrates the closed mindedness of the writers of the state framework, and it also demonstrates their intention to put forth only one point of view—the non-theistic theory of evolution.

Another answer lies in the misleading headlines, "Creation Science Banned in Schools", which swept America and were picked up by Darwinists (the dominating force in the scientific and academic community) for propaganda purposes.

The main answer, I believe, however, is that evolution was already considered and taught as established fact in the past (1950's, '60's, '70's, '80's) as the accepted paradigm. Then came the defeat of the creationists in the Supreme Court (1987) by the evolutionists. This gave them more confidence and impetus such as that reflected in the new California State framework for education.

Finally, as Dr. Philip Johnson brought out, **evolution has been defined as synonymous with science** and **Creation has been stereotyped as religion** and thus does not belong in the science curriculum.

At this point, you are probably saying, "With all the scientific evidence coming out in favor of creation science over evolution, how did the creationists get defeated in the Supreme Court? And why did the Supreme Court label Creation Science as a religious point of view?" The answer is the evolutionists attacked the creationists at their most vulnerable point—*the age of the universe.* The creationists argued for a universe of about 10,000 years in age based on their interpretation of the Bible (literal 24-hour creation days in Genesis 1) and the evolutionists for a universe of about 18 billion years. If the creationists believed and had presented their package with a universe of billions of years (as many of we creationists believe), the evolutionists could have been routed. As Dr. Johnson related in his booklet, "Evolution as Dogma", "If Creation science is admitted as a serious possibility, Darwinism cannot win!"

The problem is that a universe of 10,000 years is as unscientific as the theory of organic evolution; that is, as organic evolution is not based on established scientific fact, neither is a universe of 10,000 years of age. This is why the "young earthers" were defeated and this is why the Supreme Court ruled "Scientific Creationism" a religious point of view and not a legitimate part of science.

Because of the importance of the question about the age of the universe, we will take a closer look at it. It's the insistence of most creationists for a young universe and earth that is standing in the way of Creation Science being considered in science classes. Science teachers throw out the whole package and refer to creationists as "flat earthers" because they know of the preponderance of evidence of an old universe and earth. A few examples will suffice at this point:

- Scientists know that stars are of different ages by their mass, color and brightness. Some stars are only thousands of years old, others are billions of years old and none exceeds 18 billion years in age which is another evidence supporting a beginning of the universe and the Big Bang theory.

- Another argument is, scientists have measured and mapped out our finite universe and, calculating the speed of the expansion rate with the speed of light and measuring from the point of singularity, have again come to an age of about 18 billion years. Of course, there are many other evidences, such as from geology and archaeology.

To sum it up, evolutionists won on established scientific fact that could be won in any court of law. Valid scientific evidence points to a universe that is 16 to 19 billion years old. Science takes the position that the universe is real and not an illusion—that the size of the universe is not an illusion and that the beams of light coming from planets billions of light years away is not an illusion, that the geological strata represent billions of years and that dinosaurs roamed the earth billions of years ago.

If the universe and earth are only 10,000 years old, cosmology, physics, chemistry, geology, archaeology, etc., as we understand them, would be invalidated. The evidence of a young universe and earth is flimsiest at best and could never be won in a court of law.

The bad part of the U.S. Supreme Court debate is that creationists didn't concentrate on the real issue of the creation event versus evolution. Evolution vs. Creation was hardly even discussed!

With the clarification of the Supreme Court decision and the presentation of an "old universe", everything could be reversed. If the truth is brought out and science and social studies teachers become knowledgeable, they'll understand that Creation Science can and should be brought back into the classroom.

Many people are confused about the U.S. Supreme Court decision in 1987 regarding the teaching of science in public schools. Much of the public (as well as educators) believed the Supreme Court banned Creation Science, but what it really said was that states could not *demand* the teaching of Creation Science in public schools, then it went on to state that *all* evidences of origins should be presented in science classes. This, of course, would include any negative results such as the creationists arguments against evolution. The Supreme Court also went on to say that any science can be presented in classrooms as long as it is based on established fact. There is much in Creation Science that *is* established fact and thus should be included in science and social studies curriculums.

This could also include a first cause creative agent—as all evidence supports a beginning to the universe. A good question at this point is, "How can you educate about origins without bringing up the subject of God?" Where everything came from is a scientific question (cause and effect). Dr. Ross (astrophysicist) has related in both of his books, *The Fingerprint of God* and *The Creator and the Cosmos,* that because all the evidences come out supporting the Big Bang theory, a group of scientists at Cal Tech are now doing research on the "first cause creative agent".

The California State framework makes the following statements under the heading, "Scientific Practice and Ethics":

"Scientists have responsibilities to their colleagues and to the public. Because all observations are based on human senses and expectations, results must be reported as fully and openly as possible. Scientists also have a responsibility to limit the scope and the implications of their results, not to over-generalize their findings. *Negative results—those that do not agree with the hypothesis— must be reported along with those that do agree."*

I can fully agree with that. Isn't it interesting, that Creation Science has been excluded and none of the enormous contradictions (negative results) of the theory of evolution are included in the science framework? Is it, simply an ignorant lack of knowledge or an indoctrination conspiracy—preaching secular humanist religion?

What is "Creation Science"?

One of the major misconceptions in education is that Creation Science is the product of a few fundamentalist radicals or religious extremists and that students have to throw away their brains when considering alternative theories of origins than those which are presented in our textbooks. Creation Science in substance is *not* an attempt to preach religion but is only an attempt to expose students to true scientific and historical facts. The creationists' position is that there is not one shred of scientific evidence to support the evolution model; that is, "macro evolution"—molecule-to-man. Thus, creationists are in a battle attempting to hurdle the barrier of entrenched evolutionary-based humanist philosophy and to present things *as they are*.

Again, many evolutionists at this point would say, "But creation is religion and evolution is science." This is not so because **both** positions are belief systems and ultimately philosophical and religious in nature. You cannot go back to the beginning and apply the scientific method (observation, experiment) to prove creation or evolution. Science is based on emperical evidence—that which can be verified by repeated testing. Organic evolution, therefore in essence is not science. True science is *only* that which can be experimentally verified; we do not have access to the past. We only have the present, we cannot directly test the past using the scientific method.

If Darwinists claim Creation Science is a religious doctrine masquerading as a science, then Evolutionary Naturalism is also a religious doctrine masquerading as science since it employs the concept of non-intelligent design, atheism and the materialistic view that Nature is all that there is. This issue was actually settled in 1961 when the U.S. Supreme Court ruled that evolutionary based secular humanism is one of several atheistic religions. In *Facts & Faith*, (Spring 1994) Dr. Hugh Ross states,

> "Teaching of non-intelligent design is indeed religion— as in 'a cause, principle, or system of belief held with ardor, devotion, conscientiousness and faith'" (Webster's Third New International Dictionary).

> "The arguments for non-intelligent design presuppose the non-existence of a Creator and are therefore religiously biased.

> "My point is that the atheist, agnostic, deist and theist all are religiously biased. No one can claim to be free of religious bias. The only academically honest thing to do is to lay one's religious biases and presuppositions on the table. *If I remember right, America was born to permit the free expression of religion. I know I'm not the first to point out that many academicians (among others) today interpret the American constitution as guaranteeing freedom from religion (specifically, from theism) rather than freedom of religion. But given that the goal of some influential people is to outlaw all religious expression— except atheistic materialism—we should not be surprised.*"

What Does the Weight of Evidence Support?

While it is true that we cannot directly observe everything that happened in the past, it is also true that cosmologists, geologists, biologists, paleontologists and archaeologists can give us valid, legitimate, scientific data relating to origins; thus, we can, and should, adduce from the present world, scientific and historical evidences for the two contrasting world views.

The accumulated evidence supporting the creationist model and refuting the evolutionary model can legally be used in the classroom and this evidence virtually eliminates the theory of evolution as a viable scientific option.

What is the Real Evidence for Evolution?

We've already seen that what evolutionists propose to teach as "evolution" and what they label as fact, is based *not* upon any incontrovertible, empirical evidence, but on flimsy and highly speculative and controversial assumptions. Two examples will suffice.

First, the most famous "proof" of natural selection is the English peppered moth. Remember? The number of black and white moth populations was dependent on industrial pollution. When the pollution was cleaned up, the trees in England lightened and the light colored moths flourished again because the birds ate the highly visible black moths.

Second, they offer mutations as proof—bacterial populations that evolve resistance to antibodies. These two examples have nothing to do with the creative process that formed the bacteria and moths in the first place and, of course, the moth remains a moth. It doesn't turn into a mosquito or anything else. But there you have it! This is what is presented as proof for evolution! Natural selection and mutations produce algae, insects, animals and humans—as well as the human brain, they claim.

We have presented here scientific evidence showing the bankrupt state of organic evolution. These evidences and the like should be presented in science and social studies classes when considering origins. The two-model approach is what creationists are battling for and they can legally have it. Evolutionists in our public schools merely **assume** their scenario to be true which excludes all creationist's arguments, and then they try to fit their flimsy data into it. This is not true scientific inquiry. A critical analysis must be made. Good science and social studies education cannot be obtained when the minds of young people are restrained and not permitted to study the alternatives. No doubt, parents would object to this type of teaching in any other area of public education. Parents want their children to learn the discipline of critical thinking.

What's the Conclusion of the Matter?

The question that needs to be asked in all classes dealing with origins is, "What model or theory best fits the data available?" or, "What would one expect to see from the data and the two different models?" In using this method, students would be confronted with the overwhelming evidence against evolution and for creation, and would also have a new basis for a true philosophy of life. Dr. Hugh Ross succinctly sums up what is at stake in the Creation/Evolution controversy. He states,

> "...if the universe is not created or is in some manner accidental, then it has no objective meaning and consequently, life, including human life, has no meaning. A mechanical chain of events determines everything. Morality and religion may be temporarily useful but are ultimately irrelevant. The Universe (capital *U*) is ultimate reality.

> "On the other hand, if the universe is created, then there must be reality beyond the confines of the universe. The Creator is that ultimate reality and wields authority over all else. The Creator is the source of life and establishes its meaning and purpose. The Creator's personality defines personality. The Creator's character defines morality."

"Does he who implanted the ear not hear?

Does he who formed the eye not see?"

Dr. David Hume, the brilliant empiricist philosopher who is usually misrepresented as the man who destroyed the arguments for the existence of God or as the man that was opposed to belief in the existence of God, states in his book, *The Natural History of Religion*:

> "The whole frame of nature bespeaks an intelligent author. No rational inquirer can, after serious reflection, suspend his belief a moment with regard to the primary principles of genuine theism and religion. The world is one vast machine and is divisible into a network of smaller and yet comparable machines that far outstrip human comprehension. Reasonable men are forced to conclude the source of everything is a superior mind or intelligence. Consider and anatomize the human eye curveting its structure and contrivance and tell me from your own feeling if the idea of a contriver does not immediately flow in upon you with a force like that of a sensation. The most obvious conclusion surely is **in favor of design.** Who can behold the male and female of each species, the correspondence of their parts and instincts, their passions and whole course of life before and after generation but must be sensible that the propagation of species is intended by nature. Millions and millions of such instances present themselves through every part of the universe and no language can convey a more intelligible, irresistible meaning than the curious adjustment of final cause. Whatever arguments may be urged, an orderly world as well as a coherent articulate speech will still be received as an incontestable proof of design and intention. The order and arrangement of nature, the curious adjustment of final causes, the plain use and intention of every part and organ, all these bespeak in the clearest language an intelligent cause or author. The heavens and earth join in the same testimony, the whole chorus of nature raises one hymn to the praise of its creator."

Men of Science Who Believed in Creation

- Francis Bacon...originator of the scientific method.

- Robert Boyle...the father of chemistry.

- Johann Kepler...the father of astronomy.

- Copernicus and Galileo...gave accurate concepts of the universe. They destroyed the geocentric (earth-centered) theory of our solar system and established the heliocentric (sun-centered) theory. Galileo also developed the telescope.

- Isaac Newton...considered the greatest scientist who ever lived, discovered the law of gravity and wrote books defending the literal accuracy of scripture.

- Michael Faraday...developed the disciplines of electromagnetic and field theory.

- Samuel Morse...invented the telegraph.

- Charles Babbage...developed the first true computer system.

- Matthew Maury...regarded as the father of hydrography and oceanography.

- Louis Pasteur...biochemist and bacteriologist, developed pasteurization process.

"We fit into the plans of the Great Architect...else we would not have a sense of our own responsibility" —Robert A. Millikan...Nobel Prize-winning Physicist.

"All good scientists stand in awe and wonder at creation. Only matter-of-fact scientists who are either inarticulate or brute mechanics might not have this sense of awe"—Seymour Hutner...Microbiologist.

"For myself, faith begins with a realization that a supreme intelligence brought the universe into being and created man. It is not difficult for me to have ethic faith, for it is incontrovertible that where there is a plan there is intelligence—an orderly, unfolding universe testifies to the truth of the most majestic statement ever uttered—'In the beginning God'" —Dr. Arthur Compton, Nobel Prize winner in physics.

"So many fall back on the explanation—'the law of chance', Whose law? For me, I prefer the belief in a creator, divine, supernatural. I cannot accept chaos" —George Lechler, Anthropologist.

Dr. William Swann, a leading authority on cosmic radiation stated,

"The man of science likes to separate fact from speculation. Now viewing the universe as a whole, I cannot escape the fact that it is of intelligent design. By this, I mean that the universe shows on a magnificent scale the same kind of inter-relationship of its working and efficiency of its planning as an engineer strives to achieve in his smaller undertakings."

Wernher von Braun, the brilliant German rocket expert stated,

"Why do I believe in God? Simply stated, the main reason is this: anything as well ordered and perfectly created as is our earth and universe must have a maker, a master designer. Anything so orderly, so perfect, so precisely balanced, so majestic as this creation can only be the product of a divine idea. There must be a maker; there can be no other way.

"My experience with science led me to God. To be forced to believe only one conclusion—that everything in the universe happened by chance—would violate the very objectivity of science itself."

In the First Century, the Apostle Paul put it this way,

"For since the creation of the world God's invisible qualities—His eternal power and divine nature have been clearly seen, being understood from what has been made, so that men are without excuse" (Romans 1:20).

Chapter 10

The Real Identity of America

Biblical reformation faith, is the foundation of our country. It was the original root and foundation of America—the faith that catapulted America to greatness. The move away from this fact began in 1947 when the Supreme Court declared that the state must be neutral in religious affairs. Thus began the de-Christianizing of American classrooms. We have secularized teachers' textbooks. Unjustified censorship of the Bible and our religious history is destroying America's basic values and ethics. Consequently, Americans have been, and are being brainwashed and are ignorant of our true origins. Alan Bloom stated, "Our youth have no sense of tradition" and he sadly concludes, "They have impoverished souls."

Biblical Reformation Faith

Today, it is often said that we are no longer a Christian nation and, considering the churches of America, many are ignorant or confused as to what the original reformation faith of our founders was. I believe it is essential that we rediscover that faith, because of the cultural and moral collapse we are presently witnessing, causing the disintegration of the American family as well as American institutions.

"Who you are is who you were" —Amistad, the movie

"There can be no building without rebuilding memory

and without building monuments to those who built us."
                                        —Russian poet Yevgeny Yevtushenko

The prominent minister Dr. D. James Kennedy, of the Coral Ridge Presbyterian Church in Florida in a speech entitled "America Adrift", poignantly identified the present problem and critical condition of America. He stated,

> "Our nation today…, is like a ship cut adrift with no rudder, compass or goal. We don't know where we're going because we don't know from whence we came; or another similitude is that we are like a child who is struggling to find his identity because he doesn't know his parents or his lineage." Dr. Kennedy further states, "Why doesn't the average American have a solid identity? Simply because our Christian roots have been expunged from our culture and institutions and most important, *they are no longer taught in our schools and have been taken out of our textbooks. In order for us to rediscover our identity and discern our destiny, we must again rediscover our true origins."*

Let us look at the nature of the Protestant Reformation itself— a revolution that many historians call the greatest political and social upheaval in history and definitely the greatest schism in the history of the Christian church.

My analysis of this generational revolt and the nature of reformation faith itself draws from R. C. Sproul (editor of the *New Geneva Study Bible—Bringing the Light of the Reformation to Scripture*) and his book, *Faith Alone;* from Roland H. Bainton in his book, *Here I Stand;* from Paul Johnson in his article, *The*

Almost Chosen People, taken from *The Wilson Quarterly* (Winter 1985); from the book, *The Light and the Glory*, by Peter Marshall and David Manuel; from the book, *A Woman Rides the Beast*, by Dave Hunt; and finally, from the tape, *America, You're Too Young to Die* by David T. Moore, Pastor of the Southwest Community Church, Palm Desert, California.

Causes of the Protestant Reformation

In the 16th century, the Roman Catholic Church was not only a religious system, but a political and economic power as well. It replaced the Roman Empire and became known as the Roman Catholic Empire.

No doubt, there were many causes for the break-up of this empire. The Reformation was not just a religious revolt. The following points will suffice.

- **Political**—Nationalism was a growing force in the 16th century and the people of the newly-formed countries in Europe were beginning to see Rome, Italy, as a foreign country and the Pope as something like a dictator of that country ruling them.

- **Economic**—People were becoming disgruntled about sending money to an Italian Pope (taxes, alms, etc.). They were also becoming increasingly disturbed by the fact that Rome owned much of the land in their own country; in fact, Rome, a part of the feudal and manored system, owned a third of the land in Europe.

- **Troubles of the Papacy**—People became alarmed and confused because of the power grabs in Rome. In 1309, a French Pope, Clement I, moved the Papacy from Rome to Avignon, France, where it remained for 70 years. This period was called the "Babylonian Captivity". Soon, they had two Popes, one in France and one in Rome. Then, in time, there were three Popes, all claiming to be the Vicar of Christ. The common people and nobles alike were asking, "Who's the true Vicar (deputy) of Christ on earth?" "Who has authority over our souls?"

- **Corruption**—People knew of the immoral lives of the clergy and of the abuse of money—the buying and selling of church offices, such as the position of bishop. Money was the thing that mattered in obtaining such a position whether or not a person was qualified or even had any religious training. Along with such examples of corruption (and there were many more), possibly the most heinous crime was the selling of salvation—indulgences (pardons for sin). Because of the promise of the Pope and indulgence preachers, people began selling their possessions.

Money was rolling in as the church told the people they could buy their relatives out of purgatory or spend less time in purgatory themselves. A small alms might lessen time in purgatory by five years, a large amount by maybe 30,000 years. The Pope's peddlers of indulgences were not always consistent in telling the people that they should also confess their sins and live contrite lives. Even worse, if you were a rich bishop, for example, and you wanted to commit adultery, it was possible to pay beforehand.

Martin Luther posted his 95 theses against the sale of indulgences, sparking the Reformation. Luther was especially appalled about the exploitation of the poor, illiterate peasants. They were selling their possessions and flocking to the "salesmen". At the beginning, Luther only wanted to stop the abuse of indulgences. But in time, he was beginning to doubt the whole system. Peddler Johann Tetzel—"Hear the cries and screams of your poor parents and relatives. 'Have pity on us. Free us from these flames.' As soon as the coin in the coffer rings, the soul from purgatory springs."

- **Spiritual**—Because of all the abuses of the church, there was a spiritual vacuum among the people. Also, with the Renaissance (rebirth of learning) and the scientific revolution in full force (Copernicus, Galileo), people were beginning to question and doubt the Church.

Many people of the newly-formed countries were thinking about forming their own state church, but they were in a quandary as to how to accomplish this. Remember, this period in history was called "the age of faith".

The dilemma of the people (nobility and common people) was this: "How can we leave the one true church, founded by St. Peter, that has the keys to the kingdom of heaven? There's no salvation outside the church!" Ex-communication was greatly feared by all because this meant eternal hellfire. By what authority could they leave? A catalyst was needed and that catalyst was Martin Luther, and the authority for such a break from the church was the Bible.

Many scholars believe Martin Luther was a genius. Starting out as a lawyer before becoming a monk, he was acknowledged as one of the brightest legal minds in Germany with a brilliant future. But one day on horseback, riding in the forest in a terrible storm, he was almost struck by lightning and was knocked off his horse. In his "Damascus road experience", he cried out, "Help me Saint Anne; I shall become a monk!"

Life in the Monastery

Luther struggled for about five years as a monk, as the life of monkery didn't give him peace. He was constantly plagued with guilt. Because of his work ethic, Luther became a Latin, Hebrew and Greek scholar and an expert on the Bible, but he still had no peace from his indoctrination in Roman Catholicism. Also, having a brilliant, legal mind and applying it the Old Testament law of God, he clearly understood the biblical teaching of the holiness of God. His frustration was his inability to be holy and to keep the law of God. He was so haunted and tormented that he stated he visualized Christ as a stern judge with lightning bolts in each hand before whose presence he would certainly perish.

Luther became an over-conscientious, neurotic monk attempting to follow the Roman Catholic plan of salvation of righteous living and sacramental works. The sacraments were thought of as something like a ladder to heaven. The Church taught (as all world religions teach) that one has to earn salvation by good works. But even doing this, there was still no assurance of salvation.

"If ever a man could go to heaven through monkery, it was I. No one was as austere or dedicated as I was. No one denied himself as much as I did in pursuing righteousness," he said. Luther attempted almost everything to have peace with God —self-flagellation, wearing hair shirts, sleeping without blankets, long hours of prayer and meditation, and starving himself.

Many modern psychologists believe Luther was on the brink of insanity as he confessed his sins to his father confessor daily, which would last from one to four hours at a sitting. The superiors of the monastery were frustrated and exasperated at hearing hour after hour of Luther's confession of trivial sins. When the father confessors saw Luther coming, they would generally hide.

The Pilgrimage to Rome

But in this time of desperation, a unique opportunity presented itself. The Superior of the order of monks gave Luther and a fellow monk permission to make a pilgrimage to Rome to represent their order in an important meeting. Luther was ecstatic about having the opportunity to visit the Holy City—the capitol of Christendom. Rome also had more sacred relics and shrines than any other city in Christendom. Going to Rome and seeing the relics (bones of St. Peter, hay from Jesus' crib, pieces of the cross, etc.) was one of the chief ways of getting indulgences. This meant a greatly reduced time in purgatory; in fact, seeing Rome's relics was worth more than a million years less time in purgatory. Luther excitedly exclaimed, "Oh, that my father and mother were dead." He really meant it! He wanted to give them the benefits of his soon-to-be-gained indulgences. He finally decided to give the merits of his pilgrimage to his deceased grandfather.

Going to Rome shook Luther to the foundation of his faith. The Church at this time in history was at the height of corruption. With shock, bitterness and disillusionment, Luther saw priests give Mass five times as fast as the priests in Germany, just to get through it. Priests also flagrantly and openly displayed their immoral lives. There were houses of prostitution all over Rome. Priests regularly visited the brothels and openly engaged in homosexual relationships. There were so many illegitimate children in Rome that it became known as "the city of bastards".

Luther, "the personification of piety", a zealot for righteousness, was in a crisis of faith, broken and filled with doubt. He decided to visit the Lateran Church in Rome. The steps of this sacred site were supposed to be the ones Jesus walked on. Luther crawled on his knees, saying the Rosary on the way up to the shrine where Christ was supposed to have been judged by Pontius Pilate. He wrote that when he got to the top, with no one around, he said, "Is it really true?" Luther was now beginning to doubt the whole sacrament of penance.

Back from Rome, Luther was more confused and frustrated than ever and still obsessed with guilt and a phobic preoccupation with the wrath of God. Unable to find peace, he was once asked, "Luther, do you love God?" Luther replied, "Love god? You ask me if I love God? Sometimes I hate Him!"

The Superior of the monastery, wondering what to do about Luther and knowing of his keen intelligence and work ethic as well as his giftedness as an orator, told the shocked Luther that he was to be main theologian of the monasteries of Germany. Luther reluctantly accepted.

"Plan one" not working, Luther began further in-depth studies of the scriptures following the advice of his Father Superior. In doing this, he was led to his "tower experience". Luther was astounded at how far the church had strayed from the original teachings of the apostles as well as the early church fathers. He was beginning to realize that the church, by adding pagan traditions to the scriptures, had distorted and, in fact, perverted the gospel. The same accusation of Jesus to the Jewish Pharisees applied to the Catholic Church. "They [the Pharisees] tie up heavy loads, hard to bear, and place them on men's shoulders...." "...you shut up the kingdom of heaven to men's faces..." (Matthew 23:4, 13). "By your traditions you have made void [of none effect] the Word of God" (Mark 7:13). As Jesus said, by adding their traditions, the Church, in essence, had "locked up" the kingdom of heaven from the common man.

As already related, the Catholic Church's plan for salvation was the sale of sacramental works. It was actually salvation by installments. But even with all this, there was still no assurance of salvation.

More frustrating, the Church taught that no one could ever perform enough good works to go to heaven. So, everyone had to spend some time in purgatory (a place not mentioned in the Bible, by the way). There they would be tormented by fire until pure enough for heaven. Luther, vividly understanding all this and that there was no biblical foundation for these church teachings, was now ready for his tower experience.

The Gospel

Knowing of Luther's tower experience and his restoration of the true biblical gospel is important in order to understand the Pilgrims' and Puritans' concept of the gospel and their general frame of reference. To enjoy the freedom of the gospel, to make this the foundation of their lives and the new government and to spread the gospel to the heathen was the main motive of our founders' coming to the New World.

About five years after his trip to Rome and extremely knowledgeable about the Bible, Luther was still blind to the truth of the gospel. He was still "homogenizing" church teachings with the Bible. The Catholic Church taught that Church tradition was equal to the Bible and he had not yet separated the two.

By this time, he had been ordained as a priest of the Church and a doctor of religion. Because of his brilliance in theology, Prince Fredrick of Saxony brought him to the town of Wittenberg to be the Professor of Religion at the new university. It was at this time Luther had his "tower experience".

The Just Shall Live by Faith

"For I am not ashamed of the gospel of Christ, for it is the power of God to salvation for everyone who believes … for in it the righteousness of God is revealed … as it is written, the just shall live by faith." (Romans 1:16, 17)

Remember, Luther at this point had not found himself, nor did he understand the gospel. He had been indoctrinated in Catholicism since he was a child and although he knew the scriptures in four languages, because of his background, he was blinded to the truth of the gospel.

Luther needed a mentor and that mentor would be the brilliant theologian and Church Father who lived about a millenium before him—St. Augustine (4th century).

The Tower Experience

"and the Righteousness of God is Revealed from Heaven"

One night in the tower of the university, Luther was preparing his first lecture on the first chapter of Romans. In reviewing the commentaries of church theologians of the past, he happened to come across an essay written by St. Augustine on Romans 1:16, 17. Augustine stated, when St. Paul said, "... and the righteousness of God is revealed from heaven," he was not talking about the inherently righteous nature of God, but about **a righteousness God freely gives to those who have no righteousness.**

When that theological truth burst into his consciousness, Luther went into total shock and cried, "What? You mean Paul here is not talking about God's own righteousness, but the righteousness God freely gives to a believer?" He later wrote, "I understood the gospel for the first time in my life—that the ground of my justification is not in my own righteousness but the righteousness that is given to my account. When I understood, the gates of paradise swung open and I walked through." He shouted, "I have found the gospel and nobody can take it away from me, not emperors or popes, not church councils or princes. I have the gospel, 'The just shall live by faith!'"

In this tower experience, Luther was transformed and relieved of his neurotic guilt. He had finally found his long sought-after peace with God. He also knew in that moment that the Church had perverted the gospel.

Biblical Reformation Faith

Luther's new-found gospel literally turned the medieval world "upside down" and also became the foundation and frame of reference of our early founders.

R. C. Sproul in his book, *Faith Alone—The Evangelical Doctrine of Justification*, analyzes Martin Luther's and John Calvin's theological perspective of Justification by Faith (the gospel). Concerning the central issue of the Reformation, Dr. Sproul states,

> "It is probably safe to say that virtually every delegate to the Council of Trent would have affirmed that justification is by grace.

> "The same can be said of the next affirmation: 'We are justified ... *through faith*.' Again, Rome has always insisted that faith is a necessary condition for justification. What they denied historically is that it is a *sufficient* condition. The Reformation was waged, not over the question of justification by faith but over the issue of justification by faith *alone*. It was the *sola* of *sola fide* that was the central point of dispute."

Betrayal of the Gospel?

Dr. Sproul makes use of the word, forensic. Forensic means the legal character of an issue. There's forensic medicine, forensic jurisprudence, etc. Here we are considering the legal character of justification. Forensic justification was the fiery issue of the Reformation. Is a doctrine that denies the forensic character of justification or the concept of the imputation of the righteousness of Christ really the gospel? Dr. Sproul states,

"The Reformers viewed justification as being forensic, resting on **God's judicial declaration** that the sinner is counted as just or righteous by virtue of the imputation of the righteousness of Christ. To be declared just on the sole grounds of the imputation of Christ's righteousness was to them the very essence of the gospel."

The central theological issue of the Reformation was, "Are we redeemed **solely** by the righteousness of Christ or does it demand a mixture of the righteousness of Christ added to the believer's own inherent righteousness?" The Roman Catholic Church's Council of Trent (just after the start of the Reformation) took the latter position.

Luther and Calvin

Dr. Sproul states,

"Martin Luther came to the conclusion that the central issue was *sola fide*. Hence his well-known assertion that *sola fide* is '... the article with and by which the church stands, without which it falls'. Luther said of justification: 'The article of justification is the master and prince, the lord, the ruler and the judge over all kinds of doctrines; it preserves and governs all church doctrine and raises up our conscience before God. Without this article the world is utter death and darkness.'

"Elsewhere Luther wrote: 'If the article of justification is lost, all Christian doctrine is lost at the same time.'

"Luther was not alone in regarding justification by faith alone with such singular importance. John Calvin, likewise, attached crucial importance to it:

"The doctrine of Justification ... is the principal ground on which religion must be supported, so it requires greater care and attention. For unless you understand first of all what your position is before God, and what the judgment [is] which He passes upon you, you have no foundation on which your salvation can be laid, or on which piety towards God can be reared.

"Both Luther and Calvin expressed the singular importance of justification with the metaphor of a *foundation.* Of course, both men understood that the biblical metaphor of foundation is that of the prophets and apostles, a foundation that is laid in Christ, the Chief Cornerstone.

"But their use of the image of foundation is linked to the central importance of the gospel itself. It is basic (foundational) to salvation inasmuch as it contains the essence of **how** a person is redeemed. It is not merely the foundation for a building, edifice or institution; it is foundational to religious life and piety."

Dr. Sproul quotes James Buchanan in his book, *The Doctrine of Justification,* on the central issue of what caused the Reformation. He states,

"In his introduction to James Buchanan's classic work, *The Doctrine of Justification,* J. I. Packer comments on Luther's formula *articulus stantis et cadentis ecclesiae*:

"By this he meant that when this doctrine is understood, believed, and preached, as it was in New Testament times, the church stands in the grace of God and is alive; but where it is neglected, overlaid, or denied, as it was in medieval Catholicism, the church falls from grace and its life drains away, leaving it in a state of darkness and death. The reason why the Reformation happened, and Protestant churches came into being, was that Luther and his fellow Reformers believed that Papal Rome had apostatized from the gospel so completely in this respect that no faithful Christian could with a good conscience continue within her ranks."

"It is entirely by the intervention of Christ's righteous-ness that we obtain justification before God. This is equivalent to saying that man is not just in himself, but that the righteousness of Christ is communicated to him by imputation, while he is strictly deserving of punishment" —John Calvin.

We'll conclude with Dr. Sproul's use of forensic justification —the imputation of righteousness for mankind's atonement.

"Reformed theology insists that the biblical doctrine of justification is *forensic* in nature. What does this mean? In the popular jargon of religion, the word *forensic* is used infrequently. The word is not foreign, however, to ordinary language. It appears daily in the news media, particularly with reference to criminal investigations and trials. We hear of 'forensic evidence' and 'forensic medicine' as we listen to the reports of criminologists, coroners and pathologists. Here the term *forensic* refers to the judicial system and judicial proceedings....

"The link between these ordinary usages of *forensic* and its theological use is that justification has to do with a *legal* or *judicial* matter involving some type of declaration. We can reduce its meaning to the concept of a *legal declaration*.

"The doctrine of justification involves a legal matter of the highest order. Indeed it is the legal issue on which the sinner stands or falls: his status before the supreme tribunal of God.

"When we are summoned to appear before the bar of God's judgment, we face a judgment based on perfect justice. The presiding judge is himself perfectly just. He is also omniscient, fully aware of our every deed, thought, inclination and word. Measured by the standard of his canon of righteousness, we face the psalmist's rhetorical question that hints at despair: 'If you, LORD, should mark iniquities..., who could stand?' (Ps. 130:3 NKJV).

"The obvious answer to this query is supplied by the Apostle Paul: 'There is none righteous, no, not one ...' (Rom. 3:10).

"By imparting or imputing Christ's righteousness to us sinners, God reckons us as just. It is 'as if' we were inherently just. But we are not inherently just. We are 'counted' or 'reckoned' just by imputation.

"This is the point of Luther's statement that we are 'at the same time just and sinner' (*simul iustus et peccator*). We are just by imputation even while sin still remains in us, though it does not reign in us.

"Calvin goes on to say: '*To justify*, therefore, is nothing else than to acquit from the charge of guilt, as if innocence were proved. Hence, when God justifies us through the intercession of Christ, he does not acquit us on a proof of our own innocence, but by an imputation of righteousness, so that though not righteous in ourselves, we are deemed righteous in Christ.'

"In the atonement, Christ satisfies the negative side of God's justice. Here, again by imputation, Christ pays the penalty due for our sins. He receives, for us, the punitive wrath of God that our sin deserves. He takes the consequences of our demerits, our unjustness. He receives the judgment due our guilt. In this regard God's justice is satisfied.

"The atonement is vicarious because it is accomplished via imputation. Christ is the sin-bearer for his people, the *Agnus Dei* (Lamb of God) who takes away (expiates) our sin and satisfies (propitiates) the demands of God's justice. The cross displays both God's justice (in that He truly punishes sin) and His grace (because He punishes sin by providing a substitute for us)."

"Christ redeemed us from the curse of the law, having become a curse for us..." (Galatians 3:13).

The Catholic plan of salvation in reality **denied the finished work of Christ** on the Cross. Paul states in Romans 3:24, "Being justified freely by His grace through the redemption that is in Christ Jesus, whom God set forth as a propitiation (covering) by His blood through faith...."

Redemption means "to buy back" or to be "paid in full". The redemption of mankind took place on the Cross and procured for the believer the free gift of righteousness or justification. The Catholic Church program of works to earn salvation contradicted the biblical concept of redemption and was the antithesis of the Apostle Paul's gospel, as Paul states, "To him that **worketh not** but **believeth** [trusts] Him who justifies the ungodly, his faith is counted to him as righteousness...." Paul also said, in Galatians 2:21, "I do not frustrate the grace of God; for if righteousness comes through the law, then Christ died in vain."

Christ is Our Righteousness

Luther first discovered the biblical gospel in Romans 1:19, 20, "The just shall live by faith." This means that the moment one has true faith, submitting to the lordship of Christ, God gives that person the benefits of forgiveness of sins (past, present and future) and the gift of eternal life. In other words, without works, God imputes to the believer the righteousness of Christ.

Imputation means to transfer to or to credit (as in a legal sense) to one's account the righteousness of Christ. To put it another way, justification (acquittal by a judge) takes place in the instant of true faith as a person's sins are imputed to Christ on the cross and the believing sinner receives the cloak of righteousness—the righteous covering of Christ (II Corinthians 5:21).

Luther (for assurance) continually returned to Ephesians 2:8, 9: "For by grace (God's love and mercy, His unmerited favor) you have been saved (past tense) through faith and that not of yourselves, it is the gift of God, not of works lest any man should boast."

The gospel couldn't be any clearer, but remember that Luther had been indoctrinated in Catholicism from birth and the common people of that day didn't have access to a Bible. In time, however, the German people would have the Bible, again thanks to Martin Luther. After his ex-communication from the Church, Luther went into hiding and there translated the Latin Bible into every day German. Previously, only the professional clergy could read the Bible; now, the people could read it for themselves.

"Abraham believed God and it was reckoned over to him as righteousness" (Genesis 15:6).

Salvation has always been by grace through faith alone— even in the Old Testament as the above verse states. In the Old Testament, people looked forward to the Cross and in the New Testament, people look back to the Cross (Romans 4).

The Prince of Peace (Isaiah 9:6)

"Therefore having been justified by faith, we have peace with God through our Lord Jesus Christ, through whom also we have access by faith into this grace" (Romans 5:1).

Again from Paul's writings, Luther received assurance that the war was over. He was no longer tormented by guilt and no longer felt frightened and estranged from a holy God. He now had peace with God.

"Therefore... " (Romans 5:1)

When Paul uses the word "therefore" in his epistles, he's talking about the conclusion of the matter or the results (in this case) of "justification by faith". At the moment of trusting faith, a believer has peace with God and also, as the verse states, access to the very presence of our holy God. Hebrews 4:16 states,

> "Let us therefore come boldly [without fear] to the throne of grace that we may obtain mercy and find grace to help in time of need."

In other words, at the moment of conversion, a believer can come to the very throne of God in prayer because he or she has been covered by the righteousness of Christ. Paul stated, "I labor day and night to present every man perfect in Christ."

These biblical breakthroughs ran like wildfire all over Germany as Luther's pen wrote the glorious liberating gospel in the language of the people. This was the time of the invention of the printing press and soon Luther's ideas spread all over Europe.

The Catholic church, fearing a revolution, became alarmed and Luther was summoned by the Church to the town of Worms to meet the Emperor and face a Church Council. On the way to the City of Worms, great crowds followed his two-wheeled cart, crying, "Go, Martin, go!" Luther had become a national hero as people crowded into the city, standing on buildings, towers and balconies. The people of Europe were now ready to break from the Roman Catholic Church.

> "Let goods and kindred go. This mortal life also.
> The body they may kill. God's truth abideth still.
> His kingdom is forever!"
>
> —from A Mighty Fortress is Our God by Martin Luther

The Church, without allowing Luther to give a defense, demanded that Luther recant his beliefs or face excommunication. Excommunication (according to the Catholic Church) not only meant eternal hellfire but also possibly execution. John Huss had previously been burned at the stake.

Luther was frightened and asked for 24 hours to think about it. The Church reluctantly granted his request. The next day after hours of prayer, Luther was ready to sacrifice his life for the cause of the gospel. The inquisitor of the Council rose to his feet and loudly said, "Luther, do you recant? Give us a straight answer!" Luther struggled to his feet and humbly said these words, "I can't recant, my conscience is held captive by the Word of God. Unless I'm convinced by sacred scripture, I can't recant, for even popes and councils can err. Unless I'm convinced by sacred scriptures or evident reason, I can't recant. To act against one's conscience is neither right nor safe. Here I stand; there's nothing else I can do. God help me." These solemn words of Luther echoed all over Europe and the Reformation was on.

The gospel, then, was the heart and soul of the Protestant Reformation, liberating millions and causing one of the greatest social and political revolutions in history. The gospel was the power and strength of the Reformation and the "energizer" of the first settlers that sent them to the New World to provide the very foundations of the institutions of our country.

Chapter 11

Teaching Our Heritage in the Public Schools

The erroneous stereotype of the original American Settlers now being presented in our textbooks is that they were a chance accumulation of adventurers, deists, aristocrats, convicts, blue-blood, self-righteous bigots who chased witches, and religious outcasts seeking their own economic gain. While there were such among them (as in most movements), the real motivation of the first Americans was *biblical reformation faith*. They came to America to freely exercise their faith and to set up "the Kingdom of God" that had fallen apart in the Old World. They believed they were (like the ancient Israelites) a covenant people. This solemn pact with God meant that they were under His providential call to spread the gospel and to be "a light to the nations" or, as John Winthrop said, "... a city on a hill".

Also, as with the ancient Israelites who were delivered from Egyptian bondage, the early Americans were people of content-ment and great consolation and were filled with thankfulness because they believed they had been freed, not only from the guilt and condemnation of sin, but also freed from external tyranny—no pope, no king, no state church. This was the real identity of our founders.

The Gospel—Foundation of American Institutions

Luther's newfound freedom changed him inside and out. Then, it began to change everything in his world—society, business, education, families, government and church affairs. The cultural revolution that Luther started created the greatest personal freedom the world had ever known, making Martin Luther one of the beacons of Western Civilization.

In Luther's day, the common people were uneducated and their lives were controlled by an elite group of priests, nobles and kings. Luther started events that changed all of this. He showed that every man is a priest and king over his own mind, body and possessions. Man is not to be ruled by corrupt oligarchies. Instead, man is to live by divine providence and written law based on the Bible.

The Belief in the Providence of God

"I will instruct and teach you in the way that you should go; I will guide you with my eye" (Psalm 32:6).

The Christian commitment of our founders and their belief in the providential leading of the God can easily be documented from primary sources such as essays, speeches, diaries and historical examples. These sources demonstrate that our founders believed that the only way this nation could survive and be prosperous is if its people were dependent on God. In contrast, most Americans today—products of our educational system—believe our founding fathers intended to establish a secular nation. Nothing could be further from the truth. Our founding fathers had every intention of establishing America as a Christian nation.

It is commonly taught in our public schools that most of our founders were nominal church goers, agnostics or deists. A deist is a person who believes that God created all things, then left the scene. In other words, He's not here and He doesn't interfere in the affairs of men, consequently there's no use to pray. The evidence does not support these erroneous and damaging concepts. Our founders were surrounded by ample evidence of Divine Providence and did not fail to give God the credit for both special providences and their godly institutions.

William Bradford, in his *History of the Plymouth Plantation*, tells of the Pilgrims' complete reliance on Divine Providence in the midst of their many tragedies.

> "But these things did not dismay them (though they did sometimes trouble them) for their desires were set on— the ways of God, and to enjoy His ordinances; but they rested on His providence and knew whom they had believed."

Before setting foot in the New Land, the Pilgrims formed the Mayflower Compact, called "the birth certificate of America". Contained in this document was a statement of the purpose for the Pilgrims' coming to the New World, "We came for the glory of God and enjoyment of the liberties of the Gospel."

When all the colonies got together for the first time to form the New England Confederation, they made this statement:

> "Whereas we all came together to America for the one and same end and aim, to advance the Kingdom of our Lord Jesus Christ and to enjoy the liberties of the Gospel in freedom and peace."

George Washington—the father of our country as most Americans know, was the man who led us through the Revolutionary War and the formation of our government and Constitution. In diaries and letters, he gave constant reference to

God's providence in his life and the life of the nation. These excerpts demonstrate that Washington was much more than a nominal church goer, a liberal or a deist.

"By the miraculous care of providence, that protected me beyond all human expectations, I had four bullets through my coat and two horses shot from under me and yet escaped unhurt."

— July 18, 1775 - letter to his brother after

Braddock's disaster, French and Indian War

"It is the duty of all nations to acknowledge the providence of almighty God, to obey His will, to be grateful for His benefits and humbly to implore His protection and favor."

— Thanksgiving Proclamation, October 3, 1789

The Declaration of Independence written July 4, 1776, which mentions the name of God four times, concludes with a similar testimony by stating:

"With a firm reliance on the protection of divine providence...."

"We shall not fight alone, God presides over the destiny of nations, the battle is not for the strong alone. Is life so dear and peace so sweet as to be purchased at the price of slavery? Forbid it, Almighty God! Give me liberty or give me death" —Patrick Henry (March 23, 1775, just prior to the American Revolution).

I am not aware of **any** high school textbook which gives the context of Patrick Henry's statement, "Give me liberty or give me death!" Is this sectarianism by omission?

Slogan of the Revolutionary War—"No King but Christ"

The Wilson Quarterly (Woodrow Wilson International Center for Scholars—Smithsonian Institute, Winter 1985), in an article entitled *The Almost Chosen People* by Paul Johnson, documents the fact that the Revolutionary War was inspired by Protestant preachers. After Jonathan Edwards' first sermon, churches all over America were preaching revolution.

"The coming American Revolution was in essence the political and military expression of a religious movement, the Great Awakening (ca. 1720-50). Certainly those who inspired it and carried it through believed that they were doing God's will. The man who first preached the Revolution, Jonathan Edwards (1703-58), believed strongly that there was no real difference between a political and a religious emotion, both of which were God-directed."

George Washington at Valley Forge

"Let my heart, gracious God, be so effected with your glory and majesty that I may fulfill these weighty duties which you've required of me. I have called upon you to pardon me and forgive me of my sins. Thank you for the sacrifice of Jesus Christ offered on the cross for me. You gave your son to die for me and have given me assurance of my salvation." —Washington's personal diary, Valley Forge

"O most glorious God I acknowledge and confess my faults in the weak and imperfect performance on the duties of this day. I have called on thee for pardon and forgiveness of sins but so coldly and carelessly that my prayers are become my sin and stand in need of pardon. I have heard Thy holy word but with such deadness of spirit—that I have been an unprofitable and forgetful

hearer... but, oh God—Who art rich in mercy and
plenteous in redemption, mark not, I beseech thee, what I
have done amiss, remember that I am but dust, and remit
my transgressions, negligences and ignorances, and cover
them all with the absolute obedience of Thy dear Son,
that those sacrifices which I have offered may be
accepted by thee, in and for the sacrifice of Jesus Christ
offered upon the cross for me."

— Sunday Evening Prayer, Valley Forge

"Direct my thoughts, words and work, wash away my
sins in the immaculate blood of the Lamb, and purge my
heart by the Holy Spirit. Daily frame me more and more
into the likeness of Thy Son Jesus Christ.

— Monday Morning, Valley Forge

Benjamin Franklin (a so-called deist) was the founding father
who set the precedent for having prayer every time Congress met,
reminding those present that it was their continuous prayers during
the Revolutionary War that gave them the victory.

The constitutional convention met to form a new government
just after the Revolutionary War. In the summer of 1787,
desperation and a deadlock had descended upon the constitutional
convention and men from various states were planning to leave.
As the convention was already adjourned in dissension, Benjamin
Franklin addressed George Washington with the following
request:

"How has it happened, Sir, that we have not hitherto once
thought of humbly appealing to the Father of lights to
illuminate our understanding? In the beginning of the
contest with Great Britain, when we were sensible to
danger, we had daily prayers in this room for divine
protection. Our prayers, Sir, were heard and they were
graciously answered. I have lived, Sir, a long time and
the longer I live, the more convincing proofs I see of this

truth—that God governs in the affairs of men. And if a sparrow cannot fall to the ground without His notice, is it probable that an empire can rise without His aid? We have been assured, Sir, in the sacred writing that 'except the Lord build the house, they labor in vain that build it'…. I firmly believe this…."

James Madison (chief architect of the constitution, called "the Father of the Constitution") said,

"We have staked the whole future of American civilization not upon the power of Government, far from it. We have staked the future of all of our political institutions upon the capacity of each and all of us to govern ourselves, to control ourselves, to sustain ourselves according to the Ten Commandments of God."

Above the Chief Justice of the Supreme Court today sits the American eagle symbolically standing above the Ten Commandments, protecting them. Today, of course, the Supreme Court(1980) has outlawed the posting of the Ten Commandments in classrooms. Their absurd reasoning was this: "If the Ten Commandments were posted in the classroom, students might be induced to read them, and in reading them, might meditate upon them, and in meditating on them, might be induced to obey them — this is not acceptable."

A good question to ask is, "What has happened to America?"

Biblical Roots of Our Institutions

"We do not have a government armed with the power capable to deal with human passion. Our Constitution was made only for a religious and moral people. It is wholly inadequate to govern any other way" —John Adams.

"The highest glory of the American Revolution was not freedom but it connected in one indissoluble bond the principles of civil government and the principles of Christianity" —John Quincy Adams.

Not only is it a lie to say that our founders were only nominal church goers or deists but it is also false to say that our institutions were mainly the product of the Enlightenment. American institutions in their beginnings (Pilgrims and Puritans—the 13 Colonies) were all biblically oriented. The founders (by and large) were Protestant followers of Luther and Calvin—men who broke from the Roman Catholic Empire and returned to the Bible and the original teachings of the Apostles. By checking out the Church affiliations of the signers of the Declaration of Independence and framers of the Constitution, you will find that 53 of the 55 were Orthodox Protestant Bible- believing Christians. *That's why there are scripture verses on all the monuments in Washington D.C.!*

The Wilson Quarterly (Winter 1985), in an article entitled *The Almost Chosen People*, states,

"Even those most strongly influenced by the secular spirit of the Enlightenment acknowledged the centrality of the religious spirit in giving birth to America. As John Adams put it in 1818: 'The Revolution was effected before the war commenced. [It] was in the minds and hearts of the people; a change in their religious sentiments of their duties and obligations.' He saw a religion, indeed, as the foundation of the American civic spirit:

"One great advantage of the Christian religion is that it brings the great principle of the law of nature and nations, love your neighbour as yourself, and do to others as you would that others do to you, to the knowledge, belief and veneration of the whole people.... The duties and rights of the man and the citizen are thus taught from early infancy.'"

The Reformation brought about the greatest explosion of education the world has ever seen. Martin Luther, John Calvin, John Knox and other reformers are credited by education historians as the men who laid the foundation for modern education. They reasoned that all people should have the ability to read the Bible.

> "The philosophy of the classroom in one generation will become the philosophy of the government in the next."—Abraham Lincoln

> "The use of the Bible as the ultimate source of religious truth renders general education a necessity."—Martin Luther

Our founding fathers, believing that the Protestant biblical heritage of our country was vital to our survival, created the first public education system in the history of the world with the main purpose of teaching children how to read the Bible. The Bible, in fact, was **the only textbook** at the beginning of our public education system and our first colleges were institutions which had the purpose of preparing men to teach the Bible and prepare for the ministry.

- Harvard was founded by the Pilgrims and stated their purpose as, "Everyone shall consider the main end in life and studies to know God and Jesus Christ which is eternal life."

- Yale was founded because Harvard was slipping spiritually and was too expensive. In 1828 the school sent out the "Yale Band" to evangelize in the state of Illinois.

- Princeton University was founded during the Great Awakening. The faculty was required to be convinced of the necessity of religious experience for salvation.

- Dartmouth was founded to evangelize the Indians and Christianize the English youth.

- Brown University was founded by Baptists to train missionaries. The first president was a missionary from The Society for the Propagation of the Gospel in Foreign Parts.

- The University of Pennsylvania held its first sessions in a building erected by Benjamin Franklin for Whitfield's congregation. The school was guided by Whitfield's counsel and inspired by his life.

- The textbook for preparing men to be lawyers was *Blackstone's Commentary on Law*. It was the legal text for 160 years. After each law, all the scriptures were printed to prove the law was just. John Finney, one of the great evangelists in the history of our country, in studying to be a lawyer and using Blackstone's textbook, was actually converted and decided to go into the ministry.

Biblical Roots of Our Constitution

Not only is it a lie that our founders were nominal Church goers or deists and our institutions were mainly the product of the Enlightenment, but it is also untrue that our Constitution was mainly a product of the Enlightenment. Scholars today would agree that our Constitution is one of the most amazing documents ever written. A few years ago, political scientists of the University of Houston asked the question, "How has the American Constitution withstood the test of time? Why has it not gone through massive revision? It's so short and it's over 200 years old, what's the answer to its greatness?"

These political scientists made a ten-year study of 15,000 writings of the founders, attempting to find the source of the greatness of the U.S. Constitution. They found that the three most quoted men were Montesque, Blackstone and Locke. But to their surprise, the Bible was quoted four times more than Montesque, twelve times more than Blackstone, and six times more than Locke. More incredible than this, 34% of the writings of the founding fathers were direct quotes from the Bible and 64% were quotes of men who were quoting the Bible. In other words, 98% of the quotes the founding fathers used in forming our Constitution were based on the Bible. This evidence further documents the fact that our founders were not agnostics or deists but were Bible-believing Christians and their intention was to create a Christian democracy with Bible-based institutions. Also, this evidence demonstrates that *the foundation of our country was not the Enlightenment, and in essence, not even the Constitution, but the Bible.*

An article in *Newsweek* magazine (1984) confirmed this fact—

"It has now been discovered by scholars that the Bible even more than the Constitution is the founding document of America."

The Wilson Quarterly (Winter 1985), in an article entitled *The Almost Chosen People*, states:

"No one who studies the key constitutional documents in American history can doubt the central and organic part played by religion in the origins and development of American republican government. The Fundamental Orders of Connecticut (1639), the first written constitution in the modern sense of the term, puts forth in its introduction that the state owes its origin to 'the wise disposition of divine providence' and that 'the word of God' requires 'an orderly and decent Government

established according to God' to 'maintain and preserve
the liberty and purity of the Gospel.'"

"For the Lord is our judge, the Lord is our law giver,

the Lord is our king" (Isaiah 33:22).

The preceding verse was used by our founders in developing
the three branches of our federal government (Executive, Legislative and Judicial). The separation of powers and rotation of
offices along with the system of checks and balances in the three
branches, came from the biblical premise of the fallen nature of
man (Jeremiah 17:9, Romans 3:23). James Madison, chief
architect of our Constitution with its checks and balances stated
that men were not angels and politicians could not be trusted.

The founders were all aware of the biblical premise of the dual
nature of man which says on one hand, man is great, capable of
benevolence and genius (as history records) because he is created
in the image of God. On the other hand (as history also bears out),
man is capable of monstrosities. This balanced biblical view
drove the framers of the Constitution to develop a form of
government that would neither depend blindly upon the will of the
masses nor give absolute power to one man.

Lord Acton has succinctly stated, "Power corrupts and
absolute power corrupts absolutely." The first Americans, the
Pilgrims and Puritans, were of this very frame of mind as
illustrated by the fact that before they made a permanent
settlement, the Mayflower Compact was formed with elected
officials and a list of laws that they all agreed to obey.

"All men are created equal"

The idea that all men are created equal—the foundation of what America is all about, came from the restored Reformation biblical premise of "... salvation by faith alone" (the gospel) and the individual priesthood of all believers (Ephesians 2:8,9; I Timothy 2:5).   In other words, Luther and Calvin in the Reformation restored the biblical teaching that salvation is a matter between God and man alone—all men must come the same way through faith not through works, priests, ecclesiastical structures, popes or kings—and when they do, they are all equally priests and Christ is their high priest. Thus, the peasant is equal to the pope and kings are not exempt from God's laws. He is like any other citizen—"all men are created equal".

The equality of all men was also made to apply to people of other religions and ethnic groups. Patrick Henry stated,

"It cannot be emphasized too strongly or too often that this great nation was founded not by religionists, but by Christians, not on religions, but on the Gospel of Jesus Christ! For this very reason, peoples of other faiths have been afforded asylum, prosperity and freedom of worship here."

Concerning the equality of all people in the framework of our Protestant Christian nation, Marshall Foster, in his book *The American Covenant*, quotes the eminent theologian and professor, Charles Hodge, of Princeton seminary (1876). He states,

"The proposition that the United States of America are a Christian and Protestant nation is not so much the assertion of a principle as a statement of a fact. That fact is not simply that the great majority of the people are Christians and Protestants, but that the organic life, the institutions, laws and official action of the government, whether that action be legislative, judicial or executive, is, and of right should be, and in fact must be, in accordance with the principles of Protestant Christianity.

"When Protestant Christians came to this country they possessed and subdued the land. They declared Christianity to be part of the common law of the land. In the process of time, thousands have come among us who are neither Protestants nor Christians. All are welcomed, all are admitted to equal rights and privileges. All are allowed to acquire property and to vote in every election, made eligible to all offices, and invested with equal influence in all public affairs. All are allowed to worship as they please, or not to worship at all, if they see fit. No man is molested for his religion or for his want of religion. No man is required to profess any form of faith, or to join any religious association."

It can be categorically stated at this point that the biblical philosophical base of this country has produced the greatest country in the history of the world. No other country has enjoyed the equality and freedom that this country has enjoyed. The First Amendment demonstrated that our founding fathers intended to achieve full religious freedom for all people. It can also be categorically said, in the context of a Christian nation, there has been more religious liberty for more people than has ever existed in any other nation on earth.

Separation of Church and State?

"Much has been written in recent years concerning Thomas Jefferson's reference in 1802 to 'a wall of separation between church and State.' ...Jefferson's figure of speech has received so much attention that one would almost think at times that it is to be found somewhere in our constitution." —Baer vs. Cole Morgan, 1958 Supreme Court case.

Another lie perptuated in our public schools is that there is a wall of separation between church and state. Our public education system and the media have done a "good job" in that polls have indicated that 67% of Americans believe that the statement of separation of church and state is contained in the Constitution. It is **not in our Constitution** or in the First Amendment. It is (or was) in the Russian Constitution. The real intention of the founding fathers was that America was not to have a state Church—that no Christian denomination would be "king-pin" over the others like they had in England. All Christian denominations were to be equal. The real intention of our founders was—"Church and state hand in hand."

- First amendment—Congress shall make no law respecting the establishment of religion or prohibiting the free exercise thereof.

The concept of a "wall" of separation first came about during the presidency of Thomas Jefferson. A group of Baptists heard a rumor that the government was going to establish one national church—the congressional church. They appealed in fear to Jefferson who, responding in a letter, stated to them that this was not so. Jefferson assured them that the first amendment stated in essence that there could be no national church and that the government could not run the church. There was no problem, though there was some debate through the years, until 1947 when the Supreme Court violated the intent of the founding fathers and took out of context, Jefferson's reply to the Baptists. They stated that there was a "high wall" of separation between state and church. *This meant in essence—according to the Supreme Court —that you could not have religious values in public affairs, including education.*

From that time forward, moral absolutes were taken out of public affairs and public schools because they had a religious basis and all religious activities were also taken out. The original purpose of the Supreme Court was to interpret the Constitution, but they began to intrude into the legislative branch of our government with their secular humanist bias.

R. C. Sproul, in his book *Knowing Scripture,* states,

"Historically, the United States of America has a special agency that theoretically functions as the supreme board of hermeneutics for our land. That agency is called the Supreme Court. One of its primary tasks is to interpret the Constitution of the United States. The Constitution is a written document and requires such interpetation. Originally, the procedure of interpreting the Constitution followed the so-called grammatico-historical method. That is, the Constitution was interpeted by studying the words of the document in light of what those words meant when they were used at the time of the formulation of the document.

"Since the work of Oliver Wendell Holmes, the method of constitutional interpretation has changed radically. The current crisis in law and public confidence in the nation's highest court is directly related to the underlying problem of method of interpretation. When the Court interprets the Constitution in light of modern attitudes, it in effect changes the Constitution by means of re-inter-pretation. The net result is that in a subtle way, the Court becomes a legislative rather than an interpretive agency."

What Did Jefferson Really Say and Believe?

"The First Amendment has erected a wall of separation between church and state, but that wall is a one directional wall. It keeps the government from running the church, but it makes sure that Christian principles will always stay in government.

"Indeed, I tremble for my country when I reflect that God is just: that his justice cannot sleep forever"—Thomas Jefferson.

Is this separation? Are these the words of a *Deist*?

The First Amendment was first presented in Congress on September 1, 1789 at which time congress was considering approximately twelve different versions, two of which were:

- "Congress shall make no law in preference to any one denomination over another."

- "Congress shall make no law establishing one religion over another."

These quotes clearly show that Congress' only concern was over the establishment of a state church like the one they revolted against in England. Today, the First Amendment is being taken out of context and interpreted to mean the separation of church and state.

John W. Whitehead, a respected Constitutional lawyer and author, gives the following clarion paraphrase to the First Amendment of the U.S. Constitution in modern English language:

"The Federal government shall make no law having anything to do with supporting a national denominational church, or prohibiting the free exercise of religion."

Theologian and philosopher, Francis Schaeffer, states,

"We must smash the lie of the new and novel concept of the separation of religion and the state. This lie is totally against the meaning of the First Amendment. The First Amendment was for two things: a. That there should be no established church for the entire thirteen colonies; and b. That the state would never interfere with the freedom of religion."

What Should Be Taught in Our Public Schools?

As the colonists began to move to the west, the question was, how the western states should be governed. The Northwest Ordinance of 1787 provided for the governing of these territories.

The ordinance became famous because of its contribution to the growth of democracy. Public education was encouraged according to the general belief of the founding fathers that it was a necessary condition for the successful working of a representative government.

What kind of education did the founders envision? The Northwest Ordinance declared that,

> "Religion, morality and knowledge being necessary to good government and the happiness of mankind, schools and the means of education should forever be encouraged."

It is interesting to note all the debate which has taken place in recent years, and the books and essays on what the founding fathers really meant by the First Amendment and the question of separation of church and state. The answer can easily be found by understanding the frame of reference of the founders who formed the amendment and the context in which it was written. We already know the founders were mainly Bible-believing Christians, and the context can also easily be discerned, so we can know exactly what they meant. How? The Congress which gave us the First Amendment was also the Congress that gave us the Northwest Ordinance two years later, and stated that *religion, morality and knowledge* should be taught in our public schools.

Founding father, Benjamin Russ, in 1791, published twelve reasons the Bible should not be taken out of public schools and prophetically said, in conclusion,

> "If we take the Bible out, we will have an explosion of crime. We would then waste all kinds of time and money punishing criminals."

Founding father and educator Noah Webster, stated,

"All the miseries, vice, crime and evils will come to our country if we despise and neglect the precepts found in the Bible."

George Washington, in his farewell address, gave three warnings for America's survival, which are not in textbooks today. Excerpts from this most significant speech used to be memorized in public schools:

- "The two foundations for political prosperity are religion and morality.

- "You can't accept the tenet that you can have morality without religion.

- "The Bible is the only basis for security, for property, life and freedom."

What did the Supreme Court Say?

The Supreme Court, 1731:

"Whatever strikes at the root of Christianity tends manifestly to the dissolution of civil government" — Rex vs. Woolston.

The Supreme Court, 1796:

"By our form of government, the Christian religion is the established religion of all sects and denominations of Christians where we are all placed on the same and equal footing."

In the House Judiciary Committee Report from 1853 (the Trinity Decision), the Supreme Court had examined all the documents that had anything to do with the founding of America from the pilgrims to that time, and stated,

"Had the people during the revolution had a suspicion of any attempt to war against Christianity, that revolution would have been strangled in its cradle. At the time of the adoption of the Constitution and its amendments, the universal sentiment was that Christianity should be encouraged, but not any one denomination. In this age there is no substitute for Christianity. That was the religion of the founders of the republic and they expected it to remain the religion of their descendants. The great divider, the conservative element of our system, the thing that holds our system together, is the belief of our people in the pure doctrines and the divine truths of the Gospel of Jesus Christ."

The Supreme Court, 1892:

"Our laws and our institutions must necessarily be based on and must include the teachings of the redeemer of mankind. It is impossible for it to be otherwise. In this sense, to this extent our civilization and our institutions are emphatically Christian."

Such convictions for America being a Protestant Christian nation have persisted almost to the present. John W. Whitehead gives a summary of the U. S. Supreme Court's historic understanding of the relationship between Christianity and the government in the United States. He states,

"In 1892, the United States Supreme Court made an exhaustive study of the supposed connection between Christianity and the government of the United States. After researching hundreds of volumes of historical documents, the Court asserted, 'These references add a volume of unofficial declarations to the mass of organic utterances that this is a religious people ... a Christian nation.' Likewise in 1931, Supreme Court Justice, George Sutherland, reviewed the 1892 decision in relation to another case and reiterated that Americans are a 'Christian people' and in 1952, Justice William O.

Douglas affirmed, 'We are a religious people and our institutions presuppose a Supreme Being.'"

"Non-Sectarian Without Being Non-Religious"

America's common national creed, then, made biblical reformation faith the central and organic part of the origins and development of American republican government. A study of the original state constitutional governments demonstrates that America was to be non-sectarian without being non-Christian (this, of course, included public education). It is true the first colonists tried to create their own theocratic communities, but the sectarian violence of the Old World convinced most Americans of the evils of a state church. However, none of our founders doubted that a core of religious belief was essential to an American democracy.

The Wilson Quarterly (Winter 1985), in an article entitled *The Almost Chosen People* by Paul Johnson, states,

> "Because Protestant religious establishments were popular, not hierarchical, a distinctive American religious tradition began to emerge. There was never any sense of division in law between laymen and cleric, between those with spiritual or social privileges and those without. America was born Protestant and did not have to become so through revolt and struggle against a Catholic Church or an ecclesiastical establishment. In all these respects it differed profoundly from the Old World. America's common national creed was to grow out of a set of Protestant assumptions."

John Adams wrote, "Our constitution was designed for a moral and religious people and no other!" George Washington warned that America was not a secular state and that secular morality was not enough. In analyzing the speeches of both

Lincoln and Washington, it can be demonstrated that they believed firmly that God was the final arbitrator of public policy and that the providential plan and the working of democracy were organically linked. The philosophers of the Enlightenment were important in our struggle for independence (Locke, Voltaire, Rouseau—the natural rights of man) but they were secondary to the biblical frame that America was to develop. Even Jefferson and Franklin (products of the Enlightenment and often quoted as being deists) appeared to have given little importance to their positions in the forming of our government. By their quotes it can be demonstrated that their world view was subordinate to the overwhelmingly biblical Christian frame America was to develop.

Thomas Jefferson, who was not a Christian, stated the following concerning the Bible,

> "I have always said, and always will say, that the studious perusal of the sacred volume will make better citizens, husbands, and better fathers."

The Bible then was the foundation and strength of the original American republic and source of the early American's reformation faith, work ethic, basic morality, marriage, family and other traditional values. *Today only a skeleton remains.*

"Without God, everything is permissible, crime is inevitable."
—Dostoyevsky

The first major blow to our Judeo-Christian heritage and the consequent deterioration of America began when the Supreme Court in 1947 stated there was a high wall of separation between church and state. This meant you couldn't have religious values in public affairs, including education. With this came the expelling of Bible instruction, prayers, the posting of the Ten Commandments, and the celebration of Christmas and Easter. The most detrimental of all to our students is the almost complete elimination of the historical facts of our Christian roots. To fill this vacuum, came evolution-based secular humanist philosophy.

Soon afterward in our educational institutions, in place of biblical truth came the myths of the 1960's. In the heyday of the heroes of secular humanism—Darwin, Freud, Nietzsche, Camus, Marx and Sartre—and continuing to the present, the following myths flourished: God is dead, the Bible is myth, man is not depraved but good (or neutral), morals are relative and finally, "there is nothing". The famous existentialist Jean Paul Sartre coined this phrase in a speech at U.C. Berkeley. All of this meant that mankind is free from God, the Bible and Judeo-Christian heritage but without a foundation for meaning or morality. Man must "heroically" become an independent, autonomous, productive, self-actualizing person (Existentialism).

When I attended a secular college in 1959 and '60, this was the exact mentality. In science classes, evolution was taught as a fact and Man was seen as nothing more than a biological animal. Thus, mankind was free from religion and superstition. In psychology classes, the thinking was that mankind is good (or neutral) and thus free from negative Puritanism with its guilt and repression of sex. It was taught that "abstinence will only make you sick—so let your glands be your guide. Don't suppress your normal drives. If it feels good do it."

Soon after this, in the '60's came the "flower children" revolting against the Judeo-Christian heritage and, without hypocrisy, acting out the new philosophy of nothingness they were taught. Smoking pot, having free sex and trying to find peace became the scenario.

In the 70's and 80's, with the same frame of reference of man's goodness, we went into the decade of the "me generation"—"I love me, I have a duty to myself to perform, forget the Judeo-Christian 'others first.'" This meant, if need be to gain self fulfillment ("to find yourself"), leave your wife or husband and children. Mankind with a deceiving, fallen nature and with a great capacity to rationalize evil, felt emancipated from the responsibilities of society. With the new obsession with self, the thinking now was, "Be true to yourself. You only live once, don't be cheated. You only go around once in life, so get all the gusto you can."

People were reading books like *I'm O.K. You're O.K.*, *Looking Out for Number One* and *Winning Through Intimidation.* Radical individualism, relative values and morals, and the gospel of greed (get money at any cost) was the message of the 70's and '80's. As a result of the obsession with self, America is lost and confused. Also, as Dostoyevsky predicted, without God, everything is becoming permissible and crime is becoming rampant—the sign of our disintegrating culture.

Most Americans today believe as they were taught, that we are a secular nation and that this was the intention of our founders. This is because we've been brainwashed by a generation of secular textbooks and teachers.

Dr. D. James Kennedy, Minister of the Coral Ridge Presbyterian Church in Florida, quoted Dr. Paul Vitts, Professor of Psychology at New York University, who led a blue ribbon panel to examine some 60 or 80 history and social studies textbooks, used widely throughout the United States. The panel was shocked to find that almost everything religious and spiritual as well as the Christian history of this nation has been expunged. Dr. Vitts stated, "It seems like the writers of the textbooks have a positive paranoia when it comes to the Christian religion."

Further evidence for the attempt to secularize America can be demonstrated by an objective examination of current school textbooks. For example, a $73,445 study was completed by the U.S. Department of Education (1986). The following are excerpts from the study:

"An examination of textbooks used in public schools in this country finds that they virtually ignore religion as an element of American life and discount traditional family values. Social studies texts, intended to introduce youngsters to contemporary U.S. society, contain no mention whatever of ordinary religious activities, such as praying or going to church. The dominant theme is the denial of religion as an actual part of American life.

"The general finding is that public school textbooks have a strong liberal bias and present a biased representation of both religious and traditional values. Both basic readers and social studies texts are so written as to represent a systematic denial of the history, heritage and values of a very large segment of the American people. For instance the first-through-fourth-grades social studies texts, in addressing the family, commonly define it as "the people you live with" and never use the words "marriage," "husband," "wife" or "homemaker". There is not one textual reference to marriage as the foundation of the family. Not only this but also, there was not one portrayal of a contemporary American family that clearly featured traditional sex roles. Countless references are made to mothers and other women working outside the home in such occupations as medicine, transportation and politics, but in no cases indicating that a mother-homemaker is an important job. Moreover, only money, status and enjoyment are presented as motivations for work with no indication that many work out of concern for others or because of the intrinsic value of certain kinds of work. The absence of any concern for non-material values was so extreme that not one discussion of a family budget included any money for charity, or money for others in need. Giving money to a church was never mentioned. While the social studies texts through the fourth grade omit any specific reference to typical religious activity, one text mentions the rural Amish, while others cited Indian rain dances and prayer to 'Earth Mother.'"

*"In a reference to the Pilgrims' first Thanksgiving, no
mention is made of God to whom the thanks were given.
In several world history textbooks for the sixth grade, the
life of the Moslem founder, Mohammed, gets much more
coverage than the life of the founder of Christianity,
Jesus. One of the strange characteristics of many of the
texts was their failure to mention the Protestant Reformation, and in cases when they do, to omit the issues
involved in it. Some kind of repression or denial of
Christianity is demonstrated by how these texts treat the
Christian religion."*

The above study is candid proof that the history of the United
States of America is not only being slanted, but it's actually being
altered by secular humanists. While a number of reasons are
behind such selective editing, such as producing textbooks that
meet with legislative approval and that supposedly are not
offensive in conforming to contemporary views, the major impetus
is to promote secular humanist philosophy by omitting the real
Christian roots of America. This is actually no different from the
Neo-Nazi movement who today attempt to alter history to
convince people that the Holocaust never occurred. While some
educators argue that the secular humanist movement is only an
attempt at neutrality (separation of church and state), the above
evidence contradicts this notion. Also, the end result of 30 to 40
years of secular indoctrination is evident all around us today. Most
of the general populous is secularized and ignorant of our heritage.

Who are Secular Humanists?

In the United States, after the Scopes "monkey trial" and
acceptance of the theory of evolution, humanism began to take the
form of a non-theistic religion committed to replacing the Bible
and the Christian frame of America. Its "creedal formulation" is
contained in The Humanist Manifesto I (1933) and II (1973)
signed by several hundred leading secular thinkers. Its
membership organization, the American Humanist Association

was founded in 1941. In the fall of 1980, 61 prominent scholars and writers issued the Secular Humanist Declaration. *It denounces absolute morality and calls for an emphasis on science and reason. The declaration reflects the two earlier manifestos and depicts supernatural religion and divine revelation (the Bible) as enemies of the rational process.* This is the philosophy that is now in control of public education.

Secular Humanists have even given a code of ethics (which they have successfully imposed on the public) saying such things as gambling, pornography, abortion and all sexual activities between consenting individuals (not necessarily adults—there is no regard to gender or age) is acceptable.

Psychologists, in interviewing rapists, serial killers and other sex offenders, determined that the liberal code of ethics which now dominates our schools and the media, has contributed largely to the epidemic of sex offenses.

Most people realize there is something wrong in our schools as we continue to fall behind and what we are doing simply isn't working. While new creative and innovative advances such as restructuring techniques and methods of teaching has improved the quality of teaching, the foundational problem of secular humanist philosophy hasn't been addressed. Also, the many new movements and extracurricular programs that have emerged, giving such remedies as self-realization, high self-esteem and the power of positive thinking, are helpful but, alone, are nothing more than putting Band-aids on symptoms.

Future predictions for the American family and the fate of our children are not reassuring as studies following current trends project that by the year 2000, the traditional family as we have known it, may become obsolete. Within this context, if America is to survive, our educational system must not only get back to teaching students the truth about our original Christian roots but also teach the traditional family values which formed our country in the first place. While extracurricular programs are important, this essential knowledge should be given priority in the classroom, "the meat and potatoes of education." For over 30 years, students have been given a steady diet of secular humanism in our classrooms. It is time that they be given the truth about America's real identity.

The subtle omission of valuable information (although not as blatant) could be compared to Hitler's burning of the books in his attempt to make Germany homogeneous in thinking. This vivid example in history and what we are presently witnessing and what we are part of, should drive us to our senses to re-think educational content and research techniques, especially as they relate to our Bible-based Protestant roots. Educators who continue to follow the status quo are simply perpetuating the opposite of what they are supposed to be propagating which is an unbiased presentation of facts. This would include all areas of education which, according to our founders, was not only secular knowledge but **religious and moral teaching as well.**

No doubt, the problems in America are monumental and complex, but the place to start is to find out what disease or diseases are killing us and go from there. America has been, and is being fed a pack of lies—lies concerning our origins (evolution and its ramifications) and lies concerning the roots and true nature of this country.

Doesn't history mean research and investigation—a search for the truth of what really happened? Isn't it about time to doubt the party line being fed to us? What has happened to our educational system? Isn't it true that we are sacrificing truth in following this present erroneous "Zeitgeist"—that it's leading us down the path of destruction? Isn't it about time to get our religious heritage back into textbooks and, most important, isn't it about time to re-investigate the book that was the source of our greatness?

It is time to bring the Bible back into the classroom. The Bible was the original foundation of our government and basis of morality and restraint of behavior. Our founding fathers warned and predicted that if we take the Bible out of the classroom, we'll have moral collapse. Their prophecies have come true and our students (as well as our country) are the victims.

"The reason that Christianity is the best friend of government is because Christianity is the only religion in the world that deals with the heart" —Thomas Jefferson, author of *The Declaration of Independence*.

"In regard to the Great Book, I have only to say that it is the best gift which God has ever given to man. All the good from the Savior of the world is communicated to us through this book. But for it, we could not know right from wrong."—Abraham Lincoln.

"Every thinking man, when he thinks, realizes that the teachings of the Bible are so interwoven and entwined with our whole civic and social life that it would be literally—I do mean literally—impossible for us to figure what that loss would be if these teachings were removed. We would lose almost all the standards by which we now judge both public and private morals; all the standards toward which we, with more or less resolution, strive to raise ourselves."—Theodore Roosevelt

"If religious books are not widely circulated among the masses of this country, I do not know what is going to become of us as a nation. If the evanglical volume does not reach every hamlet, the pages of corruption and licentious literature will; if the power of the gospel is not felt through the length and breadth of the land, anarchy and misrule, degradation and misery, corruption and darkness will reign without mitigation or end."—Daniel Webster

"We must keep the Bible in the classroom because it is the foundation of our morals and behavior in America"

—Fisher Ames, the founding father *who gave us the words for the First Amendment.*

Chapter 12

The Time Has Come

"The idea of evolution rests on pure belief"
—Dr. Herbert Nilsson

What's the conclusion concerning organic evolution and its product, secular humanist philosophy? Having seen where the knowledge explosion has led us, concerned citizens should now realize that the contest between creationists and evolutionists is over. **The accumulated scientific evidence supports Special Creation and renders evolution to be false.**

It's been demonstrated that mutations and natural selection, over millions and billions of years, did not bring about all living organisms—"molecule-to-man." In fact, there's no evidence for these processes creating anything new at all as demanded by Neo-Darwin, "Macro-Evolution" Theory. Also, ingenious design features in nature (as well as in the universe) demonstrate the scientific impossibility of blind, random, accidental evolution. Finally, the geological strata, the history of the origin of life on planet earth, demonstrates "explosions" of thoroughly developed life, stasis, extinction, no transitional forms, then new explosions all of which agrees with the sequence of creative events as related in the book of Genesis.

Suffice it to say, there has been no "thread of life". The historical and scientific record supports Special Creation by an all-powerful, personal being of infinite wisdom as stated in the Bible. Evolutionists, if honest, and after studying the evidence should realize that in holding to their position, they have actually moved into the realm of religion. Not only that, their faith is pure speculation and their religion is nothing more than a "blind leap of faith".

The tragedy of it is that this so-called "theory" doesn't even qualify as a good hypothesis and yet it is being taught as fact in our educational institutions. That means, when the theory of evolution is fully implemented in California and America, this damaging "substitute religion" will be taught to our students throughout their entire educational career—Elementary, Junior High, High School and college—unless something happens to bring about a change. In other words, all the false "issues" that dominate modern thought, existentialism, humanism, relativism, Freudianism, hedonism will continue to be perpetuated even though they are outdated and based on the incorrect assumptions of atheism and evolution.

Californians (as well as all Americans) should be alarmed to the extent of taking action because their children have been and will be fed proven lies about the most crucial questions of human existence — Who am I? What does it mean to be a human being? Where did the universe and earth come from? What's the meaning and purpose of human existence? Why are we here?

A Time to Question, A Time to Act

Hendrick H. Hanegraff, president of the Christian Research Institute International, in a letter to his supporters July 14, 1994 expresses his extreme concern for America's students. He states,

"As you read this letter, day by day, year by year, students across North America are being subtly seduced by an outrageous lie. And that's not the half of it.

"This deception has persisted for decades, disguised as 'science.' Its consequences have been incomprehensibly tragic, and the toll is mounting. I'm talking about the farce of EVOLUTION.

"By causing countless children—from elementary schools to universities—to believe in evolution, 'science' has deftly eliminated man's need for God in the minds of millions. And the damage being done reaches far beyond the classroom."

Haven't we had enough evidence given by eminent scientists against evolution and for creation and a creator, and haven't we had enough examples from past history and from our own present dilemma of where this foundational lie is leading us? Isn't it about time to heed the words of Alan Bloom, "To question conventional wisdom—to challenge conventional perspectives?" Our country and kids are already in a crisis situation and yet our state framework on science has made the strongest statement in support of this bogus, atheistic theory. Unless there is an about face, our educational system will continue to accelerate with a new boldness the propagation of this devastating doctrine.

"Where is the wise man? Where is the scribe? Where is the debater of this age? Has not God made foolish the wisdom of the world?" —I Corinthians 1:20

The apostle Paul in quoting this verse, was actually quoting Isaiah in the old testament. Isaiah was asking the idol worshipping Egyptians just after they had fallen, "Where are your wise men now? Where has your wisdom led you?" This principle of following man's wisdom and the disastrous results can be verified by a study of the collapse of Communism. We could see the same thing happen in America as we continue to self-destruct.

The Spiritual Crisis in America

The *Wilson Quarterly* (Winter 1992), in an article entitled "The Fragility of Liberalism" by Christopher Lasch ,states,

> "In the very hour of its greatest triumph, in the very nation that has been its champion, liberal capitalism is in an alarming state of decay. 'The signs of impending breakdown are unmistakable,' warns Lasch, an iconoclastic historian and author of *The True and Only Heaven* (1991). 'Drugs, crime, and gang wars are making our cities uninhabitable. Our school system is in a state of collapse. Our political parties are unable to enlist the masses of potential voters into the political process.' And the emerging U.S. dominated global culture, far from reflecting a regard for human dignity and other liberal values, is 'the culture of Hollywood, rock and roll, and Madison Avenue...a culture of hedonism, cruelty, contempt, and cynicism.'"

The real need in America, as the Carnegie report related in "Crisis In The Classroom" is not new teaching strategies or new programs. The problem is that we are in **a spiritual crisis.** Our kids in the classroom (and America in general) have lost the meaning and purpose of life, and along with this an understanding of what is right and wrong, what is good and bad, what is true and false.

Anyone viewing TV today would admit we are like the ancient Greeks, whom Paul addressed in I Corinthians 1:20, except on a greater scale. With a relativistic philosophical frame of reference (like the Corinthians and Athenians who were lovers of philosophy) we are being bombarded with every "wind of doctrine" known to man of what it all means and how to solve our problems. We have hundreds of points of view given in self-help books, on news broadcasts and talk shows as America sits in confusion, alarm and disagreement, sinking deeper and deeper in despair. A good question to ask is the same one the apostle Paul presented to the Greeks of Athens and Corinth in his day: Where are our wise men today? Where has and is human wisdom leading us? If we are honest, we'll admit we have lost our way and we need to get back to our roots.

"But we're a pluralistic nation!"

Many people, at this point, are undoubtedly saying, "We admit, initially we were a Christian nation, but let's face it, we are now a country of many races, religions and ethnic groups. We can't go back, pluralism is the key word for today." My immediate response would be, "Is it working? Are we better off today without God?" For all practical purposes, we are a secular nation now (so-called pluralism) and look at our big, sick, crime-infested cities; look at our schools that are turning into jungles, with gangs, weapons and drugs. Is "the right of privacy" working? Is it possible in trying to please everybody, we are shooting at everything but hitting nothing? A true candid picture of America is that our culture, institutions and people are simply confused and disintegrating—and at a very fast pace!

Secondly, how did we get our pluralistic culture in the first place? It came through our founding fathers, our Judeo-Christian heritage. By following the precepts of the Bible, its gospel message and the concept of natural law that presupposes a creator, our founders formed the Constitution and produced the first true democratic experiment in history. The U.S. Constitution gave religious liberty to all, equality of races ("... there is neither Jew nor Greek") and equal opportunity to all; all of which provided the "right of dissent" and healthy debate which is a vehicle for arriving at truth—hence, pluralism.

No doubt, because of human nature, our democracy has had its failures and hypocrisies but has any other empire or nation in the noble quest of human dignity and liberty surpassed our country? Now, **in the name** of pluralism, we're actually **losing** our pluralism. With the elimination of our Judeo-Christian heritage, we are now seeing not only the moral decline of our country, but a loss of our pluralistic freedoms as well.

The "Multiculturalists"

Under the banner of such labels as "multiculturalism" "pluralism", "affirmative action", "diversity training", etc., the secular humanists—many of them are the same group of leftists that rebelled in the 60's—are leading the culture war. They are attempting to strip America of its Judeo-Christian roots and impose a dictatorship of their own values.

This same movement, which considers itself "politically correct", is destroying diversity and pluralism and in essence is violating the Constitution by pushing freedom *from* religion— with all its disastrous results—instead of freedom *of* religion.

Richard Bernstein, author of the book *Dictatorship of Virtue*, adds light to the present cultural war—as cited in the *Wilson Quarterly* (Autumn 1994). Alan Wolfe (university Professor of Sociology at Boston College) summarizes Bernstein's book as follows:

> "New York Times correspondent Richard Bernstein, who at one time reported from France, believes that America's current battles over multiculturalism are 'the dèrapage (rough translation: the 'slippery slope') of the civil rights movement.' Just as Robespierre's insistence on virtue led to terror, Bernstein cautions, so the campaign to root out racism and sexism in school is the

first step on the road to Maoist style thought control. (Bernstein also worked in China.)

"Bernstein certainly finds enough examples to justify his alarm. At the University of New Hampshire, a writing instructor's illustration of a simile—'belly-dancing is like Jell-O on a plate with a vibrator under the plate"— was defined as sexual harassment by university bureaucrats, in part because of methods of investigation that 'bear a chilling resemblance to those of true dictatorships.' The University of Pennsylvania tells students that if 'you are perceived to be racist, sexist, heterosexist, ethnocentric, biased against those with religions different from yours, or intolerant of disabilities, you must be willing to examine and change that behavior.'

"In Bernstein's view, the multicultural police—academic reformers charged with implementing affirmative action policies and complying with feminist concerns— are ambitious, power-seeking and ruthless. Most disturbing, they have come to dominate academia as a kind of 'bureaucracy of the good'. Convinced of their virtue, they are intolerant of those who disagree with them and oblivious to anyone else's rights. 'The whole point of the liberal revolution that gave rise to the 1960's was to free us from somebody else's dogma.' Bernstein writes, *'But now the very same people who fought for personal liberation a generation ago are striving to impose on others a secularized religion involving a set of values and codes that they believe in, disguising it behind innocuous labels like "diversity training" and "respect for difference."'*

"'Not only are the Multiculturalists authoritarian,' says Bernstein, 'but they are also hypocritical. They actually detest traditional cultures. They want everyone to speak in one tongue — the language of the Left (which, ironically, is Western and hegemonic). *And they hate the one country, the United States, that has done more than any other to make diversity real.*'"

What Can We Do?

When you're physically ill, you go to the doctor to get a correct diagnosis in order to apply the proper treatment. If the doctor, not trying to upset you, tells you that you just have the flu instead of the early stages of cancer—disaster is going to occur. America has the early stages of cancer—the cancer of evolution-based secular humanism.

"The wind and dust, blowing through the window created this beautiful portrait of an ocean scene!"

A good example of the destructive effect of the cancer of secular humanist thinking and philosophy which says, "Don't bother me with facts", occurred on a recent TV talk show I heard. The person who called into the show first stated that he was an atheist and a happily married man with children. He also stated that he liked the program and respected the intelligence of the spokesperson and the fact that he was knowledgeable, but was confused as to why he believed in God. The spokesman answered that his brother who was a specialist in medicine, convinced him one day by explaining the ingenious engineering and workings of the human body.

The caller replied, "Well, that's just an evolutionary coincidence."

The spokesman asked, "Are you educated?"

The caller replied, "Yes."

The spokesman followed by saying that his answer confirmed what is being taught in our public schools and in our colleges. The spokesman then gave the young atheist two illustrations to

consider. He stated, "If you were in the mountains and an ava-
lanche occurred and the huge rock formation at your feet perfectly
spelled out 'hello' would you consider it a coincidence or
planned?"

The caller stated, "A coincidence."

He then said, "If you took a rocket ship to Venus and found a
computer there, would you say a computer maker put it there, or
was it simply a product of evolution?"

The caller stated, "Evolution!"

Another good example of the moral, spiritual and philosophical confusion of the average American, took place at Yale
University a few years ago. The president of Yale in a speech to an
assembly of educators, stated, "We need an intellectual and moral
renovation of the students of America."   The reply of the
audience?—he was booed and hooted with shouts, "Whose
morality are you going to impose?"

Alan Bloome (Chapter Seven) related that the intellectual and
moral crises in America are one. He said that the malignant
relativism, the dominant force in the American university, is
destroying the ideas of moral truth, wisdom and greatness.

The Wilson Quarterly (International Center for scholars),
Winter 1998, in their cover page feature article, presented three
pertinent essays by eminent college philosopher/scientists
debating the question, "Is Everything Relative?" Neo-Darwinism,
axiomatic truth, was the dominant theme of the debators as the
word evolution (organic, biological, genetic, cultural) was
repeated at least 37 times on the pages of the essays. In essence,
the rhetoric was concerned with how to get out of the relativist
dilemma of our day without God. The editor of the Wilson
Quarterly, Jay Tolson, introduced this question, warning that the

generally-accepted and long-taught subjective relativism is now reaching a dangerous stage in America. He states,

> "Reports on the relativist muddle abound, but none capture the situation better than do two articles in a recent issue of the *Chronicle of Higher Education*. One tells of a class of 20 students at a small West Coast college who were asked to read Shirley Jackson's short story, 'The Lottery'. After lengthy discussion, the instructor was shocked to learn that not a single student would 'go out on a limb' and condemn the ritual human sacrifice depicted in the story. An exceptional case? Hardly. The other Chronicle account is even more unsettling. According to its author, a philosophy professor at a distinguished East Coast college, the students in his courses were 'unable morally to condemn [the Holocaust], or indeed to make any moral judgment whatever.'
>
> "These two cases are not aberrations. They are symptomatic of a doctrinaire relativism that forecloses any serious discussion of absolutes or universals. The 'absolutophobia', as the author of the second article calls it, leads to a kind of moral idiocy, and as he rightly asks, 'Isn't it our responsibility as teachers to show, by directly confronting the confusions underlying absolutophobia, that students need not be inflexibly dogmatists in order to have a moral ground on which to stand?' Yet, even if they wanted to, where might teachers turn to find such a ground? That is the philosophical conundrum."

It Is Time to Get Involved

The founders of our country gave us an unshakeable philosophical and moral basis, and produced a country unparalleled in the history of the world. No other country has had such success and power in providing intellectual and spiritual leadership for the rest of the world or has enjoyed such prosperity, liberty and freedom of expression. But in the last quarter of a century, atheists and humanists have secularized our country which has resulted in confusion and a moral collapse. With the breakdown of our culture, we are creating a situation where we could eventually lose our freedom.

The first of our freedoms to go could be our religious freedom, since our religious heritage is already being expunged from our culture and institutions. Isn't it time for Christians to get involved—before it's too late? Remember, it was Jonathan Edwards who first preached revolution from the British. He believed strongly that there was no difference between a political and a religious emotion—both were God-directed.

Charles Finney said,

"The Church must take ground in regard to politics...the time has come that Christians must vote for honest men, and take consistent ground in politics or the Lord will curse them...God cannot sustain this free and blessed country, which we love and pray for, unless the Church will take right ground. Politics are part of a religion in such a country as a part of their duty to God...God will bless or curse this nation, according to the course Christians take in politics."

The impact of change is demonstrated on a personal level— one person at a time. The following excerpts from Frank Pastore's conversion experience, taken from a tract entitled *One Pitch from Humility*, illustrate the personal change that takes place when an individual faces the reality of truth. Frank Pastore is now director of Talbot Impact Ministries at Biola University:

"Like most people, I just wanted to be rich and famous. I really believed that if I were, I'd be happy and fulfilled. So when the Cincinnati Reds drafted me out of Damien High School in 1975, I was on the fast-track to 'success'.

"Over the course of my first 9 years with the Reds, I accumulated all the trinkets of a 'successful young professional'. I had a great career, bought the right status symbols, married a beautiful girl, had the perfect children, avoided drugs and alcohol, earned the respect of my peers and became known as a morally 'good person'. Although I may have had all the external components of success, internally something was still missing - there was a big hole in my life and I didn't know how to fill it. As time went on, I tried putting more stuff into the hole but that didn't seem to help, the void only grew deeper and more painful.

"Then on June 4, 1984, in Dodger Stadium, cruising along to a 3-1 victory with 2 outs in the 8th inning, I made the pitch that forever changed my life. Dodger Steve Sax rocketed a 2-2 fast ball off my right elbow and my world changed in one brief but painful instant. For 20 years my identity was in being a baseball star, my security and self-esteem were determined by my athletic performance. Suddenly, all that was threatened. As I clutched my wounded elbow, my immediate response was to cry out, "Why God? Why!?" I knew my arm would never be the same. My career, as I had known it, had come to an end.

"Later that night, in the chaos of my thoughts, I once again had the urge to pray, but it seemed rather foolish and silly. From the first grade on I had been taught to doubt the existence of God: the universe had just 'popped' into existence out of nothing, evolution was a 'scientific' fact, there was no Creator. My whole life, I had been fed a steady diet of secular propaganda. 'God' was a crutch for intellectual weaklings, an excuse for mediocrity and failure, a placebo for psychologically imbalanced people, and even a myth for injured professional athletes. 'If there is a God, He doesn't love me, He hates me! He's destroyed my life and left me nothing!' I said to myself, 'It's pointless to pray if no one is listening,' so I didn't even try.

"Four days later, I finally accepted one of the recurring invitations to attend the Red's Bible Study held at Tommy Hume's house. I didn't want to go to study the Bible, but to discredit it. I hated the fact that my naive Christian teammates clung to the infantile idea of a loving Creator whom they called 'Father' while I who knew better, was miserable. I arrived at the study wounded, bitter and armed with every argument I could think of to mock religion and the Bible. The instant the study was underway, I unloaded. I launched all my hostility and pain in a barrage of blasphemy, thoroughly overwhelming the guys as I attacked everything holy and sacred for nearly an hour.

"When I finally stopped, the Red's Chaplain, Wendel Deyo, feigning defeat, said 'Wow, I've never thought about those things before. I certainly don't want to believe anything that isn't true. Maybe you could help us.' 'Sure!' I said gullibly, 'How?' Wendel laid the trap, 'If I give you some books to read, will you critique them and get back to us so we too can learn the truth?' 'I'd be glad to,' I said, swallowing the bait. He gave me three books: *Mere Christianity* by C.S. Lewis, *Scientific Creationism* by Henry Morris and *Evidence That Demands A Verdict* by Josh McDowell. I immediately set out on the 'easy' task of disproving the Bible and Christianity.

"As I read, I was stunned—the mounting evidence for the truth of Christianity was overwhelming! Oddly, I became filled with both love and anger. I loved this historical Jesus I was meeting for the first time, but I was angry that I had been deceived my whole academic life by teachers who never told me of all the problems with the theory of evolution, nor of the evidence for the resurrection. I came to realize that naturalistic evolution isn't science, its science fiction! That was the myth, not Christianity!

"It was only one month after making that fateful pitch that I acknowledged Jesus Christ for Who He Is: Creator, Savior and Lord. In spite of the injury and all the uncertainty at that point in my life, when I asked Him to forgive me of my sin and fill me with His Spirit, the void I had been trying to fill my whole life was finally filled.

"I share this story with you because I hope you can learn from my experience. For 27 years I was an evolutionist, and the way I competed in the survival of the fittest was by throwing baseballs. Money is how we keep score in the 'jungle'. Today, the more you make, the higher you are on the food chain. Jesus taught me that life's true meaning is beyond the pursuit of Pride, Power and Possessions. Real fulfillment begins with knowing God, and deepens as you walk with Him daily.

"Evolution and external success kept me from seeking God for 27 years. What's it going to take in your life? After all, like me, you're only one pitch away from humility."

"See to it that no one takes you captive through philosophy and empty deception, according to the tradition of men, according to the elementary principles of the world, rather than according to Christ. For in Him all the fullness of Deity dwells in bodily form, and in Him you have been made complete, and He is the head over all rule and authority" (Colossians 2:8-10).

The following are excerpts taken from William J. Bennet's book *The De-valuing of America*, subtitled *The Fight for Our Culture and our Children* (1992). Dr. Bennett served as Director of the Office of National Drug Control Policy under President George Bush and served as Secretary of Education and Chairman of the National Endowment for the Humanities under President

Reagan. In his book, he elucidates on the nature of our cultural war and the fight to save our children.

> "Sociologists tell us that when groups of like-minded people gather, they do so with tacit understandings. There are certain things that don't have to be discussed if they are already settled in advance. *There are certain words or phrases that are accepted without examination; these are considered 'argument closers'. Among many academics, liberal segments of the media and intellectuals, these words are 'fundamentalist', 'born again' and 'the religious right'. In their minds, these words put an end to the argument. Any serious nod in the direction of spokesmen for 'the religious right' is guaranteed to call forth not simply criticism but also ridicule, and an attitude of intellectual superiority. Anyone who actually takes 'the religious right' seriously on anything automatically forfeits his intellectual respectability.* But while in office I took seriously the concerns of people such as Paul Weyrich, Phyllis Schlaffly, James Dobson and my colleague Gary Bauer, and I'm glad that I did.

> *"The fate of our democracy is intimately intertwined— 'entangled', if you will—with the vitality of the Judeo-Christian tradition....* The attitude that regards 'entanglement' with religion as something akin to entanglement with an infectious disease must be confronted broadly and directly.... It would be—it is tragic indeed to find that the passing of old-fashioned suspicion of particular religions has been followed, with barely an interruption, by a new suspicion of our broad religious tradition on the part of secularized elites, far more sophisticated, a bit better disguised, but no less divisive, no less reprehensible, no less damaging [than the old divisions between Protestant and Catholic, Gentile and Jew].... *The Judeo-Christian tradition is not a source of fear in the world; it is a ground of hope....* *No one demands doctrinal adherence to any religious*

beliefs as a condition of citizenship, or as proof of good citizenship here. But at the same time, we should not deny what is true: that from the Judeo-Christian tradition come our values, our principles, the animating spirit of our institutions. That tradition and our traditions are entangled. They are wed together. When we have disdain for our religious tradition, we have disdain for ourselves.

"Public schools should not indoctrinate anyone in any particular set of sectarian beliefs. One must always recognize that in a public setting, there are people of different beliefs. But *this does not mean we have to stop teaching history, stop teaching what we know to be true, stop teaching the difference between right and wrong, or disparage the efforts of deeply committed religious people to have their ideas respected.* I have no doubt that the real irritation of those on the religious right is not that their particular creed is not embraced by the schools, but that often their creed is the only one singled out for contempt.

"*So be it. Reclaiming our institutions is less a political opportunity than a civic obligation. It involves hard work.* But it is work of immense importance. At the end of the day, *somebody's* values will prevail. In America, 'we the people' have a duty to insist that our institutions and our government be true to their time-honored tasks. In some instances that means that the American people must roll up their sleeves and work to ensure that their institutions and government reflect their sentiments, their good sense, their sense of right and wrong. *This is what a democracy—a government of, by, and for the people— is all about. The debate has been joined. But the fight for our values has just begun.*"

Robert Vernon, former assistant chief of police, L.A.P.D. in his book *L.A. Justice* (1993), elaborates on the present cultural war and gives his advice on how we can save our culture and our

children. Police officer Vernon, for 40 years, had a reputation of
being a very competent and committed professional and was in
line to become the next Chief of Police. In the '90's however, after
the Rodney King incident, he was a victim of a "witch hunt"—an
inquisition by the arrogant, liberal, left elitists (secular humanists).
In his book, he relates how his religious freedom was violated and
by "smearing techniques" (unsubstantiated rumors), he was forced
to retire from the police department.

Because of his faith as an Evangelical Christian, he became a
victim of character assassination. He was considered by the left
wing elitists as not being "politically correct" and was falsely
portrayed as a radical, religious fanatic who favored "born again"
Christians and made unwise political and on-the-job decisions
because of his "mysticism". The following is an excerpt from an
interview given to a reporter of the L. A. Times newspaper,
attempting to trap Bob Vernon. It's an excellent example of our
"upside down" collapsing culture attempting to take away
religious freedom as well as destroy a virtuous and committed
public servant:

> "'Do you bring your faith to work with you?' the reporter
> asked. 'In other words, does your religion have any
> influence on your decisions here at work? Is your
> on-the-job performance affected by your faith?'
>
> "'Yes,' I answered, 'I hope my faith is evident in my
> behavior and decisions here at work.'
>
> "My answer shocked him. He was visibly taken back by
> what he surmised was an admission of guilt. He made
> sure his recorder was working and positioned his pen at
> his note pad. He couldn't conceal his excitement as he
> prepared to take down my confession.
>
> "'Yes, Chief,' he said. 'Could you give me some
> examples of how you have allowed your faith to affect
> your work?'

"'Well, I hope I have a reputation for telling the truth. I hope I'm known to keep my word. I trust I've established a pattern of working well past the required commitment. I've tried to pursue excellence in all I do. My desire is to have my troops feel I have demonstrated my support for them.'

"'That's how I hope my faith has intersected with my work. I hope people have observed that I'm a sincere, diligent, compassionate servant. I hope they've seen actions that cause them to believe that.'

"I could see the disappointment in his eyes. That wasn't what he had hoped to hear.

"'Okay, Chief,' he tried again. 'I understand. What I was wondering is if you talk about your religion at work. Do you talk about the gospel when you perceive people have a need of it?'

"'The city of Los Angeles pays me to be a police administrator, not a preacher. When I'm on duty, I try to be the best police executive I can possibly be. I think that's demonstrating my faith. If I were to preach on duty, I would be breaking faith with my employer. I think I would be abusing my authority to do so. I hope my life *preaches*.'

"Once again, I could see he was disappointed. 'Bill,' I said, 'my belief about God's leading in my life is not really dramatic or mystical. I accept the biblical admonition to submit to authority. I believe that principle implies that God will usually lead me through a chain of command. In other words, He often uses human instruments to give me guidance.'

"'Of course, there's one important caveat. If the authority over me asked me to violate a specific command from God, I would have to refuse. By the way, he has never asked me to violate one of those basic principles.'

"Disappointment was written all over his face. He was hoping he would hear some dramatic revelation. My answers were too ordinary. They didn't fit the mold of a mystic or a fanatic. The interview ended abruptly."

"Woe to those who call evil good and good evil; who put darkness for light, and light for darkness; woe to those who are wise in their own eyes, and prudent in their own sight" (Isaiah 5:20,21).

Dr. Earnest F. Young, anthropologist, artist and educator in a tract, "Pop Culture and the Art of Fruit Inspection", sums it up for us. He states,

> *"Science research has moved beyond nineteenth century 'modern' materialism and has entered a post modern era of rediscovery, of breakthroughs in cosmology, among many other fields, that verify biblical revelation. At the same time, the leaders and shapers of Western culture are moving in the opposite direction, toward relativism, subjectivism, naturalism, mysticism, and other destructive isms, propelled by the old untruths of 'modern' (nineteenth century) science.*

"How bad are our recent defeats? Far worse than most of us can imagine. The Constitution and the will of the voters can no longer be counted on to defend against irrational, immoral change; they have been effectively neutralized by a process called 'judicial review'. The court system now uses separation of church and state not just as a wall but as a weapon to blast God and religious values out of every aspect of public life, including health and education.

"The one great 'sin' our popular culture acknowledges is disapproval of almost anything—homosexual relations or any sexual relations outside of marriage, euthanasia, pornography, etc.,—except religious faith, especially Christian faith, and of such life-essential concepts as objective truth and moral absolutes.

"In fact, disapproval of religious faith is moving into a new phase: active hostility. The media are stirring up fear of the supposed theocratic goals of the religious right. Christians, especially pastors and evangelists, are repeatedly depicted as fools or villains, and every scandal makes headlines.

"A less visible, perhaps more insidious hostility is expressed in the nation's classrooms, starting with college and trickling all the way down to kindergarten. The emerging philosophy is called 'deconstruction', and it is exemplified in the latest 'whole language primary reading instruction' for tomorrow's elementary schools. Teachers in training are taught that since there is no such thing as Truth, and since original meanings are impossible to determine due to cultural change, children should invent their own meanings from any given text and develop their ideas from there.

"What can you and I do? For one thing, we can be good stewards of our resources, including our political resources. We would do well to take all the opportunities yet available for expressing our views and exerting our influence for good. The more united we are, the greater our impact will be."

Back to the Bible

England today is a second or third rate power but at one time in history she was unequaled, not only in military power but in economic, democratic and spiritual leadership. When Queen Victoria was asked by an African prince the secret of England's greatness, she presented him with a Bible and said, "This is the secret of England's greatness."

Gladstone, former Prime Minister of Great Britain in the 1800's and one of the greatest statesman and legal minds of history said,

> "Talk about the questions of the day! There is but one question, and that is the Gospel. That can and will correct everything. I am glad to say that about all the men at the top of Great Britain are Christians.... I have been in public position fifty-eight years, all but eleven of them in the Cabinet of the British governments, and during those forty-seven years have been associated with sixty of the master minds of the century, and all but five of the sixty were Christians."

John Adams, our second President, said,

> "I have examined all (that is, all of Scripture) as well as my narrow sphere, my straightened means, and my busy life will allow me; and the result is that the Bible is the best book in the world. It contains more of my little philosophy than all the libraries I have seen, and such parts of it I cannot reconcile to my little philosophy, I postpone for future investigation."

President John Quincy Adams said,

> "I speak as a man of the world to men of the world: and I say to you: search the scriptures. The Bible is the book above all others to be read at all ages and in all conditions of human life; not to be read once or twice through and then laid aside, but to be read in small portions every day."

Daniel Webster made this statement:

> "If there be anything in my style or thoughts to be commended, the credit is due to my kind parents for instilling into my mind an early love of the Scriptures."

In closing, let's consider the advice of Abraham Lincoln, who was possibly our greatest president and considered one of the wisest of all our presidents. The *Los Angeles Times* (November 19, 1993) contains an article on Lincoln by Ronald D. Rietveld entitled "A President for the Ages". The following is an excerpt from the article:

> "While we see Lincoln primarily as a war President (Civil War freeing of slaves), we must not forget that the Lincoln Administration and the Republican Congress were instrumental in the most fundamental changes in the American economy: banking, tariff, land policy and the creation of the land grant universities, positioning the United States to be a great industrial exporting power.... How could Lincoln accomplish so much in the midst of such violent bloodshed? As a leader, he had remarkable spiritual qualities. His speeches, which he wrote mostly himself, manifest an awareness of God and divine providence in the midst of the contest and have become masterpieces of literature."

Abraham Lincoln said, "I know there is a God, and that He hates injustice and slavery. I see the storm coming, and I know that His hand is in it. If He has a place for me—and I think He has—I believe I am ready. I am nothing, but truth is everything. I know that I am right because liberty is right, for Christ teaches it, and Christ is God.... I may not see the end, but it will come, and I shall be vindicated; and these men shall find that they have not read their Bible aright."

The Wilson Quarterly (Winter 1985), in an article *The Almost Chosen People*, states concerning Lincoln,

> "No one ever reflected more deeply on the relationship between religion and politics than Lincoln, the archetypal American statesman.

> "When Lincoln issued the Emancipation Proclamation in 1863, he appealed both to world opinion and God for approval. Lincoln confided to his Cabinet that the timing was determined by divine intervention in the Battle of

Antietam. Secretary of the Navy Gideon Welles noted in
his diary:

"'He remarked that he had made a vow—a covenant—
that if God gave us the victory in the approaching battle,
he would consider it an indication of the Divine will, and
that it was his duty to move forward in the cause of the
slaves. He was satisfied it was right—and confirmed and
strengthened in his action by the vow and its results.'"

In the farewell address of Lincoln at Springfield, Illinois on
February 11, 1861, he said.

"I now leave, not knowing when or whether ever I may
return, with a task before me greater than that which
rested upon Washington. Without the assistance of that
Divine Being who ever attended him, I cannot succeed.
With that assistance I cannot fail."

The following is an excerpt from a speech given by Lincoln on
April 30, 1863. It is equally applicable for America today.

"We have been the recipients of the choicest bounties of
heaven. We have been preserved these many years in
peace and prosperity, we have grown in numbers in
wealth and power as no other nation has grown, but we
have forgotten God. We have forgotten the gracious
hand that preserved us in peace and multiplied and
enriched and strengthened us. We have vainly imagined
in the deceitfulness of our heart that all these blessings
were produced by some superior wisdom and virtue of
our own. Intoxicated with unbroken success, we have
become too self sufficient to feel the necessity of
redeeming and preserving grace. Too proud to pray to
the God that made us. It behooves us then to humble
ourselves before the offended power to confess our
national sins and to pray for clemency and forgiveness
upon us."

Appendix A

Days of Genesis	Sequence of Creative Acts	Geological Development	Geological Timetable
		Matter, the universe, earth	Cosmic Era
Day 1 Gen. 1:1-5	The Heavens and the Earth Earth Darkness Unformed condition Light	Dark, diffuse nebulae Earth in molten condition All oceans in atmosphere Sun begins to radiate as a star	Azoic Era
Day 2 Gen. 1:6-8	Expanse or sky space between water on the Earth and clouds	Water begins to collect, condense Clouds and oceans form Oxygen develops (atmosphere)	
Day 3 Gen. 1:9-13	The Earth out of the sea Vegetation (algae and plant life)	Cooling of Earth's surface Continental shields form and come out of the water	Archaeozoic Era

Day 4 Gen. 1:14-19	Luminaries made to appear	Earthquakes-mountain ranges form Tropical hothouse, plants By condensation, the cloud envelop thins or breaks, making light visible	Proterozoic Era
Day 5 Gen. 1:20-23	Out of the sea-sea monsters Moving & flying creatures	Invertebrate life of all kinds-fish, amphibians and insects (swarms of living creatures)	Paleozoic Era Cambrian Devonian Carboniferous
Day 6 Gen. 1:24-31	Animal life of all kinds Cattle, creepers, beasts Man and Woman	Reptiles-land, sea & air (dinosaurs) Mammals of land, sea & air. True birds & non-domestic carnivors Adam and Eve	Cenozoic
Day 7 Gen. 2:1-3	The Sabbath rest	No new "kinds" or orders	Psychozoic Era

Appendix B

Bogus Evidences for a Young Universe

"Scientific creationists" who hold to a 24-hour creation day insist that the evidences for the age of the universe and the earth are inconclusive and that there is, by contrast, a considerable body of evidence supporting a young age. Here they are sadly misguided and are misguiding many whose science education and biblical training are inadequate to aid them in evaluation. All of these so-called "evidences" of youthfulness, when investigated closely involve one or more of the following problems:

- faulty assumptions

- faulty data

- misapplication of principles, laws and equations

- ignorance of mitigating evidence

Ironically, these fallacious arguments, when corrected, provide some of the strongest evidences available for an old universe and an old earth. Consider these examples taken from Dr. Ross' book, Creation and Time, chapter 10, *Is There Scientific Evidence for a Young Universe?*:

A: The continents are eroding too quickly.

Erosion measurements show that the continents are lowered by wind, rain, etc., at a rate of 0.05 mm per year. At this rate, the continents—averaging about 800 meters in elevation—would disappear in about 16 million years. Since continents do still have considerable elevation, the earth must be younger than 16 million years.

Response: The fallacy here lies in the failure to recognize that lava flows, delta and continental shelf buildup (from eroded material), coral reef buildup, and uplift from colliding tectonic plates are occurring at rates roughly equivalent to, and in a few cases far exceeding, the erosion rate. The Himalayas, for example, are rising as much as 15 mm per year.

Sample Argument B: The earth's magnetic field is decaying too rapidly.

The strength of the earth's magnetic field has been decreasing steadily since measurements were first taken about 150 years ago. Based on the field strength of a typical magnetic star (certainly exceeding any conceivable value for the earth) and on the observed rate of decay, some creationists have calculated that the decay process must have begun no more than 10,000 years ago. Thus, the earth's age must be 10,000 years or less.

Response: The oversight in this argument is that the earth's magnetic field does not undergo steady decay but rather follows a "sinusoidal" pattern. That is, the field decays, builds up, decays, builds up, etc. The proof for this pattern lies in ancient geologic strata found throughout the world. The rocks reveal that the earth's field reverses its polarity about every half million years—the reversal process itself lasting roughly 10,000 years.

Sample Argument C: The sun burns by gravitational contraction and is, therefore, relatively young.

Before the discovery of nuclear energy the only explanation astronomers could offer for the enormous energy output of the sun and other stars was gravitational contraction. Given the diameter and energy output of our sun, we can calculate that its maximum age would be 100 million years—if it were generating energy only by this process. When some measurements indicated a slight decrease in the sun's diameter, a number of creationists were quick to conclude that the sun's energy source must indeed be gravity, rather than nuclear fusion; and, thus, the sun's age must be less than 100 million years.

Response: Again, the argument overlooks significant data. First, it has been shown that if a body of our sun's dimensions were experiencing gravitational contraction, the temperature, pressure, and other conditions at its center would be such as to ignite nuclear fusion. Furthermore, various measured characteristics of the sun, including its effective temperature, luminosity, spectra, radius, and mass, all indicate that the sun certainly is burning by nuclear fusion and that this fusion has been proceeding for about 5 billion years.

As for the observed decrease in the sun's diameter, the measurements cited were later found to be at odds with other visual measurements. The conflict has since been laid to rest completely by the much more precise work of Barry LaBonte and Robert Howard, published in *Science*, volume 214 (1981), pp. 907-909. Their measurements, within a limit of 0.1 arc seconds, show no change in the solar radius over the years from 1974 to 1981.

Sample Argument D: Galaxy clusters are not widely enough dispersed.

In order for a cluster of heavenly bodies to remain together, the gravity of the system must be sufficient to overcome the velocities of the individual bodies within it. Armed with measurements of velocities and masses, astronomers can calculate (a) the dispersal time for clusters whose total mass is too small for gravitational containment, and (b) the relaxation time (the time required for the bodies to assume randomized velocities) for clusters whose total mass is large enough for containment. Some creationists point out that when such calculations are applied to galaxy clusters, the lack of galaxy dispersal indicates an age for the clusters much less than a billion years.

Response: The problem with this argument is that these calcuations for dispersal and relaxation times are applicable for point sources only. Galaxies are not point sources. In fact, their diameters are less than one order of magnitude smaller than the average distances between them, within a given cluster. Therefore, these dispersal-time calculations are meaningless.

By comparison, however, stars in a cluster are point sources; the average distances between them are at least seven orders of magnitude greater than their average diameters. When dispersal and relaxation time calculations are applied to star clusters in our galaxy, many clusters show their ages to be greater than two billion years.

(Author's Note: For additional materials, contact Reasons to Believe, P. O. Box 5978, Pasadena CA 91117, or call (626) 335-1480.)

Appendix C

Points of Discussion

The Sabbath Day Rest

> "Remember the Sabbath day to keep it holy, for in six days the Lord made the heavens and the earth but He rested on the seventh day." Exodus 20:10-11

There are those who interpret the fourth commandment as positive proof that the "days" of Genesis were twenty-four hours. Gleason Archer (renowned Hebrew scholar) disagrees, stating,

> "By no means does this demonstrate that 24-hour intervals were involved in the first six days any more than the eight-day celebration of the Feast of Tabernacles proves that the wilderness wanderings under Moses occupied only eight days."

For agricultural land, the Sabbath rest was a twelve-month rest period to restore the land (Leviticus 25:4) —for human beings, a 24-hour rest period is needed. God, who is non-temporal and immutable, is not subject to biological cycles. His days and rest periods are completely flexible just as are His creation days described in Genesis 1. The emphasis here is a pattern of one-out-of-seven, not day and night.

The seven days of our calendar week simply follow the pattern established by God. This is the same usage as the High Priest who served in a sanctuary which was a copy and shadow of that which is in heaven (Hebrews 8:5). The human and the temporal are always copies and shadows of the divine. God's workweek (the days of Genesis) are not the same for mankind and the land, nor must they be the same in Creation.

Death and the Days of Creation

> "Sin entered the world through one man and death through sin, and in this way death came to all men, because all sinned."
>
> Romans 5:12

The heated controversy over this question is caused by the interpretation that says that there was no death **of any kind** prior to Adam's fall into sin, and therefore, only a brief time could have transpired between creation of the first life forms and Adam's sin; however, we need to remember that some life forms cannot survive for even three hours without food. The mere ingestion of food by animals requires the death of plants or other animals.

This erroneous interpretation assumes that plants and animals die because of Adam's sin, but it is a legitimate question to ask, Are all birds, fish, mammals and plants condemned to death because of Adam's sin ... or is this simply God's natural order of things? Notice, the verse says that death " ... comes to all **men for all sinned.**" There is no biblical evidence that animals, who are driven by instinct, sin.

Death comes to humans in three forms as a result of Adam's fall:

- Spiritual death—broken fellowship with God (Eph. 2:1)

- Physical death—(Heb. 9:27)

- Eternal death—judgment and eternal separation from God (the second death).

"And you He made alive who were dead in trespasses and sins."

Ephesians 2:1

In addressing Christians in Ephesus, Paul speaks of their spiritual rebirth from the dead condition of their past sinful lives. All humans coming from the loins of Adam (the first man) are born sinners by nature. Adam passed on to his descendants, a predisposition for sin and a rebellious heart—the determination that, "I'll do it my way!" Mankind cannot know or please God in this unregenerate state. The implications of Adam's fall are that humans are not sinners because they sin, but rather they sin because they are born into the world as sinners. Only by a spiritual rebirth can the curse of Adam be reversed, but there appear no grounds to deny physical death for non-human life prior to this.

When God spoke to Adam in the garden, He was warning him of the disaster that would occur if he disobeyed His command. God said, "In the day that you eat of it, you shall surely die" (Genesis 2:17). In that moment of disobedience, Adam instantly died—he was immediately denied fellowship with God—but he remained alive physically for many years.

Only humans are sinners and only human beings as spiritual creatures, can experience spiritual death through sin. Dying spiritually meant that Adam broke his harmonious fellowship with God by his rebellious act against Him. In disobedience, he and his offspring introduced the inclination to do one's own will, to have one's own way above God's way.

"Since by man came death, by man came the resurrection of the dead. For as in Adam all die, even so in Christ shall all be made alive."   I Cor. 15:21-22

From this Scripture, it is clear that Paul is not referring to death in general for all creatures, but only to creatures (humans) who are spiritually dead. Paul is also saying that by faith in Christ, people can be " ... made alive in Christ ... " and escape the judgment of all who are still identified with Adam (Romans 5:12,18,19).

There is no biblical foundation for the concept that there was no physical death for animals before Adam sinned. To cling to short days for Creation on this basis is not sustainable. This argument does not rule out Creation days of great length.

Bloodshed and the Doctrine of Atonement

There are also those who assert that there was no shedding of blood before Adams' sin. They propose that God brought in death and bloodshed as the basis of the Gospel message because of sin. This is precarious since it is possible that the death of plants and animals existed before Adam's time and if so, it destroys this whole basis for redemption.

Again, **men are sinners,** not animals who have nothing to do with mankind's redemption. For example, the blood sacrifices instigated after Adam's sin were only types and shadows of Christ's sacrifice for redemption. Hebrews 10:1-4 states that the blood of animals cannot take away sin. The penalty for sin is spiritual death. Soulish animals cannot atone for spiritual creatures and sin is a spiritual matter between God and man. The Atonement had to be made by Christ who is a spiritual being. There is no biblical foundation to assume that there was no blood shed by animals before Adam's fall.

BIBLIOGRAPHY

Adler, Mortimer *Truth in Religion* Collier Books, New York 1990

Arthur, Chester A. *An Introduction to Paleobotany* McGraw-Hill, New York 1947

Asimov, Isaac. *In the Game of Energy and Thermodynamics You Can't Ever Break Even.* Smithsonian Institute Journal 1980

Bainton, Roland H. *Here I Stand* Meridian Press New York NY 1995

Behe, Michael, *Darwin's Black Box — The Biochemical Challenge to Evolution*, The Free Press, New York, NY, 1996

Bennet, William J. *The De-Valuing of America* Summit Books New York 1992

Bernstein, Richard *Dictatorship of Virtue* Gilson Quarterly (Autumn 1994)

Bloom, Alan. *The Closing of the American Mind.* Insight Magazine. May 11, 1987

Boardman, William W. Henry M. Morris. *Science and Creation.* Creation Science Research. San Diego, California. 1972

Bradley, Walter. *Theories on Life Origins Take New Directions, Facts & Faith* 1993

Carr, William. *Hitler.* The Bath Press. Great Britain. 1986

Crick, Francis. *Life Itself* New York; Simon and Schuster 1981

Darwin, Charles. *Origin of Species*. Barrow J.W. ed. Classic Penguin books. 1968

DeBeer, Gavin. *Homology: An Unsolved Problem*, Oxford: Oxford University Press, 1971

Denton, Michael. *Evolution: A Theory in Crisis*. Burnet Books. Great Britain. 1985

De Young, Don *Thinking About the Brain* Impact (February 1990)

Dobzhansky, Theodosius. *Genetics and the Origin of Species* New York: Columbia University Press 1951

Downs, Robert B. *Books That Changed the World.* Mentor Books, New York, New York 1956

Durant, John *How Evolution Became a Scientific Myth New Scientist,* 1980

Eccles, John *The Self and the Brain, Wilson Quarterly* 1980

Eckhardt, Robert B. *Population, Genetics and Human Origins, Scientific America* 1972

Eldridge, Niles *Punctuated Equilibria, Paleobiology*, V.3, Spring 1977

Encyclopedia Britannica *Haeckel*, 15th Edition vol. IV

Everest, Alton *Modern Science and the Christian Faith* Scripture Press, Chicago IL 1950

Fix, William R. *The Bone Peddlers* New York, MacMillan 1987

Geisler, Norman L. *Origin Science.* Baker Book House, Grand Rapids, Michigan 1948

Geisler, Norman L., and Howe, Thomas *When Critics Ask* Victor Books SP Publishing Inc. (1992)

Geisler, Norman L. and Brooks, Ronald M. *When Skeptics Ask* Victor Books SP Publishing Inc. 1825 College Avenue Wheaton Illinois 60187, (1990)

Gish, Duane T. *Evolution: The Fossils Say No!* Creation-Life Publishers. San Diego, California, 1972

Gish, Duane T. *Speculation and Experiments Related to Theories on the Origin of Life.* Institute for Creation Science San Diego, California 1977

Gould, Stephen J. *Ever Since Darwin* Burnett Books 1978; *Is A New and General Theory of Evolution Emerging?*, *Paleobiology* vol. 026 1980

Graham, Billy *Storm Warning* Word Publishing, Dallas TX 1992

Grasse, Pierre-Paul. *Evolution of Living Organisms.* Academic Press; New York, 1977

Haller Jr., John S. *Outcasts from Evolution! Scientific Attitudes of Racial Inferiority 1859-1900.* 1972

Halverson, Dean C. *The Compact Guide to World Religions* Bethany House Publishers, Minneapolis MN 1996

Ham, Ken *The Lie: Evolution.* Master Books Creation Life Publishers El Cajon, California 92022, 1987

Ham, Paul S. and Kenneth A. Taylor, *The Genesis Solution.* Baker Book House. Grand Rapids, Mich., 49516, 1991

Henry, Carl F. *Evangelicals at the Brink of Crisis* Word Books, Waco TX 1967

Hitchcock, James *What Is Secular Humanism?* Servant Books, Ann Arbor, Michigan 1948

Hitching, Francis. *The Neck of the Giraffe: Where Darwin Went Wrong* Ticknor and Fields, New Haven, CT 1982

Hoyle, Fred *Hoyle on Evolution, Nature* vol 294 1981

Hunt, Dave—
    A Cup of Trembling Harvest House Publishers, Eugene, Oregon, 1995
    A Woman Rides the Beast Harvest House Publishers, Eugene OR 1994

Huse, Scott M. *The Collapse of Evolution*. Baker Book House. Grand Rapids, Michigan, 1983

Johnson, Paul. *The Almost Chosen People*. Wilson Quarterly. Winter, 1985, p78ff.

Johnson, Phillip E. —
>   *Evolution as Dogma* Haugton Publishing Co. 1990
>   *Darwin on Trial* Haugton Publishing Company 1989
>   *Defeating Darwinism by Opening Minds* InterVarsity Press 1997

Keith, Arthur, Sir. *Evolution and Ethics*. New York, Putnam. 1974

Kelso, A. J. *Origin and Evolution of the Primates* New York 1974

Kitts, David B. *Paleontology and Evolutionary Theory* 1974

Kofahl. Robert E. and Segraves, Kelly L. *The Creation Explanation*. Harold Shaw Publishers, Wheaton, Illinois 1975

Kofahl. Robert E. *Handy Dandy Evolution Refuter* Beta Books, San Diego, California 1980

Kristol, Irvin. commentary *Wilson Quarterly* Autumn 1991

Lasca, Christopher. *The Fragility of Liberalism*. The Wilson quarterly (Winter, 1992)

Leakey, Richard *Lucy*, *Weekend Australian* 1983

Lewin, Roger *Thread of Life* Smithsonian books Washington D.C. 1982 *Bones of Mammals Fleshed Out*, Science vol 212 1981

Lipson, H.S. *A Physicist Looks at Evolution*, *Physics Bulletin* vol 31 1980

Looy, Mark *I Think, Therefore There is a Supreme Thinker*, *Impact* 1990

Marshall, Peter J.. Manuel Jr., David B., *The Light and the Glory*. Fleming H. Revell Company. Old Tappan, New Jersey, 1977

Maslow, Abraham *The Psychology of Being* Van Nostrand Reinhold Company New York 1968

Mayr, Ernst *The Nature of the Darwinian Revolution Science*, vol. 176. June 2, 1976

McDowell, Josh *Reasons Skeptics Should Consider Christianity* Living Books, Tyndale House Publishers, Inc., Wheaton, Illinois, 1981

McGee Jr., Vernon J. *Genesis Volume 1* Griffin Printing Glendale, California 1975

Missler, Chuck *The Divine Watchmaker? - The Accidental Watch* Personal Updaate (July 1996)

Morris, Henry M. —

> *The Bible and Modern Science* Moody Press, 1956
>
> *Biblical Cosmology and Modern Science* Craig Press, New Jersey 1970
>
> *The Genesis Flood* The Presbyterian and Reformed Publishing Company Philadelphia, Pennsylvania 1970
>
> *What is Creation Science?* Creation-Life Publishers Inc. San Diego, California 1982
>
> *The Troubled Waters of Evolution* Creation-Life Publishers Inc. San Diego, California 1982
>
> *The Logic of Biblical Creation,* Impact, July 1990

Moreland, J.P. *Christianity and the Nature of Science*—A Philosophical Investigation, Baker House Books, Grand Rapids, Michigan, 1998

> *Sealing the Secular City,* A Defense of Christianity, Baker House Books, Grand Rapids, Michigan, 1987

Nilsson, Herbert *Synthetische Artildung* Lund Sweden 1954

Norman, J.R. *Classification and Pedigrees: Fossils in a History of Fishes* Dr. P.H. Greenwood Third Edition 1975

Olson, E.C. *The Evolution of Life* New American Library New York 1965

Patterson, Colon *Evolution* London British Museum 1978

Ramm, Bernard L. *Questions About the Spirit* World Books Publishers, Waco, Texas, 1974

Raup, David M. *Conflicts Between Darwin and Paleontology, Field Museum of Natural History Bulletin* vol 50 January 1979

Restak, Richard M. *The Brain, Wilson Quarterly* 1980

Ridley, Mark *Who Doubts Evolution?, New Scientist* vol 90 1981

Romer, A.S. *Vertebrate Paleontology* Chicago University Press 1966

Ross, Hugh —

The Creator and the Cosmos NavPress Colorado Springs, Colorado 1993

The Fingerprint of God Promise Publishing Company Orange, California 92865, 1991

Creation and Time NavPress Colorado Springs, Colorado 1994

Big Bang Gets New Adjectives - Open and Hot Facts and Faith (First Quarter 1998)

Pond Scum Defies Evolution Facts and Faith (Summer 1994)

Eve's Secret to Growing Younger Facts and Faith (First Quarter 1998)

Theories on Life Origin Take New Directions

Facts and Faith (Winter 1992, 1993)

New Developments in Martian Meteorite Facts and Faith (fourth Quarter 1996)

Sagan, Carl *Cosmos* Random House New York 1980

Sartre, Jean Paul *The Words of Jean Paul Sartre* Fawcett Crest Books Greenwich, Connecticut 1966

Saur, Erich *The Dawn of World Redemption* William B.Eerdmans Publishing House Grand Rapids, Michigan 1951

Saur, Erich *From Eternity to Eternity* William B. Eerdmans Publishing House Grand Rapids, Michigan 1954

Schaeffer, Francis —

Genesis in Time and Space Inter-Varsity Press Downers Grove, Illinois 60515

The God Who Is There InterVarsity Press Downers Grove, Illinois 1968

Shapiro, Robert *Origins: A Skeptics Guide to the Origins of Life on Planet Earth* Summit Books New York 1985

Simons, Elwyn *The Origin and Radiation of the Primates* N.Y. Academy of Science 1969

Simpson, George Gaylord *The Major Features of Evolution* Columbia University Press New York 1953

Sproul, R. C.—

Faith Alone. Baker Books. Grand Rapids, Michigan, 49516, 1995

The New Geneva Study Bible—Bringing the Light of the Reformation to Scripture, Thomas Nelson Pub., 1995

Knowing Scripture InterVarsity Press, Downers Grove, Illinois, 1997

Stahl, Barbara J. *Problems in Evolution* McGraw Hill New York 1974

Stanley, Steven M. *A Theory of Evolution Above the Species Level* Natural Academy of Science U.S.A. Vol 72, 1975

The New Evolution, John Hopkins Magazine June 1982

Sunderland, D. Luther *Darwin's Enigma* Zondervan Publishing House Grand Rapids, Michigan 1984

Swinton, W.E. *The Origin of Birds* Academic Press New York 1960

Tolson, Jay *Is Everything Relative?* The Wilson Quarterly (Winter 1998)

Uhlenberg, Peter and Eggebeen, David *The Declining Well Being of American Adolescents, Wilson Quarterly* Winter 1986

Wald, George *The Origin of Life*, Scientific America vol. 191, 1954

Watson, Lyal *The Water People, Science Digest* vol. 90 May 1982

Wyson, R.L. *The Creation-Evolution Controversy* Inquiry Press Midland, Michigan 1984

Yockey, Hubert P.—

A Calculation of the Probablity of spontaneous bi-ogenesis by Information Theory 1974

Information Theory and Molecular Biology Cambridge Publishing Company, New York, 1992

Young, Robert M. *The Darwin Debate, Marxism Today*, v. 26 April 1982

Zuckerman, Lord Solly *Beyond the Ivory Tower* Taplinger Publishing Co. New York 1970